☆ *The Confederate General* ☆

Volume 3

The Confederate General

Volume 3

Gordon, George W. to Jordan, Thomas

William C. Davis, Editor

Julie Hoffman, Assistant Editor

A Publication of the
National Historical Society

Library of Congress Cataloging-in-Publication Data
The Confederate General / William C. Davis,
   editor; Julie Hoffman, assistant editor.
      p. cm.
     ISBN 0-918678-65-X (v. 3) : $29.95
     Contents: v. 3. Gordon, George to Jordan, Thomas.
     1. United States—History—Civil War, 1861-1865—
Biography. 2. Confederate States of America. Army.—Biography. 3. Generals—Confederate States of America—Biography. 4. Generals—Southern States—Biography. 5. Generals—United States —Biography.
I. Davis, William C., 1946-   .   II. Hoffman, Julie.
  E467.C76   1991
  973.7'42'0922 [B]   91-8508
(B)   CIP

Editorial Assistant, Eleanor Mauck
Designed by Art Unlimited
Printed in the United States of America

✶ Contents ✶

✯ *George Washington Gordon* ✯

A handsome, and previously unpublished, early portrait of Gordon as a brigadier, taken sometime between August and December 1864. (Alabama Department of Archives and History, Montgomery, Ala.)

Born in Giles County, in Middle Tennessee, on October 5, 1836, Gordon was reared and received his rudimentary education in rural Texas and Mississippi. He completed his education at the Western Institute of Nashville, where he studied engineering under the future Confederate Major General Bushrod R. Johnson. After graduating in 1850, Gordon became a surveyor. He remained in this profession until the commencement of the Civil War, at which time he tendered his services to his native state.

Assigned in 1861 to the 11th Tennessee Infantry as drillmaster, Gordon joined his regiment subsequent to its organization and accompanied it on its march to East Tennessee, where it formed part of the command of Brigadier General Felix K. Zollicoffer. Gordon was soon elected captain of Company I, and by July 3, 1862, he had advanced to the rank of lieutenant colonel. The unit continued to serve in East Tennessee, now assigned to Brigadier General Carter L. Stevenson's brigade of Major General Edmund Kirby Smith's command.

During a skirmish near Tazewell, Tennessee, in the vicinity of Cumberland Gap, two soldiers of the 16th Ohio Infantry became confused, and instead of retreating with their outnumbered comrades, they advanced toward the Confederate lines. They happened upon Gordon, took him prisoner, and, moving by a circuitous route, managed to return to their lines with their prisoner.

Gordon was exchanged and promoted to colonel prior to the end of October 1862. The 11th Tennessee at that time constituted part of Brigadier General James E. Rains' brigade of Major General Carter L. Stevenson's division. Reassigned to Major General John P. McCown's division, the brigade joined General Braxton Bragg's Army of Tennessee in time to participate in the Battle of Murfreesboro. On December 31, the opening day of that engagement, Gordon sustained a serious wound while gallantly leading his regiment through the cedar thicket. His efforts formed part of the Confederate effort to turn the enemy's right flank.

Gordon remained in the Army of Tennessee for the remainder of his military service. Transferred to Brigadier General Preston Smith's brigade of Major General Benjamin Cheatham's division of Lieutenant General Leonidas Polk's corps by July 31, 1863, the 11th found itself after the reorganization following the Battle of Chickamauga in September under Brigadier

Since Gordon spent most of his tenure as a Confederate brigadier in a Federal prison, it is quite possible that portraits like this and the one following were made shortly after his July 1865 release. (Library of Congress)

General Alfred J. Vaughan, Jr., in Major General Thomas C. Hindman's division of Lieutenant General William J. Hardee's corps.

Between January 20 and February 20, 1864, Vaughan's brigade returned to Cheatham's division, which now formed part of Hardee's Corps. The 11th remained in this situation throughout the Atlanta Campaign, although following the Battle of Kennesaw Mountain June 27, 1864, Gordon took command of the brigade. Promoted brigadier general on August 16, 1864, to rank from August 15, Gordon commanded the 11th, 12th, 13th, 29th, 47th, and 154th Tennessee regiments.

During the invasion of Tennessee, Gordon's brigade formed part of Major General John C. Brown's division of Lieutenant General Alexander P. Stewart's corps. At the Battle of Franklin on November 30, Gordon led members of his division in what proved to be the deepest penetration of the Union center. The unsuccessful charge ended for Gordon when he found himself wounded and a prisoner of war. Transferred east, he remained a prisoner in Fort Warren, Boston harbor, until the end of the conflict, and was there when the Confederate Senate confirmed his appointment on February 20, 1865. Sixteen of the high-ranking Confederate officers imprisoned there, including Gordon, expressed their deepest regrets to Union Lieutenant General Ulysses S. Grant about the assassination of President Abraham Lincoln on April 16, 1865.

Released from prison in July, the dashing twenty-nine-year-old Gordon began rebuilding his life by studying law at Cumberland University at Lebanon, Tennessee. He began practicing law at Pulaski but soon relocated to Memphis, where he labored as an attorney for several years. He also managed to acquire a substantial plantation in Mississippi. When yellow fever struck Memphis in 1873, Gordon remained in the city to nurse the victims. His first marriage ended tragically three years later, when his wife died during their honeymoon in New York City.

Gordon began a career in politics in 1883, when he became a state railway commissioner. Two years later he secured an appointed position in the Department of the Interior. Between 1885 and 1889 he served as an Indian agent in Arizona and Nevada. Returning to Memphis in 1889, Gordon became superintendent of the city's schools in 1892. He remarried in 1899.

In 1906 Gordon won election to the U.S. Congress, making him the last Confederate general to be a member of that body. Reelected in 1908 and 1910, he served on the committee on military affairs and was noted for writing all his letters himself, never having become accustomed to dictating them.

Always active in the affairs of Confederate veterans, Gordon had been among the forty-five "Founders of Southern Historical Society" in New Orleans on April 21, 1869. In 1910, and again in 1911, the United Confederate Veterans elected Gordon their commander-in-chief. He suffered from exposure at a reunion of that organization and, failing to recover, died in Memphis on August 9, 1911, survived by his wife. He was buried in Elmwood Cemetery.

Lawrence L. Hewitt

Brock, R. A., ed., *Southern Historical Society Papers*, Vol. XVIII (Richmond, 1890).

Faust, Patricia L., ed., *Historical Times Encyclopedia of the Civil War* (New York, 1986).

Very probably an early postwar portrait in uniform. (Museum of the Confederacy, Richmond, Va.)

⚝ *James Byron Gordon* ⚝

Born in Wilkesborough, North Carolina, on November 2, 1822, James B. Gordon graduated from Emory and Henry College in Virginia, then farmed and entered the mercantile business in his native Wilkes County, where his Scottish ancestors had settled about 1724. In 1850 he was elected to the state legislature, subsequently serving a number of terms.

When North Carolina seceded in 1861 after the firing on Fort Sumter, Gordon enlisted as a private in the Wilkes Valley Guards. His comrades elected him lieutenant, and upon the organization of the 1st North Carolina Cavalry in July, Gordon was appointed its major. The regiment, under Colonel Robert Ransom, was transferred to Virginia and assigned to the brigade of J. E. B. Stuart. On November 26 near Vienna, the regiment participated in its initial action with Gordon leading the command in a charge. Less than a month later, on December 20, at Dranesville, Stuart's brigade fought a spirited engagement.

In spring 1862, Gordon secured promotion to lieutenant colonel when Laurence Baker succeeded Ransom as colonel of the regiment. The 1st North Carolina participated in the Peninsula and Seven Days' campaigns during May and June. On July 25 Stuart reorganized his mounted command, assigning the North Carolinians to the brigade of Wade Hampton.

Gordon and the regiment earned distinction throughout the major campaigns and cavalry raids during the summer and fall of 1862. At Second Manassas, Antietam, and in Stuart's Dumfries Raid,

Gordon demonstrated bravery, intelligence, and leadership. By the spring of 1863, the forty-year-old North Carolinian seemed destined for higher rank.

At Brandy Station on June 9, 1863, Hampton's brigade fought savagely in the swirling battle. The North Carolinians rode in the thick of the combat, crushing the flank of a Union brigade. Less than a month later, on July 3, at Gettysburg, the regiment once again fought valiantly. When Baker replaced a wounded Hampton, Gordon assumed command of the regiment.

During the Confederate withdrawal from Gettysburg, Stuart's cavalry screened the army's rear. At Hagerstown, Maryland, on July 5, Gordon led his regiment and part of the 5th North Carolina Cavalry in a counterattack that routed the Union brigade of Judson Kilpatrick. Stuart later cited Gordon for this action, writing that the colonel exhibited "under my eye individual prowess deserving special commendation." Gordon had earned his colonelcy, and when Baker suffered a severe wound on July 31, Stuart and Robert E. Lee urged Gordon's elevation to brigade command.

On September 28, 1863, Gordon was promoted to brigadier general, effective immediately, and assigned to command, accepting on October 5, of the so-called North Carolina Brigade—the 1st, 2d, 4th, and 5th cavalry regiments. Within days Gordon led his brigade in

This Vannerson and Jones carte-de-visite of Gordon was taken in Richmond sometime between September 1863 and May 1864. (Museum of the Confederacy, Richmond, Va.)

the Bristoe Campaign. He suffered a wound at Auburn Mill on October 13 but retained command and, in Stuart's words, "continued, by his brave example and marked ability, to control the field." Six days later at Buckland, Gordon again distinguished himself. During the Mine Run Campaign in November, he had a horse shot from under him in an action near Parker's Store.

Gordon led his brigade in the Overland Campaign, May 4–June 12, 1864. When the Union cavalry under Philip Sheridan raided toward Richmond, Stuart's horsemen intercepted them north of the city. On May 12 at Meadow Bridge, Gordon fell mortally wounded, dying in Richmond on May 18. His remains were carried to Wilkesborough and interred.

Gordon was one of a handful of non-Virginians in Stuart's cavalry corps who had distinguished himself. At every level of command he had performed capably, with marked distinction on a few occasions. Had he lived, Gordon might have attained higher rank during the war's final months. Wade Hampton, who had replaced the fallen Stuart, knew Gordon well, and the attrition in the officer ranks offered opportunity for such solid officers as James Gordon.

Jeffry D. Wert

Freeman, Douglas Southall, *Lee's Lieutenants: A Study in Command* (New York, 1942–44).

Hill, D. H., *North Carolina*, Vol. IV in Evans, *Confederate Military History*.

Longacre, Edward G., *The Cavalry at Gettysburg* (New York, 1986).

Gordon looks slightly younger and less weary in this portrait, one of only two known of him. (U.S. Army Military History Institute, Carlisle, Pa.)

⋆ *John Brown Gordon* ⋆

A handsome, previously unpublished profile of General Gordon as a brigadier, presumably prior to May 1864. (Museum of the Confederacy, Richmond, Va.)

Gordon, whose rise from the rank of captain to major general marks one of the most impressive achievements in the history of the Army of Northern Virginia, was born on a plantation in Upson County, Georgia, on February 6, 1832. Though his father prospered as a planter and a minister in their community, he moved Gordon and his eleven siblings to Walker County in northwestern Georgia around 1840. Gordon enrolled in the University of Georgia in 1850, achieved senior standing in two years with one of the highest grade point averages in his class, but inexplicably withdrew from the university before receiving his diploma.

Moving to Atlanta in 1854, he studied law and passed the bar. Few clients sought his counsel, however, and in 1856 Gordon accepted a position in his father's coal-mining enterprise, which operated in the tristate area of Tennessee, Alabama, and Georgia. He quickly became wealthy and launched a political career. A staunch Democrat, he spoke passionately about Southern rights. His oratorical skills earned the respect of yeomen in Alabama, despite their lack of enthusiasm for Gordon's prosecession sentiments.

At the outbreak of the war, Gordon raised a company of mountain men, called the "Raccoon Roughs." His command entered active service in the 6th Alabama Infantry, where he was unanimously elected major on May 14, 1861. Ordered to the Virginia theater and assigned to Richard S. Ewell's brigade near Manassas, Gordon failed to see any significant fighting. His rank was upgraded to lieutenant colonel on December 26, 1861; four months later, on April 18, 1862, Gordon was promoted to colonel of the 6th Alabama after which his regiment was transferred to Robert E. Rodes' brigade.

During the Peninsula Campaign, March to August, 1862, Gordon took over the brigade after Rodes was wounded on May 31 at the Battle of Seven Pines. He then made his presence felt on the battlefield of Gaines' Mill (June 27) and Malvern Hill (July 1), setting an example of personal leadership characteristic of his entire military career. His aggressiveness, controlled by a sound tactical sense, secured the loyalty of his troops and the accolades of his superiors. One of his soldiers recalled that Gordon "had a way of putting things to the men that was irresistible, and he showed them at all times that he shrank from nothing in battle."

Remaining near Richmond until late August 1862, Gordon returned to his regiment on the eve of the Maryland Campaign. His performance in the fighting at South Mountain on September 14 and at Sharpsburg three days later demonstrated that he was a rising star in the army. Posting a desperate defense along a farmer's lane near Sharpsburg, he was struck by five bullets during the course of the day. A well-deserved brigadier general commission, dated November 1, 1862, effective immediately, waited for his signature at headquarters, though he did not formally accept it until he rejoined the army on March 30, 1862. With this boost in rank, he also received command of a brigade in Jubal A. Early's division. "Not to promote him," Edward Porter Alexander observed later, "would have been a scandal."

For some reason the Senate failed to confirm Gordon's appointment, but after Chancellorsville, on May 11, 1863, he was reappointed, and finally confirmed January 25, 1864, to rank from May 7, 1863.

During the Chancellorsville and Gettysburg campaigns in the spring and summer of 1863, Gordon handled his brigade reasonably well. Moreover, he earned the esteem of his new command. Some of his men asked Lee that Gordon permanently remain with their brigade. Six feet tall, narrow of frame, and possessing perfect posture, Gordon could inspire confidence in his troops with his image alone. Henry Kyd Douglas thought he was "a picture for the sculptor," and Jedediah Hotchkiss believed Gordon to be "the very personification of a hero." The Georgian had a much different view of himself, however. Writing to his wife during Lee's raid into Pennsylvania, he called himself "your big old Ugly."

The Overland Campaign of 1864 brought Gordon everlasting fame and elevated him into the upper echelons of

Gordon appears to be a colonel in this subtle image. Certainly his collar stars so indicate, though the button arrangement might be that of a major general. His youthful face, however, suggests that this is an 1862 image. (Tulane University Library, New Orleans, La.)

The Winchester, Virginia, firm of Lupton & Brown made this standing image of Gordon as a brigadier, though Gordon spent more time in Winchester after his promotion to major general in May 1864, meaning he probably did not change his tunic buttons. (Courtesy of Mark Katz)

the Army of Northern Virginia. At the Wilderness on May 6 he delivered a crushing blow to the right flank of Grant's line. On May 12, when the Federals pierced the Confederate line at the "Mule Shoe," Gordon, commanding a division, directed a savage counterattack that saved the army from disaster. For his herculean efforts he received a major-generalship on May 14, 1864, this time effective and confirmed immediately, and command of Edward Johnson's decimated division.

In early summer 1864, Gordon, serving under Jubal Early in the II Corps, pushed down the Shenandoah Valley and into Maryland, colliding with Federals at the Monocacy River on July 9. The death of one of his colonels in this battle devastated Gordon, who exclaimed: "Oh Lord why am I spared & so many & so good men are taken around me." Deeply religious, he held the conviction that God's hand altered human affairs. This belief served as a powerful source of inspiration and allowed him to fight with a reckless abandon. After failing to take Washington, D.C., Gordon and the rest of Early's Corps retired to the Shenandoah Valley, where they were defeated handily at Third Winchester on September 19 and Fisher's Hill on September 22.

A month later at Cedar Creek, the Confederates retaliated in one of the most spectacular flanking maneuvers of the war. Gordon's troops forded a river twice and tramped across a mountain before pitching into unsuspecting Federals, who scampered off the field. The Union army rallied, however, because droves of hungry Confederates pillaged the abandoned Northern camps. Gordon's inability to control his men at Cedar Creek outraged Early. Their relationship, always stormy, erupted into open hostility over the incident, and their bitterness toward each other lingered into the postwar years.

Gordon returned to the defenses of Richmond in December 1864 at the head of the II Corps, but he never received promotion to lieutenant general. Nevertheless, Lee considered him one of his most trusted subordinates, and assigned Gordon the critical task of defending the Southside Railroad. Lee also selected Gordon to oversee the army's final offensive movement against Grant—the attack against Fort Stedman on March 25, 1865. The plan was well conceived but poorly executed. Still, as one Confederate wrote: "A great compliment was paid Gen. Gordon in selecting him to command this assault." Gordon played a prominent role during the retreat to

A far more striking standing pose of the gallant general, showing the slouch hat he preferred to the regulation kepi. (Cook Collection, Valentine Museum, Richmond, Va.)

The lines in his face suggest that Gordon posed for this image late in the war. (National Archives)

Appomattox, including April 12, when he rode at the head of the Confederate column at the formal surrender ceremony.

Gordon's postwar career was as successful as his life in the military. Serving two and a half terms in the United States Senate (1873–80 and 1891–97) and one term as governor of Georgia (1886–90), Gordon advocated home rule and furthered white interests. He also developed a number of business interests before retiring in 1897. He then embarked on a speaking schedule as well as accepting the post of commander-in-chief of the United Confederate Veterans. In 1903, he published *Reminiscences of the Civil War*. Dripping with romanticism and full of half-truths, Gordon's recollections reflect his desire to foster harmonious relations between the two sections. Gordon died on January 9, 1904, in Miami, and was buried in Oakland Cemetery, Atlanta.

Peter S. Carmichael

Eckert, Ralph Lowell, *John Brown Gordon: Soldier, Southerner, American* (Baton Rouge, 1989).

Gordon, John B., *Reminiscences of the Civil War* (New York, 1903).

Tankersley, Allen P., *John B. Gordon: A Study in Gallantry* (Atlanta, 1955).

A view of the man who "...shrank from nothing in battle," a youthful-looking Gordon poses with arms crossed and the stoic look of major general on his face. (Virginia Historical Society, Richmond, Va.)

This is the determined face of the man who commanded half the Army of Northern Virginia at the end. (National Archives)

☆ *Josiah Gorgas* ☆

The only known wartime image of General Gorgas shows him as a colonel, presumably taken prior to November 1864. (Library of Congress)

On July 1, 1818, in Dauphin County, Pennsylvania, a future Confederate general was born. Josiah Gorgas matriculated at West Point's United States Military Academy in 1837 and finished sixth in his class in 1841 with a promising career ahead of him. He selected the artillery, and his first assignment was to the Ordnance Department, where he remained until his resignation in 1861. The army sent him abroad 1845–46 to study European artillery developments, and then when war with Mexico erupted, he returned to go to the land of the Montezumas. Promoted to 1st lieutenant on March 3, 1847, he was present during the siege of Vera Cruz, and thereafter commanded its ordnance depot, supplying Winfield Scott for his march on Mexico City.

After the war Gorgas went on to command a succession of U.S. ordnance arsenals and was in charge at Mt. Vernon in Alabama when he met and married the daughter of a former governor in December 1853. This liaison with a prominent Southern family probably explains his later decision to abandon his Northern heritage and side with the Confederacy, as it did with several other "Yankee" Confederates like John C. Pemberton and Samuel Cooper. Gorgas gained promotion to captain in 1855, transferred briefly to Maine for a posting, then was sent to Charleston, South Carolina's arsenal until 1860.

When secession came, Gorgas was serving in his native Pennsylvania, but as soon as Fort Sumter was fired on, he submitted his resignation and moved his family back to his wife's native Alabama. From there he offered his services to the Confederacy. President Jefferson Davis immediately made him chief of the

Ordnance Department, with the rank of major, and Gorgas would hold that position for the rest of the war.

All of Gorgas' prewar experience in the Old Army came into play as he performed his primary duty of equipping the soldiers, cavalrymen, and artillerymen of the South. At once he recognized that the Confederacy's manufacturing capabilities were too limited for its needs, and that most of its arms would have to come from abroad. He sent purchasing agents to England to buy rifles, cannon, ammunition, and all the other attendant equipment necessary, paying with cotton and tobacco when he had no money. At the same time he quickly took advantage of the arms captured when many U.S. arsenals fell into Southern hands, and especially made use of any manufacturing machinery left behind undamaged or repairable. He established new arsenals like those at Augusta and Selma, and let contracts to private firms like Quinby and Robinson, Griswold and Gunnison, and more, to make both cannon and small arms. Most particularly Gorgas worked with Richmond's Tredegar Iron Works to help make it the Confederacy's most important manufacturer of cannon, projectiles, and armor for ironclads, among other material.

Meanwhile Gorgas also turned his tireless energies to the limited mineral resources of the Confederacy. He operated lead mines like those at Wytheville, Virginia; mined copper for percussion caps and fuses; and oversaw manufacture of gunpowder, even sanctioning a program to collect "chamber lye"—human urine—for making saltpeter.

To bring his foreign purchases to the Confederacy, Gorgas bought a small fleet of blockade runners and thus became one of the most frequent and active supporters of the campaign to break the blockade. He created the Bureau of Foreign Supply to handle his imports and fathered more bureaus to deal with his domestic operations, such as the Bureau of Niter and Mining. Furthermore, he ran an efficient department within the War Department and managed to maintain good relations with a succession of secretaries of war, though privately he complained of almost all of them, especially James A. Sedden. Indeed, if Gorgas had a failing, it was that he was an habitual carper, finding fault in almost everyone, though the conditions of paucity and hardship under which he worked surely justified a less than cheerful attitude. He also wrote treatises advising commanders on how best to utilize the siege guns sent to their forts, and made an excellent impression on the field commanders of the Confederacy, few of whom ever really had to complain of inadequate arms. General Joseph E. Johnston supposedly declared that Gorgas "created the ordnance department out of nothing," and ran it wonderfully, an opinion he might have altered had he known how bitterly Gorgas criticized his generalship.

Davis, too, was impressed, and on November 19, 1864, signaled his approval by appointing him a brigadier general, Gorgas having already risen in rank to colonel. The Senate confirmed the promotion the same day, to rank from November 10. Gorgas was in Richmond when it fell in 1865 and accompanied the government for a time on its retreat, but left it at Charlotte, North Carolina, before the last secretary of war formally disbanded the War Department.

Gorgas went back to Alabama. Before long he continued his wartime occupation by taking the superintendency of the Briarfield Iron Works. In later years he turned to education, first becoming headmaster of the University of the South at Sewannee, Tennessee, and later its vice-chancellor in 1868. Two years later he took the presidency of the University of Alabama at Tuscaloosa, but failing health forced him to give up the post before long. For the rest of his years there he acted as university librarian, and on May 15, 1883, he died, aged sixty four. He was buried in Tuscaloosa.

No one has ever estimated Gorgas' contribution to the Confederacy as anything less than enormous. Stepping into a seemingly impossible task, he performed it so efficiently that at the end the Confederacy had no shortage of ordnance, only of men to use it all. As his biographer has aptly proclaimed, he literally "beat plowshares into swords," and materially influenced the longevity of the Confederacy.

William C. Davis

Evans, Clement A., *Civil History of the Confederate States*, Vol. I in Evans, *Confederate Military History*.

Vandiver, Frank E., *Plowshares into Swords: Josiah Gorgas and Confederate Ordnance* (Austin, 1952).

An outstanding previously unpublished portrait of General Govan made during the last half of the war. (Alabama Department of Archives and History, Montgomery, Ala.)

✳ *Daniel Chevilette Govan* ✳

Govan's rank is difficult to determine from the limited portion of uniform showing in this image, but he is probably a brigadier. (U.S. Army Military History Institute, Carlisle, Pa.)

Govan was born on July 4, 1829, in Northampton County, North Carolina, the son of Andrew Robison and Mary Pugh (Jones) Govan. The father, a South Carolinian, had represented his native state in the U.S. House of Representatives from 1822 to 1827. The family did not remain in North Carolina long, moving to Somerville, in West Tennessee, the year after Daniel's birth. In 1832 the Govans, following the Chickasaw Cession, headed south and settled in Marshall County, Mississippi. Daniel spent his youth on his family's "Snowdown" plantation, received his secondary education from a family tutor, and traveled east to matriculate at the University of South Carolina. He was a member of the class of 1848 but left Columbia before graduating.

In his twentieth year, Govan joined kinsman Benjamin McCulloch and others and headed for the California gold fields, traveling overland via the Southern route. McCulloch was elected sheriff of Sacramento County in 1850 and he selected the twenty-one-year-old Govan as a deputy. Govan returned to Mississippi two years later and became a planter. In December 1853 he married Mary F. Otey, daughter of James H. Otey, Tennessee's first Episcopal bishop. Soon thereafter the newlyweds crossed the Mississippi River and established a plantation in that section of Phillips County, Arkansas, that in 1873 was incorporated into Lee County.

In the hectic days of 1861 following the surrender of Fort Sumter and President Abraham Lincoln's call for seventy-five thousand volunteers, Govan raised a company of volunteers and was ordered into camp at Hopefield, Arkansas. Govan was elected captain and on June 5, 1861, his unit was mustered into Confederate service as Company F, 2d Arkansas Volunteer Infantry, Colonel Thomas C. Hindman commanding. Govan and his company accompanied the regiment to Memphis, then to Fort Randolph, and finally to Columbus, Kentucky. Mid-December found the regiment posted at Bowling Green, where on the 17th Captain Govan first saw combat near Rowlett's Station.

On January 28, 1862, Govan was promoted colonel, to rank from January 6, and commanded the 2d Arkansas on the long retreat from Bowling Green to Corinth, Mississippi. He led his regiment, a unit in Colonel R. G. Shaver's brigade, into the Shiloh holocaust. Physically exhausted by the flu, he was unable to take the field on the battle's second day—April 7. Even so, Colonel Shaver reported that the 2d and 7th Arkansas "both did good, effective service, and were well fought by their respective commanders."

Brigadier General St. John R. L. Liddell replaced Colonel Shaver as brigade commander, and it was to him that Govan looked for orders during the Kentucky Campaign, August to October 1862, and at the Battle of Perryville, October 8. Upon the return from Kentucky, Liddell's brigade was assigned to the division led by hard-fighting Major General Patrick R. Cleburne. Govan and his 2d Arkansas were in the forefront of the Confederate surge toward the Nashville Pike during the initial phase of the December 31 fighting at Stone's River. Govan and his regiment more than held their own in the following months, blunting the advance of the Union XX Corps through Liberty Gap, on June 25 and 26, 1863, before Federal successes at Hoover's Gap compelled Cleburne to break contact with the enemy and retreat to Tullahoma and beyond.

In late August 1863, General Braxton Bragg reorganized his army. General Liddell was placed in charge of a two-brigade division consisting of his old brigade, led by Colonel Govan, and Brigadier General Edward C. Walthall's Mississippi Brigade. Govan, at Chickamauga September 18–21, got his first experience commanding a brigade in a great and terrible struggle. Subsequent to the battle, Liddell wrote: "To my two brigade commanders...I am greatly indebted to their prompt co-operation in every movement and quick apprehension of the constantly recurring necessities that arise on the battlefield. I know of no more gallant soldiers, and feel honored by the command of such officers."

Liddell's division was broken up in October, and the Arkansas brigade again became part of Cleburne's

command. With Liddell again leading the brigade, Govan as before commanded the 2d Arkansas. In mid-November, Liddell went on leave and Govan fought the brigade at Missionary Ridge on the 25th and at Ringgold Gap on the 27th. After the Ringgold Gap battle, in which his division had savaged Major General Joseph Hooker's veterans, Cleburne, commending Govan and three fellow brigade commanders, wrote, "Four better officers are not in the service of the Confederacy."

On February 5, 1864, Govan was made brigadier general, to rank from December 29, 1863, and assigned command of the Arkansas brigade, which he had led at Chickamauga, Missionary Ridge, and Ringgold Gap. Liddell was transferred to duty in the Trans-Mississippi Department. Govan and his brigade, like all units in Cleburne's division, saw bitter fighting in the Atlanta Campaign (May 1–September 2, 1864). On May 14 Govan's troops repulsed a Union thrust at Resaca; at Pickett's Mill on the 27th they savaged Major General Oliver O. Howard's IV Corps; and on June 27 they held the Cheatham Hill rifle-pits north of the Dead Angle. Govan was in the forefront of the Confederate onslaught on July 22 at the Battle of Atlanta, when for several hours Lieutenant General William J. Hardee's corps surged ahead. Govan claimed the capture of seven hundred Yankees, many of them from the 16th Iowa, in the first charge and reported that when the tide turned, his men "brought off 8 pieces of artillery, several wagons loaded with ammunition and with intrenching tools." The cost had been terrible. Out of the one thousand men Govan took into the fight, one-half were casualties. (Govan was invited to attend a reunion of the 16th Iowa, September 26–27, 1883, and on doing so, he returned to the regiment its colors.)

September 1 was also a terrible day for Govan and his Arkansans. Having been rushed to Jonesborough on August 31, his troops and the Orphan Brigade held a salient angle in the Confederate line. After beating off one attack, they were overwhelmed by a second onslaught, and Govan and some six hundred of his men and eight cannon were captured by Union Brigadier General Jefferson Davis' bluecoats. Govan remained a prisoner for three weeks, being exchanged at Rough and Ready, Georgia, for Major General George Stoneman.

Govan rejoined his brigade and participated in General John B. Hood's ill-fated Tennessee Campaign,

November 29–December 27, 1864. He was with Cleburne at Spring Hill; in the charge at Franklin, in which six Confederate generals, including Cleburne, were killed or mortally wounded; and he himself was wounded at Nashville on December 16. By early April 1865 he had recuperated and rejoined the Army of Tennessee, then camped in and around Greensboro, North Carolina, and assumed command of his Arkansas brigade, which, because of its losses, had been consolidated with the Texas Brigade. He was surrendered by General Joseph E. Johnston on April 26 and on May 1 was paroled at Greensboro.

Govan returned from the war to Arkansas and resumed life as a planter near Marianna. In 1878 he authored a "Brief History of Cleburne's Division," which was finally published in 1911 as an article in the first volume of Fay Hempstead's *Historical Review of Arkansas.*

He left the plantation in 1894 when he was named by President Grover Cleveland to be an agent for the Tulalip Indian Agency, located at Tulalip in the state of Washington. Mrs. Govan died in 1896, the year before a change in administration, and the operations of the spoils system ended Govan's federal service.

The widowed general moved to Tennessee in 1898 and resided in that state and in Mississippi, with one or another of his fourteen children and their spouses, until his death in Memphis on March 12, 1911. On learning of his death, his former comrade-in-arms, Captain Irving A. Buck, wrote, "I regard him as one of the best soldiers it was my good fortune to know—a true Christian gentleman, a noble patriot, a loyal and uncompromising friend." Govan was buried in Holly Springs, Mississippi.

Edwin C. Bearss

Buck, Irving, *Cleburne and His Command* (New York, 1908).

Harrell, John M., *Arkansas,* Vol. X in Evans, *Confederate Military History.*

Memphis, *Commercial Appeal,* March 13, 1911.

Surely the finest of the portraits of General Gracie, made after November 1862, is this ambrotype. (Museum of the Confederacy, Richmond, Va.)

✳ *Archibald Gracie, Jr.* ✳

The Confederacy produced many a "hard luck" general, and the son and namesake of prominent New Yorker Archibald Gracie proved to be one of them. Born December 1, 1832, in New York City, he appeared at first to have many advantages. As a youth he was sent to Germany for studies at Heidelberg. Following his return to the United States, his family connections garnered for him an appointment to the United States Military Academy at West Point, which he entered in 1854. Archibald Gracie, Jr., graduated fourteenth in a class of forty-six in 1854 and then served the next two years in frontier duty, never rising above 2d lieutenant during his short tenure. He resigned in 1856 to join his father, who had moved to Alabama to open a mercantile business in Mobile. Futher cementing his newfound status as a Southerner, Gracie that same year married a woman from Virginia, a daughter of Richmond's prominent Mayo family. He also joined the Washington Light Infantry, a local militia company in Mobile, and thus all the usual elements were in place for turning a native Yankee into a Confederate general. It only needed the coming of the war.

With the secession crisis looming and South Carolina already out of the Union, Captain Gracie of the militia received orders from Alabama's governor to seize the Mt. Vernon Arsenal near Mobile, which he did on January 4, 1861, a week before Alabama's secession. Almost immediately afterward Gracie and his company affiliated with the newly forming 3d Alabama Infantry, but on July 12 he received a commission as major of the new 11th Alabama. It was a wrenching time for young Gracie, for when the crisis came and war broke out, his father and the rest of his paternal family returned to New York, their allegiance to the Union unwavering. Nevertheless, for the few years remaining to him Major Gracie's long-distance relations with his family were unchanged.

That fall Gracie and his regiment were assigned to Colonel Cadmus Wilcox in the Potomac District commanded by General P. G. T. Beauregard, seeing no

action of any substance in the months of "phony war" that followed First Manassas (July 21, 1861). That winter, however, he was called back to Mobile, where he helped raise a new outfit of which he was elected colonel. At first it was simply called "Gracie's Regiment" when attached to Brigadier General Samuel Jones' army of Mobile, and consisted of a mere 296 men and officers in March 1862. When raised to more strength, it became the 43d Alabama. Later that spring Gracie and his regiment were ordered to the Department of East Tennessee, where they were brigades with regiments from Tennessee and Georgia under command of Brigadier General Danville Leadbetter in Brigadier General Kirby Smith's small army. By August Gracie had risen to temporary command of a brigade, and led this command with Smith on the invasion of Kentucky. When the Confederates captured Lexington in September, Gracie briefly had command of the post there, and about this time also his command of the brigade composed of his own regiment; the 55th Georgia; the 58th, 62d, and 64th North Carolina; and a battery became permanent.

Recognizing Gracie's new position, the Confederate president appointed him a brigadier general on November 4, 1862, to rank from that same date, and Gracie accepted the appointment six days later. For a time that fall Gracie commanded the garrison at Cumberland Gap, and then held the position permanently throughout the spring and summer of 1863, his commander Major General Simon B. Buckner reporting that his was the only brigade in the department in a good condition. There was much jockeying about for position in eastern Tennessee during the summer, and Gracie's brigade changed in composition, being given the 1st, 2d, 3d, and 4th battalions of the Alabama Legion, a Kentucky battalion, the 63d Tennessee, and other assorted squadrons of cavalry and two batteries.

In the fall Gracie led most of this command into a new division commanded by Brigadier General William Preston, to join Buckner's Corps for the Chickamauga Campaign, August–September 1863. At

Chickamauga Gracie's brigade fought gallantly, suffering severe casualties. Then Gracie himself fell with a serious wound on December 14 in the later East Tennessee operations culminating in the battle at Bean's Station. Leading barely more than seven hundred and fifty men in a division commanded by Brigadier General Bushrod Johnson, Gracie took a rifle ball in his arm early in the action but went back into the field after having the wound hastily dressed.

Following his recovery Gracie went east with Johnson in the spring of 1864, joining Beauregard's command on the south side of the James River. There he was heavily engaged in the May 16 fight at Drewry's Bluff, his brigade's performance putting to the lie earlier charges that his command was riddled with traitors and members of a South Carolina "peace society." Thereafter Gracie served continually in the ensuing Petersburg Campaign (June 15, 1864–April 3, 1865), first at Bermuda Hundred, then on the north bank of the Appomattox at Fort Clinton, and by August in the Petersburg trenches themselves. Much of that month he spent in supervising boring of countershafts to locate suspected Federal tunnels and mines. Gracie temporarily commanded Johnson's division August through December but had little to do other than observe the continual sharpshooting and shelling, and report the tedium of siege life to headquarters almost every day. Gracie himself seems to have spent much time observing firsthand the enemy firing, and in the end this was his undoing. On December 2 he was peering through a field glass at the Yankee works during the usual shelling when the explosion of a shell nearby killed him instantly. After the war his remains were moved to Woodlawn Cemetery in New York City.

Gracie had been competent and capable, a good commander in his one and only pitched battle, Chickamauga, and a satisfactory subordinate to a number of difficult commanders. But fate never gave him a field on which to really test his merits.

William C. Davis

Trudeau, Noah, *The Last Citadel* (New York, 1991).

Tucker, Glenn, *Chickamauga, Bloody Battle in the West* (Indianapolis, 1964).

The more commonly known portrait of Gracie, also as a brigadier. (Medford Historical Society, Medford, Mass.)

☆ *Hiram Bronson Granbury* ☆

This is probably not a uniformed portrait of Granbury, but it is just possible that it is. In any case, no other definite uniformed image has come to light thus far. (Courtesy of Lawrence T. Jones)

On March 1, 1831, Hiram Bronson Granbury was born in Copiah County, Mississippi. Educated at Oakland College in Rodney, Mississippi, he moved to Waco, Texas, in the early 1850s. After studying law and gaining admission to the bar, he quickly secured a place of prominence in the local society. From 1856 to 1858, Granbury served as chief justice of McLennan County, an office apparently comparable to that of chairman of a county board of supervisors.

Following the secession of Texas, Granbury organized the Waco Guards. He took the company east of the Mississippi River, where it joined with nine others to form the 7th Texas Infantry Regiment. In October 1861 the men of the 7th elected Granbury their major. The regiment served in Kentucky and Tennessee prior to joining the garrison at Fort Donelson. For his role in the attempt to break through the encircling Union lines at Fort Donelson, Granbury's brigade commander, Colonel John M. Simonton, singled Granbury out from among the officers of the 7th as being among those officers of Simonton's command who "won for themselves the confidence of their command and are entitled to the highest commendation of their countrymen." Granbury's regimental commander and future Confederate brigadier, Colonel John Gregg, reported: "I must acknowledge the very efficient assistance of Major Granbury in the management of the regiment throughout the entire day."

Although captured at Fort Donelson in February 1862, Granbury was soon exchanged and on August 29 of that year was promoted to colonel of the regiment. The regiment served briefly in northern Mississippi before being transferred to the garrison at Port Hudson, where in early January it formed part of Brigadier General John Gregg's brigade. The 7th participated in the defense of the bastion on March 14, 1863, when Rear Admiral David Glasgow Farragut attempted to steam seven vessels past the Confederate guns which lined the bluff. On April 28 Granbury's regiment departed for Woodville, Mississippi, to intercept Colonel Benjamin Grierson's Illinois cavalrymen on their raid through Mississippi.

Immediately following that unsuccessful venture, the 7th rejoined Gregg's brigade and hastened to

Mississippi to counter Major General Ulysses S. Grant's crossing of the Mississippi River below Vicksburg. The 7th participated in the Battle of Raymond in mid-May before it joined the Confederate host being gathered in the vicinity of Jackson by General Joseph E. Johnston to relieve the besieged garrison of Vicksburg. Remaining in Gregg's brigade, the 7th formed part of Major General William H. T. Walker's division, which fought at Jackson and maneuvered about central Mississippi for the remainder of the summer.

Transferred to Georgia in September, Gregg's brigade formed part of Brigadier General Bushrod R. Johnson's provisional division of Major General Simon B. Buckner's corps during the Battle of Chickamauga. Although severely wounded in that engagement, Granbury remained with his regiment, which on November 12 found itself reassigned to an all-Texas brigade formed for the newly commissioned Brigadier General James A. Smith.

When Smith sustained a wound at the outset of the Union assault upon Missionary Ridge, Granbury assumed command of the brigade. In his report of the battle, Cleburne commented: "To Brigadier-Generals Smith, Cumming, and Maney, and Colonel Granbury, I return my thanks for the able manner in which they managed their commands." In a subsequent report which detailed his efforts to cover the Confederate withdrawal from Missionary Ridge, Cleburne wrote: "To Brigadier-Generals Polk and Lowry, and Colonels Govan and Granbury I must return my thanks. Four better officers are not in the service of the Confederacy." Their performance resulted in the Confederate Congress' passage of a joint resolution of thanks to "...Cleburne, and the officers and men under his command, for the victory obtained by them over superior forces of the enemy at Ringgold Gap...,by which the advance of the enemy was impeded, our wagon train and most of our artillery saved, and a large number of the enemy killed and wounded." For two hours Granbury had had his men prepared to make a bayonet charge to halt the pursuing enemy, but this action proved unnecessary.

Granbury's failure to endorse Cleburne's proposition for arming the slaves on January 2, 1864, undoubtedly had some influence on his confirmation as permanent brigade commander. Appointed brigadier general on March 5, to rank from February 29, 1864, he commanded the 6th, 7th, 10th, 15th, 17th, 19th, 24th, and 25th Texas infantry regiments. In mid-February 1864

Granbury's brigade was ordered to Mississippi to assist Lieutenant General Leonidas Polk in his attempt to prevent the Federals from completely overrunning that state. Halted in Alabama, the brigade rejoined the Army of Tennessee near Dug Gap, Georgia, during the last week of February and remained with it throughout the Atlanta Campaign, May 1–September 2.

On May 8 Granbury's Texans decisively repulsed a Union assault against Dug Gap. Between May 7 and May 20 during the withdrawal of the Army of Tennessee to the Etowah River, Granbury's brigade had two men killed and twenty-two wounded, less than any other brigade in its division or corps. Lieutenant General John Bell Hood reported that the fighting near New Hope Church on May 27 ended when "about 10 o'clock at night Brigadier-General Granbury, with his brigade of Texans, made a dashing charge on the enemy, driving them from the field, their killed and wounded being left in our hands." Major General Joseph Wheeler reported that Granbury was the only brigade commander who managed to get his infantrymen into position to make the final assault, concluding, "The difficulty of maneuvering so thin a line in a thick woods under a heavy fire will be appreciated." The Texans lost 33 men killed and 114 wounded in the engagement. Before the campaign ended, Granbury's brigade participated in the fortification and siege of Atlanta and fought in the battles of Peach Tree Creek and Jonesborough.

Following that engagement and the abandonment of Atlanta, Granbury and his brigade participated in Hood's invasion of Tennessee. On November 30 at the Battle of Franklin, Granbury and five other Confederate generals died in a futile assault. Like Cleburne, Granbury fell within a few rods of the Union breastworks. Initially buried at nearby Columbia, Tennessee, Granbury was reinterred twenty-nine years later at Granbury, Texas, a town named in his honor.

His surname is often misrepresented as Granberry, which is the way it was inscribed on his original tombstone in Columbia.

Lawrence L. Hewitt

Faust, Patricia L., ed., *Historical Times Illustrated Encyclopedia of the Civil War* (New York, 1986).

Hewitt, Lawrence Lee, *Port Hudson, Confederate Bastion on the Mississippi* (Baton Rouge and London, 1987).

⋆ *Henry Gray* ⋆

Gray was born on January 19, 1816, in Laurens District, South Carolina. He graduated in 1834 from South Carolina College, now the University of South Carolina. Gray studied law and was admitted to the bar. In the 1840s, he moved to Winston County, Mississippi, and practiced law there. He served as district attorney for several terms and then as a state legislator for one term. Gray ran for Congress in 1848 as a Whig but lost the election. During his years in Mississippi, he became friends with Jefferson Davis and Seargeant S. Prentiss. Gray moved to Bienville Parish, Louisiana, in 1851 and soon became a leading attorney in the northern part of that state. He changed his party affiliation to the Democrats and was elected to the legislature. Judah P. Benjamin beat Gray by one vote in the legislative balloting for United States senator in 1859.

When the Civil War began, Gray enlisted as a private in a Mississippi regiment. President Davis persuaded him to return to Louisiana to organize an infantry regiment. He organized the 28th Louisiana Infantry at Monroe and received his commission as its colonel on May 17, 1862. The regiment trained for several months in various camps in north Louisiana and received orders in November to join Major General Richard Taylor's army on Bayou Teche in the southern part of the state. There Gray's men became a part of the brigade commanded by Brigadier General Alfred Mouton.

The 28th Louisiana occupied Camp Bisland near Centerville and helped to construct earthwork fortifications there. A detachment of the regiment assisted in the capture of the Union gunboat *Diana* on the Atchafalaya River on March 28, 1863. During the fighting at Fort Bisland April 12–13, Gray's men held a position on the west side of Bayou Teche and assisted in repelling several enemy attacks. Gray led his men in the Confederate victory at the battle of Irish Bend on April 14. Taylor praised Gray's men for their "excellent discipline" during these actions, saying "no veteran soldiers could have excelled them in their conduct."

Gray assumed command of Mouton's brigade about April 15, when Taylor placed the latter officer in charge of the forces south of Red River. Gray continued to lead the brigade until he left the army next fall. A staff officer in the brigade wrote that Gray usually wore plain clothing during the Louisiana campaigns: "He was averse to everything in the way of display and always grumbled when he was required to make his appearance in full uniform."

The brigade participated in the various marches of Taylor's army in south Louisiana during the summer and fall of 1863 but saw little serious fighting. On at least one occasion Gray temporarily gave up his brigade command to serve on court-martial duty. He led his brigade and Colonel Joseph W. Speight's in a brief campaign along the upper Atchafalaya River in September 1863. The men assisted Brigadier General Tom Green's Texas cavalry in destroying a small Union force in the battle of Stirling's Plantation on

No photograph of General Gray can be found, and this pencil sketch is of unknown origin and date. (Warner, *Generals in Gray*)

September 29. In November Gray's brigade became part of Mouton's infantry division. For several months the men occupied camps near Monroe while acting as a supporting force of soldiers crossing weapons from east of the Mississippi River.

The brigade marched to Alexandria early in 1864 and served in the Red River Campaign, March to May. He led his brigade bravely in the Battle of Mansfield on April 8 and came through the contest unhurt, even though all three of his regimental commanders were killed. Because of its heavy losses on that day, Gray's brigade formed the army's reserve during the Battle of Pleasant Hill on April 9. However, Gray did briefly lead one of his regiments into action. Taylor recommended Gray and a number of his other colonels for promotion following these two battles. General Edmund Kirby Smith delayed Gray's appointment, saying, "His habits, I understand, are not good." Taylor again recommended Gray's promotion, and Kirby Smith appointed him as brigadier general on April 15 (several days after his other appointments) to take effect from April 8. The Confederate congress did not approve the promotion until March 17, 1865, after Davis formally approved Gray, effective May 17.

Gray again led his brigade in the engagement at Yellow Bayou on May 18, 1864. He exercised temporary division command on a few occasions during the next several months while his superior, Brigadier General Camille J. Prince de Polignac, was absent on various duties. The division marched into north Louisiana that fall in anticipation of receiving orders to cross to the east side of the Mississippi River. When this plan failed, Kirby Smith ordered the division into southern Arkansas to help defend that state while Major General Sterling Price led an invasion of Missouri.

Louisiana Governor Henry W. Allen called a special election to fill a vacancy in the Confederate Congress caused by the death of Benjamin L. Hodge. On October 17, 1864, Gray was elected to represent the 5th District, defeating John L. Lewis (a former volunteer aide of Gray's) by a vote of 1,078 to 233. This election has been seen as a repudiation of Kirby Smith, whose actions Lewis supported. Several writers have stated that Gray was an "involuntary candidate" or that he was elected "without his knowledge," but the diary of one of his staff officers shows these allegations to be incorrect. Gray left his brigade at Camden, Arkansas, on October 31 and took his place in Congress on December 28.

In assessing him as a commander, one of Gray's subordinate officers wrote that while he "was not famous for his expertness as a commander of troops [he]…was brave and fearless as a lion." This same soldier praised Gray as "kind, careful of his soldiers, [and] attentive to their wants." One author has described Gray's time in Congress: "During his brief congressional service Gray opposed any sort of peace negotiation and voted in favor of every desperation measure proposed."

After the war, he served one term in the Louisiana Senate. Gray's only son died in 1864, and his wife died later. These two events were said to have caused him to go into seclusion after his senate term ended. Gray died at the home of his daughter in Coushatta, Louisiana, on December 11, 1892, and he was buried in Springville Cemetery there.

Arthur W. Bergeron, Jr.

Bergeron, Arthur W., Jr., ed., *Reminiscences of Uncle Silas: A History of the Eighteenth Louisiana Infantry* (Baton Rouge, 1981).

Dimitry, John, *Louisiana*, Vol. X in Evans, *Confederate Military History*.

Warner, Ezra J., and Yearns, W. Buck, *Biographical Register of the Confederate Congress* (Baton Rouge, 1975).

⋆ *John Breckinridge Grayson* ⋆

For over a century no portrait of Grayson in uniform was known. This one appears to show him as a colonel, but the only Confederate rank he ever held was brigadier, so Grayson must have been careless about his insignia, like so many others. It was made between August and October 1861, probably in Florida. (Collection of State Historical Museum/Mississippi; Department of Archives and History)

There were many "hard luck" generals in the Confederate army, but few whose story is sadder than of this able and well-loved Kentuckian. John Breckinridge Grayson was born on October 18, 1806, at "Cabell's Dale," outside Lexington, Kentucky. It was the home of John Breckinridge, attorney general for Thomas Jefferson, and scion of the family that helped to dominate Bluegrass politics for more than a century. One of Grayson's cousins, who would grow up at Cabell's Dale, was John C. Breckinridge.

In 1822 young Grayson entered the United States Military Academy, graduating four years later right in the middle of his class, twenty-second out of forty-one cadets. A fellow graduate was Albert Sidney Johnston, and just two years behind Grayson was another native Kentuckian, Jefferson Davis.

Grayson would spend the next thirty-five years in the army at a succession of frontier posts. He was first commissioned a 2d lieutenant in the 2d Artillery and assigned to Fort Monroe, Virginia. In the 1830s he moved to a number of Southern forts and arsenals, then in 1835 took part in the Seminole War in Florida. For ten years afterward he served at New Orleans as a commissary until the war with Mexico erupted. By now he was a captain, and Winfield Scott made Grayson his chief commissariat during the campaign that led to the battles at Vera Cruz, Churubusco, Cerro Gordo, Molino del Rey, and more. Grayson was breveted major for his performance at Contreras and Churubusco, and lieutenant colonel for Chapultepec.

When peace came, Grayson resumed his commissariat duties, this time at Detroit, until 1855, and then in the New Mexico Territory through 1861. While in the latter post, and no doubt encouraged by the abundant idle time that officers at frontier posts found on their hands, Grayson became an active organizer of the Historical Society of New Mexico, serving as well on the society's committees for botany, and meteorology and climatology. At its organization he became its first president.

But other organizations beckoned to Grayson. Even though Kentucky did not secede from the Union in 1861, the sectional crisis pulled at his sympathies as it did with others of his family. On July 1, 1861, just as he was promoted to major and commissary of subsistence, he resigned his commission and made the long overland journey to the new Confederacy.

general was "nearly spent with consumption," so much so that he had expected him to fall dead in his presence on September 25. Others about him later believed that Grayson was "rendered *non compos mentis* by disease" and "could not have been responsible for any act that he might have done." Governor John Milton tried to intervene to prevent Grayson from being called upon for any decisions, as he soon became confined to a sickbed in Tallahassee.

By October 9 word had reached Richmond that Grayson was gravely ill, and the War Department ordered Brigadier General E. Kirby Smith to rush to Florida to assume to command. On October 18 Milton informed

Just when Grayson reached his destination is uncertain, but his old classmate Jefferson Davis was waiting for him. The President commissioned Grayson a brigadier general on August 15, 1861, to rank from that same date, and Grayson formally accepted his commission five days later. The next day, August 21, the War Department assigned Grayson to command of the Department of Middle and Eastern Florida, with headquarters at Fernandina. When he arrived on September 4, Grayson found the state in a deplorable condition. Immediately he commenced pulling down and reerecting defensive batteries guarding the harbor at Fernandina, then he started a tour of his command on September 14 to inspect conditions elsewhere. He warned Richmond in advance that Florida "will become a Yankee province unless measures for her relief are promptly made."

Unfortunately Grayson's health was soon to collapse, and may already have been poor when he took his command. When his tour took him to Apalachicola in late September, men there were worried by seeing him in "such an enfeebled state of health and constitution as almost to forbid hope of amendment." When Grayson met an old friend in Tallahassee, the friend reported on October 1 that the

Davis that "General Grayson is in a dying condition," and three days later, October 21, the general was dead. His son later had his body moved to New Orleans, where it now rests in St. Louis Cemetery No. 1. Whatever Grayson might have been to the Confederacy was destined to remain a mystery, for in his only month of active command, he was too ill to do anything but die.

William C. Davis

"Historical Society Minutes, 1859–1863," *New Mexico Historical Review*, XVIII (July 1943).

Johnston, J. Stoddard, *Kentucky*, Vol. IX in Evans, *Confederate Military History*.

Klotter, James C, *The Breckinridges of Kentucky* (Lexington, 1962).

This earlier portrait of Grayson cannot be dated exactly, though it shows him as a lieutenant colonel by brevet, and was taken in 1860 or 1861 in New Mexico. Grayson probably wore this uniform on the day of his resignation in 1861, and perhaps for a time afterward. (Museum of New Mexico, Santa Fe, N.M.)

⋆ Martin Edwin Green ⋆

The only known image of Martin Green in uniform is too indistinct for his rank or time of sitting to be determined. (Albert G. Shaw Collection, Virginia Historical Society, Richmond, Va.)

Martin E. Green was born in Fauquier County, Virginia, on June 3, 1815. In the 1830s he moved west, eventually settling in Lewis County, Missouri, where he and his brothers began a sawmill business. His brother, James Stephen Green, served as a United States senator.

When the Civil War began, Martin Green organized a military company of cavalry in northeast Missouri and eventually joined Sterling Price's army in the southwestern part of the state. He was elected colonel of the regiment and was present at the capture of Lexington. At Lexington a Missourian wrote that on one occasion Green, having no cannon balls, charged his guns with "gravel and rock."

When Brigadier General Thomas A. Harris won election to the Confederate Congress, Green took command of his division, and in a vote on December 2, 1861, officially won the position. He fought at Pea Ridge, where he commanded the 2d Division, Missouri State Guard. He was ordered to defend the crossroads northeast of Camp Stephens, and detailed to bring the baggage train to the army. Green reported that on March 8 when "within 1 mile of the battle ground on Saturday morning I met my messenger, bringing an order to return with the baggage to Elm Springs and there await further orders, unless hard pressed by the enemy, in which event I was authorized to continue the march south." On March 9 he turned over the baggage and was ordered to move the ammunition up but was forced to turn back. By the time he was able to get the ammunition to the army, it had retreated; he joined it at Walnut Grove.

On April 15, 1862, while at Des Arc, Arkansas, Green received orders to proceed to Memphis to report to

Sterling Price. He crossed the Mississippi River and picked up command of the 3d Brigade, Price's division, Army of the West. On July 23, 1862, Green was promoted to brigadier general, to rank from July 21, 1862; Sterling Price had recommended the promotion on March 19.

Green took part in the battle of Corinth, October 3–4, 1862, and at Hatchie Bridge, October 5. When General Louis Hébert was unable to take the field because of illness, the command of the division fell to Green. There had been plans to resume the attack at daylight but Hébert reported sick at 7:00 and precious time was lost in the change in command—Green was unable to put his division in motion until 9:00.

On October 20 and 22 the Army of the West was reorganized. General John S. Bowen was placed in charge of a two-brigade division with the 1st Brigade under Green. At Port Gibson, on May 1 when the battle began, John McClernand's corps clashed with Green's pickets. Green reported that his force did not exceed eight hundred men, and after being reinforced by the 23d Alabama did not number more than eleven hundred. Bowen reported after Port Gibson that "General Green's handsome repulse of the enemy's advance guard the night before the battle is worthy of special commendation."

Green took part in the fighting at Big Black River Bridge, and Champion's Hill, Mississippi, in mid-May 1863. At Champion's Hill May 16, he was left fighting the Federals when almost all others had been driven back. Green contested "every step of the enemy's advance and declared he never would have been driven back but for the fact that he had not a cartridge left." There was a problem at Big Black, and on June 24 Bowen told Green to file a report to let Pemberton know that the brigade was not the first to leave the trenches. "This should come from you," Bowen wrote, because Pemberton was equally interested "in wiping off this unmerited reproach upon the fair fame of the brave men of this division; he requests that you will set the matter right at once before events occur which may delay its rectification for a long time."

Unfortunately, three days later on June 27 Bowen reported: "General Green was shot through the head while examining the position of the enemy in front of his trenches at about 9:30 this morning. Devoted to our cause, without fear or reproach, his loss will be deeply felt by his entire command." In fact, Green had been wounded on June 25, and when the Federals had begun digging an approach in front of the trenches, Green had been unable to visit the fortifications and watch their movements on the 26th. Colonel Thomas P. Dockery reported: "On the morning of the 27th, he was in the ditches, as was his custom, reconnoitering the positions of the enemy along his front, and while looking over the parapet in front of the sap of the enemy, which was only about 60 yards distant, he was shot through the head by a sharpshooter and almost instantly killed. Here permit me to lay my humble tribute on his tomb. Missouri has lost another of her bravest champions—the South one of its ablest defenders. It was my fortune to be intimately associated with him; knew him well. He joined the army as a private soldier when the tocsin of war first sent its notes throughout the West. He served his country long and faithfully. His soldiers regarded him with that reverence due a father, and many a tear was shed at his fall. He was a pure patriot and a gallant officer, and a true Christian, divested of everything like a thirst for military flame. He acted solely from a sense of duty and right and a pure love of country, and thus inseparably entwined himself not only around the hearts of his troops, but of all who knew him."

In another account a Missouri soldier recalled that Green had been in the entrenchments nearly all the time, rarely leaving the ditches. He "was struck in the head by a musket ball and died instantly; and thus the life of this grey-haired patriot and brave chieftain was given to his country—to a cause for which he had long and devotedly struggled." Bowen died soon after, and Pemberton wrote that the two were "always faithful, zealous, and brave, they fell as became them in the discharge of their duty. General Green died with a bullet in his brain upon the lines he had so long and so gallantly defended." Unfortunately, Pemberton recorded: "Neither Brigadier General Bowen nor Green had furnished reports of the action of the Big Black previous to their death; to the former had been intrusted the defense of the *tete-de-pont*, and he had received my instructions in person; the latter had been second in command."

Green was buried in the George Marshall plot in Vicksburg's city cemetery, but the exact location of his grave is unknown. It is also impossible to determine if his body was ever transferred elsewhere.

Edwin C. Bearss

Bearss, Edwin C., *The Vicksburg Campaign* (Dayton, 1982).
Moore, John C., *Missouri*, Vol. IX in Evans, *Confederate Military History*.

✶ *Thomas Green* ✶

Tom Green was born January 8, 1814, in Amelia County, Virginia. The family moved in 1817 to Tennessee, where his father served as a justice of the Tennessee supreme court. Green attended the University of Nashville and Princeton College in Kentucky before taking up the study of law. In 1835, when he was twenty-one, he moved to Texas. He fought in the War for Texas Independence and participated in the battle at San Jacinto, where Sam Houston routed the Mexican army. As a private Green helped man the famous "Twin Sisters" in Santa Anna's defeat. In 1836 Green became assistant adjutant general of the Texas army. He was elected as a representative from Fayette County and served in the Fourth Texas Congress as well as secretary of the senate in the Sixth and Eighth congresses. Green fought in nine Indian and Mexican campaigns during the period of the Republic of Texas. In 1840 he was inspector general for the Somervell Expedition, and was a lieutenant colonel in the army when General Rafael Vasquez invaded Texas in March 1842. During the Mexican War Green served under General Zachary Taylor as captain of the 1st Texas Rifles. His company was in the regiment of John C. Hays, which during a surprise attack on Monterrey defeated Mexican cavalry and captured some artillery. In private life he served as clerk of the Texas supreme court from 1841 until the outbreak of the Civil War.

When the Civil War began Green became colonel of the 5th Texas Cavalry and took part in Henry H. Sibley's 1862 invasion of New Mexico. When Sibley became ill, he turned command over to Green, who commanded at the Battle of Valverde. Green was able to mount a successful counterattack that drove the Federals back to the safety of their stronghold, and the Confederates continued their move up the river, capturing Albuquerque and Santa Fe. At Glorieta Pass on March 28 the Texans fought a regiment of volunteers coming from Colorado. Although the

Confederates won the field, when they lost their supply train Sibley recognized that his invasion could not succeed; he did not have the means to control New Mexico, and his supplies were gone. The Confederates, with Green heading part of the troops, began a long retreat toward Texas.

After the Confederates returned to Texas, Sibley's brigade was ordered to assist John B. Magruder to retake Union-controlled Galveston. On January 1, 1863, Green led the cavalry aboard the *Bayou City* and the *Neptune*, hid his men behind cotton bales, and captured the gunboat *Harriet Lane*. A second gunboat was grounded, and the remainder of the Federal fleet evacuated under a flag of truce.

In spring 1863 Green joined Richard Taylor in Louisiana. He participated in turning back General Nathaniel Banks' march up Bayou Teche in April. After Sibley again became sick and Colonel James Reily was killed in the battle of Bisland, Green assumed command of the "Old Sibley Brigade." As a result of his performance in Louisiana, he was promoted to brigadier general on May 23, to rank from May 20, 1863.

In June Green commanded a brigade composed of the 4th, 5th, and 7th Texas Cavalry, and the Texas regiments of Phillips and Stone. During the fighting around Vicksburg and Port Hudson, Green commanded the cavalry and headed the successful mounted assault on Brashear City on June 23. Green's only serious military defeat came when he attacked a Federal post on the Mississippi, Fort Butler. In an unsuccessful attempt to seize the fort Green lost 260 men. General Taylor later wrote that "like the Irishman at Donnybrook, Green's rule was to strike an enemy whenever he saw him—a

The only known wartime portrait of Thomas E. Green appears to show him with a brigadier's buttons, though there is no insignia at all on his collar. (Albert Shaw Collection, Virginia Historical Society, Richmond, Va.)

most commendable rule in war, and covering a multitude of such small errors as the attack on Fort Butler."

After the surrender of Vicksburg and Port Hudson, Federal forces attacked the Confederate positions on the west side of the river. At Bayou La Fourche July 12–13 Green forced the Federals to retreat, losing only thirty-three to the Federal loss of 463. Throughout the summer and early fall Green continued to watch the Federal movements on the west side of the Mississippi. On September 29, 1863, he attacked a Federal outpost on the river and captured a large number of Federal troops stationed at Stirling's Plantation, near Morganza.

In October 1863 General Banks again tried to invade Texas by moving westward along Bayou Teche in southern Louisiana. Green attacked the Federal advance November 2–3 at the Fordoche and Bayou Bourbeau. This defeat was one reason Banks decided to recall his overland invasion and concentrate on other ways to subdue Texas. Richard Taylor wrote in November: "I have so frequently had occasion to commend the conduct of General Green, that I have nothing to add in his praise, except that he has surpassed my expectations, which I did not think possible. This officer has within the past few months commanded in three successful engagements—on the La Fourche, on the Fordoche, and near Opelousas—two of which were won against heavy odds. His sphere of usefulness should be enlarged by his promotion to major-general. He is now commanding a division of cavalry, and I respectfully urge that he be promoted."

When Banks tried to invade Texas by way of the Rio Grande, Green was instructed to return to Galveston and meet any Federal force landing on Matagorda Peninsula. But in March 1864 Green returned to Louisiana to stop Banks' push up the Red River. At the Battle of Mansfield on April 8 Green formed the left of Taylor's line, and the Confederates were successful in driving back the Union position. After the indecisive fight at Pleasant Hill the following day, Banks began a retreat. Green was ordered to attack the Federal fleet on the Red River in an attempt to stop its advance and keep it from providing any assistance to Banks' army. Green, accompanied by his brother-in-law, Brigadier General James P. Major, headed for the Red River to locate David D. Porter's fleet. At Blair's Landing on April 12 Green had a chance to hit some of the vessels that were struggling with low water. The monitor *Osage* was grounded in spite of Union efforts to free the vessel. Realizing his disadvantage, Green ordered the cavalry under his command to dismount and attack the fleet on foot. Commodore Thomas O. Selfridge,

aboard the *Osage*, recalled: "Then commenced one of the most curious fights of the war, 2,500 infantry against a gunboat aground." Porter maintained that the tenacity of the attacking force was the result of too much Louisiana rum, although the Texans later denied this.

During this action Green was killed. Selfridge later claimed that he had noticed an officer on a white horse about two hundred yards from the main line, and after aiming one of the guns at him, "saw him no longer. I learned after that the officer killed was their General Green." As the Confederates retreated, some of them returned to retrieve Green's body. One Southerner recalled in 1916 that enemy soldiers watched as he led a small group toward the general's body, "but as we were unharmed and showed no hostile intention, they evidently regarded us as on a peaceful mission and made no attempt to fire upon us or to interfere with us." There is some disagreement, however, over these events as another Confederate claimed that he had retrieved Green's body amid heavy firing and had personally placed it on the general's horse.

General Taylor called "the death of General Green an irreparable one." A Louisiana soldier agreed and said that "we could better have lost any other man in the Department." A soldier who served under Green wrote: "There is no one who knew Gen. Green, but would admit that he could do more with a handful of men that perhaps any other commander on the soil." He was extremely popular with his men, as Taylor noted: "Upright, modest, and with simplicity of a child, danger seemed to be his element, and he rejoiced in combat. His men adored him, and would follow wherever he led, but they did not fear him, for, though he scolded at them in action, he was too kind-hearted to punish breaches of discipline." In fact, Taylor compared him to other successful Southern cavalry commanders when he wrote: "Such able officers as Stuart, Hampton, and the younger Lees in the East, Forrest, Green, and Wheeler in the west, developed much talent for the war."

Tom Green was buried in Oakwood Cemetery at Austin, Texas.

Anne Bailey

Barr, Alwyn, "Tom Green: The Forrest of the Trans-Mississippi," *Lincoln Herald*, LXXXVIII (Summer 1986), 39–42.

Faulk, Odie B., *General Tom Green: A Fightin' Texan* (Waco, 1963).

Idem., "Confederate Hero at Val Verde," *New Mexico Historical Review* 38 (October 1963), 300–11.

Wright, Marcus J., compiler, *Texas in the War, 1861–1865* (Texas, 1965).

✶ *Elkanah Brackin Greer* ✶

A handsome full-length portrait of General Greer in uniform, quite probably taken in Texas late in the war. (Jack T. Greer Collection)

Elkanah B. Greer was born October 11, 1825, at Paris, Tennessee. He later moved to Mississippi, and when the Mexican War began joined Jefferson Davis' 1st Mississippi Rifles. In 1848 he migrated to east Texas where he established himself as a planter and merchant at Marshall. Greer was an ardent states righter and Grand Commander of the Texas branch of the Knights of the Golden Circle. He was part of a movement to lead a KGC army into Mexico in 1860, and in February traveled to New Orleans to confer with the KGC leaders.

After Lincoln's election Greer spoke at a mass meeting in Marshall, where he offered the state of South Carolina the services of his continually available regiment of Texas volunteers. When the Civil War began Greer immediately tendered his services to the Confederacy and received the first colonelcy awarded a Texan from the provisional government at Montgomery. He organized a regiment that took the unlikely name of South Kansas–Texas Regiment (although it eventually became the 3d Texas Cavalry). The regiment was mustered into the Confederate service at Dallas in June 1861 and joined Benjamin McCulloch at Fort Smith, Arkansas, in July. State authorities later complained that Greer had left the state without permission; that he had organized and removed his regiment from the state without going through the proper channels.

Greer participated in the Battle at Wilson's Creek, Missouri, August 10, 1861. During the fighting he ordered a charge, which he reported was done "with a shout for Texas. The enemy was thrown into confusion…Several of my men were killed and wounded in this charge." Greer had wanted to attack the main

Federal force but decided not to try when he realized he was not only under enemy fire but also exposed to friendly fire.

He participated the following year in the Battle of Pea Ridge, March 7–8, where he was slightly wounded. During the battle he commanded a division and had been ordered to "hold at all hazards a hill, which was the most prominent position on the battle-field." As the Confederates retreated, Greer went in search of McCulloch and James McIntosh but soon learned that both commanders were dead and he was the senior officer on the field. On March 17 Greer commanded a cavalry brigade consisting of the 3d Texas, Crump's cavalry, and McIntosh's cavalry, 1st Division, Army of the West. He was promoted to brigadier general on October 8, 1862, to rank immediately.

On June 3, 1863, Greer was assigned to duty as commandant of conscripts for the Trans-Mississippi Department. General E. Kirby Smith noted that the conscript bureau was defective and under no general supervision. "I have taken it in hand," he wrote, and "have appointed General Greer commandant for the department, and trust that, when systematized, abuses will be corrected and a force brought onto the field." Greer was considered "an officer of energy and capacity" and "his office is well arranged." He set up his office at Marshall but ran into trouble with the judiciary as he claimed that judges in Texas were granting too many exemptions from conscription. Smith reported that the difficulties Greer encountered came from "misunderstanding and collision between the State and Confederate authorities. The frontier counties under the present system are, moreover, a grand city of refuge where thousands of able-bodied men have flocked to escape service in the Confederate army. This will continue to be the case until the conscript service is uniformly administered throughout the State, without exempting any portion of her territory from its exercise."

When Nathaniel Banks moved up the Red River toward Texas in 1864, Greer was in charge of collecting all the Texas state troops at Marshall. On April 8 Greer directed that some of those men working for state officials and subject to the draft should clear up their affairs, as he planned to replace them with men "unfit" for service in sixty days. Angry post quartermasters, whose clerks and agents had deferments, began a deluge of correspondence to prevent losing their men to the Confederate army. To add to his unpopularity, Greer also had the task of collecting slaves for Confederate use, and in late 1864 was requested to produce four to five thousand men to work on the department's defenses.

In November 1864 Francis T. Nicholls arrived at Shreveport to replace Greer, but E. Kirby Smith refused to recognize the War Department's orders on the grounds that it was "improbable that a newcomer would perform the duties of the Bureau equally well." Smith wrote Richmond that Greer had "labored zealously, industriously, and intelligently in the discharge of that duty. He has made enemies, but in the face of many difficulties he has by perseverance introduced order and system, and is making his department a success. It would be unjust to a meritorious officer to relieve him by his junior at the moment he is reaping the reward of many months of labor and industry." Unfortunately for Greer, the War Department refused to suspend the order and Greer was replaced in December. Smith wrote that Greer, in the "discharge of his onerous duties," had taken the bureau from "a state of utter disorganization and confusion" and "thoroughly and completely systematized" it while showing the "firmness, justness, and impartiality that has characterized his official conduct."

In March 1865 Greer was ordered to relieve Brigadier General J. B. Robertson as commander of the Reserve Corps in the state of Texas. After the war he lived in Marshall and died on March 25, 1877, in DeVall's Bluff, Arkansas, while visiting his sister. He was buried in Elmwood Cemetery in Memphis, Tennessee.

Anne Bailey

Roberts, O. M., *Texas*, Vol. XI in Evans, *Confederate Military History*.

✳ *John Gregg* ✳

Believed to be a portrait of John Gregg, probably as colonel of the 7th Texas in 1861 or 1862. (Courtesy of Lawrence T. Jones)

On September 28, 1828, John Gregg was born in Lawrence County, Alabama, destined to spend most of his life on the move. While still a boy he went with his family to La Grange, there to study at La Grange College, followed by attendance at law school in Tuscumbia. As soon as he completed these studies, he moved to Fairfield, Texas, and promptly mixed law with politics by seeking and winning a district judgeship when only twenty-eight. Five years later, in 1861, he was sufficiently prominent to be chosen a delegate to the state convention called upon to decide secession, and Gregg voted with the majority.

Almost immediately Texas elected him to represent it in the Provisional Congress meeting at Montgomery, Alabama, and Gregg remained with it when it removed to Richmond in May. However, after the victory at Manassas July 21 he gave up his seat, instead going home to Texas to recruit and organize the 7th Texas Infantry. Inevitably the men elected him their colonel, and he led the regiment back across the Mississippi to Department No. 2, now commanded by another Texan-by-adoption, General Albert Sidney Johnston. Gregg joined the garrison at Fort Donelson and with it suffered surrender and imprisonment in February 1862.

Gregg was not exchanged for several months, but when he did get released, he and the 7th Texas rejoined the army at Grenada, Mississippi. As the defense of the Mississippi River, especially Vicksburg, loomed imminent, more brigadiers were needed, and President Jefferson Davis awarded a commission to Gregg on the day before his birthday, September 27, 1862, to rank from August 29. He was given a brigade composed of his own regiment and the 1st, 30th, 41st, and

Gregg's rank does not show, though he is clearly wearing military costume, with vest and greatcoat. (Cook Collection, Valentine Museum, Richmond, Va.)

A variant portrait made almost certainly at the same sitting as the previous portrait. (Warner, *Generals in Gray*)

50th Tennessee regiments, and a battery of light artillery.

That winter when Grant launched his first move toward Vicksburg, Gregg was posted to Chickasaw Bayou, where in the December 27, 1862 assaults on the Chickasaw Bluffs by Major General William T. Sherman, he took a small part in the Confederate defense and victory. A few days later he was sent south to Port Hudson and remained there until May, escaping Major General Nathaniel J. Banks' siege, but being sent to join General Joseph E. Johnston's tardy attempt to relieve another siege, this one at Vicksburg.

Gregg first saw action in the campaign on May 12, when his brigade stood almost alone in trying to retard the enemy's progress in the battle at Raymond. Withdrawn to Jackson, Mississippi, he linked with Johnston, but then watched with the rest of the relief force and waited for Johnston to act. When Vicksburg surrendered, Gregg participated in the battle of Jackson, but when Johnston's force was later broken up, having accomplished nothing, Gregg and others were sent to General Braxton Bragg's Army of Tennessee for what became the Chickamauga Campaign (August–September 1863).

On September 20, 1863, when Bragg's right nearly collapsed, Major General William S. Rosecrans' left under Major General George H. Thomas and forced the precipitate withdrawal of reinforcements from the Federal center, Gregg and his brigade were allotted to Lieutenant General James Longstreet's assault when he drove through the Yankee center and cut Rosecrans' army in half, putting most of it to rout. Gregg took a bad wound in the fighting, but recovered in time to rejoin Longstreet, who put him in Major General John Bell Hood's division, commanding Hood's old brigade, the 1st, 4th, and 5th Texas, and the 3d Arkansas.

Gregg was of a type that admirably fit commands such as Hood's Texas Brigade. A rugged and unrelenting fighter, he was personally without fear, even looking the role of a rugged frontiersman with his "spade" beard, high forehead, and fierce gaze. When he followed Longstreet to Virginia to rejoin the Army of Northern Virginia, he quickly enhanced his reputation for pugnacity by winning repeated mention in reports for his daring in the Wilderness (May 5–7, 1864), when Longstreet reached the field on the second day of battle and slammed into the Yankees.

From the Wilderness through Petersburg, Gregg led his brigade in all the combats of the old I Corps, until the fall fighting on the Charles City Road south of

Richmond. There on the morning of October 7, 1864, a Yankee bullet finally caught up with him, killing him almost instantly, yet another example of the terrible attrition that by this time was robbing General Lee of so many of his experienced brigade commanders. Gregg's remains were later removed to Aberdeen, Mississippi, for burial.

John Gregg never held independent command, nor did he have an opportunity to show what he might have done in the higher responsibilities of divisional command. He must be judged upon what he actually did achieve, and the record, while not extensive, shows a capable battlefield leader, esteemed by his men and his superiors alike, a man impervious to fear, and wholly committed to his cause, whether in congressional halls or on the Charles City Road.

William C. Davis

Roberts, O. M., *Texas*, Vol. XI in Evans, *Confederate Military History*.

Simpson, Harold T., *Hood's Texas Brigade* (Hillsboro, 1971).

The only known wartime portrait of Maxcy Gregg was made in 1861
or 1862, and probably shows him as colonel of the 1st South Carolina.
(Museum of the Confederacy, Richmond, Va.)

✶ Maxcy Gregg ✶

The antebellum South spawned a generation of fire-eating politicians who led their states into secession but who in a great many cases did not participate in the war that ensued. South Carolinian Maxcy Gregg waxed as fiery as any prewar Southern leader—and he also contributed military service in the field with considerable success.

Gregg was born in Columbia, South Carolina, on August 1, 1814, the progeny of decidedly Northern ancestry: His maternal grandfather had been president of Brown University and married the daughter of a prominent Rhode Island family. Young Gregg excelled in his studies at South Carolina College to such a degree that he tied with a classmate for first honors—then refused to accept either the honors or a diploma because of unwillingness to share the distinction. Gregg practiced law in Columbia for two decades and employed his inherited wealth to study classical subjects and natural phenomena. He held a major's commission during the Mexican War, but saw no fighting.

From his earliest political expression, Gregg advocated disunion and Southern nationalism. He spoke and wrote so stridently about states rights that he found himself in a small minority even in radical South Carolina. Gregg considered, for instance, "consolidation with Georgia and Tennessee…as only not quite so great an evil as consolidation with New York and Ohio." He jubilantly cast his vote in favor of secession at the state's 1860 convention. That same convention authorized creation of a regiment of volunteers for six-months service. Maxcy Gregg received the commission as colonel of the regiment, effective on the first day of 1861.

The South Carolina colonel habitually maintained an erect posture that looked military, but otherwise he did not resemble the conventional image of an officer. He was short and thickset and ruddy-complected and somewhat deaf. On horseback, however, where his stature was not noticeable, he seemed to a subordinate to present "a very soldierly appearance." A Virginia civilian who came to know Gregg called him "an elegant man," while a South Carolina colonel was particularly struck by "the force and weight of his character." Gregg seemed "austere and unbending," with a "reserved nature" and "an almost inflexible will." Despite a "grave and quiet exterior," his speech gave "the appearance of gentleness," and his smile seemed filled with "sweetness."

That complex blend of characteristics and styles did not include in its composition any real military background or training. Colonel Gregg did his best to cope with the demands of commanding his state's first regiment but betrayed his inexperience while garrisoning Charleston harbor. He discussed with a chatty woman visitor in decidedly unmilitary fashion how W. H. C. Whiting had all the brains and did all the work but Beauregard reaped the credit. One day in early March 1861, a cannon from one of Gregg's positions accidentally fired a solid shot that scored a hit on Fort Sumter. The three months of duty around Charleston offered no chance for serious error, though, and they seasoned Gregg and his 1st South Carolina.

After the fall of Fort Sumter, a call for help came from Virginia. Maxcy Gregg eagerly answered the summons; to his chagrin, nearly one-half of his troops refused to accompany him out of their home state. The five hundred or so South Carolinians who reached Richmond under Gregg's command were among the first outside defenders to arrive there. They savored the heroes' welcome afforded them by Virginia's populace.

Colonel Gregg and the 1st South Carolina soon moved to the military frontier in northern Virginia. There they fought one of the first small battles of the war on June 17 when they ambushed a Federal force riding a train near Vienna. The Federals retreated in abject rout, with a handful of casualties, and newspapers on either side of the lines made much of the tiny affair.

Gregg faced his most difficult time of the war when the six-month enlistment terms of his volunteers expired at the beginning of July and most of them insisted on returning home. Gregg bore quietly the abuse showered on the Carolinians for abandoning Virginia, and gradually rebuilt his regiment. Many of the men reformed once they had straightened out their affairs at home, and within six weeks the 1st South Carolina exceeded its allotted strength. Gregg's commission as colonel of the reconstituted regiment bore the date July 25. Meanwhile, however, the unit had missed the First Battle of Manassas. A tiff between some of his men who were returning by train and a Georgian riding with them led Gregg into a showdown with Jefferson Davis. The stubborn and contentious chief executive denounced Gregg on the basis of a garbled report and abused him intemperately in the presence of one of the colonel's staff before moderating his stand on receipt of more accurate details.

Maxcy Gregg took his regiment to Suffolk during the fall of 1861 but was soon separated from it because he received promotion to brigadier general on December 14, 1861, to rank immediately. He assumed his brigade command in the Pocataligo region of South Carolina. The small brigade included the 12th, 13th, and 14th South Carolina infantry regiments. Soon after Gregg took his unit back into Virginia during the spring of 1862, his old 1st South Carolina joined the brigade and so did Orr's Rifle Regiment. The five regiments would serve together for the rest of the war and win a reputation second to none in the Army of Northern Virginia. It became one of six brigades in A. P. Hill's vaunted "Light Division."

Gregg led his brigade into action for the first time on June 27 at Gaines' Mill during the Seven Days' Campaign. He performed with such bravery that a seasoned chronicler of the brigade called Gregg at Gaines' Mill "the sublimest spectacle I ever saw." The brigade missed all but marginal action during the rest of that campaign, and it served as a rear guard at Cedar Mountain. Perhaps the greatest performance of the war by the general and his brigade came at Second Manassas, where they anchored the Confederate left through a series of desperate Federal assaults. Holding tenaciously in the face of terrible losses, Gregg strode among his men, waving a scimitar carried during the revolution by an ancestor, and cried, "Let us die here, my men, let us die here." Many of them did, contributing much to winning the day.

Gregg and his five regiments staggered into the crisis on the Confederate right at Sharpsburg near the van of A. P. Hill's timely reinforcement of Lee's army on September 17, 1862. Gregg survived a close call at Sharpsburg when he fell apparently seriously and perhaps mortally wounded by the same volley that killed General Lawrence O'Bryan Branch. The ball that struck

Gregg's hip and nearly unhorsed him spent its momentum on a large handkerchief wadded in a pocket, however, and only resulted in an enormous black bruise.

When R. E. Lee stood against Ambrose Burnside's Union army on the ridge behind Fredericksburg in December 1862, Gregg's brigade held what seemed to be a relatively safe position well behind the front line. To its front, however, a wide gap loomed in the Confederate defensive alignment. The reason the gap existed remains debatable, but the result was crystal clear: Federals poured through it near midday on December 13 and surged through dense woods toward Gregg's reserve position. The courier sent to report the enemy breakthrough, as had been arranged between Gregg and a fellow brigadier holding the front line, was killed en route. When Federals began to swarm around his position, Gregg rode along his position in some confusion and ordered his men not to fire at what he presumed to be friends. An enemy volley swept through the woods too high to harm most of the South Carolinians but at the right level to hit Maxcy Gregg. The general fell near the left of Orr's Rifles, his rightward-most regiment, with a ball through his side and into his spine. A few minutes later triumphant Confederate reinforcements sweeping through in a counterattack noticed a badly wounded man who dragged himself painfully up by holding onto a sapling and cheered them forward, waving his cap. It was Maxcy Gregg, watching his last charge.

The stricken general held to life through December 14 at the nearby Yerby House. Stonewall Jackson paid Gregg an emotional visit and spoke to him of religious things. A. P. Hill came in and bade his subordinate farewell with a kiss on the forehead. At 5:00 A. M. on the 15th, Maxcy Gregg died. Five days later he was buried in his native place after a sermon that opened with words that Gregg might have chosen for himself: "We meet this day...to mourn—to mourn for ourselves, and for the State, the mother that has borne us all!"

Robert K. Krick

David Gregg McIntosh Papers, University of North Carolina, Chapel Hill.

Joseph Jeptha Norton Papers, University of South Carolina, Columbia.

Krick, Robert K., "Maxcy Gregg," *Civil War History*, XIX (1973).

Maxcy Gregg Papers, University of South Carolina, Columbia.

★ *Richard Griffith* ★

No uniformed portrait of Griffith is known. This one probably dates from the early 1850s, or even earlier. (Evans, *Confederate Military History*)

Born near Philadelphia, Pennsylvania, on January 11, 1814, Richard Griffith graduated from Ohio University, Athens, Ohio, in 1837. Shortly after graduating, he moved to Vicksburg, Mississippi, where he became a teacher. When the war with Mexico broke out, Griffith enlisted in the 1st Mississippi Rifles. Soon elected 1st lieutenant, he held the post of regimental adjutant throughout the conflict. In that position he formed an affectionate and lasting friendship with the regiment's commander, Colonel Jefferson Davis, who commended him for his performance at the battle of Buena Vista.

Following the Mexican War, Griffith engaged in banking in Jackson, Mississippi, and served as a U.S. marshal. In 1857 he received an honorary master's degree from his alma mater. When John J. Pettus was inaugurated governor of Mississippi on November 21, 1859, Griffith was grand marshal of the elaborate ceremonies, which included a procession that extended from the executive mansion to the capitol. Griffith held the office of state treasurer for two terms, and was so employed when his adopted state of Mississippi seceded in January 1861.

Not surprising in this case, the Northern-born and Northern-educated Griffith cast his lot with the Confederacy and soon found himself adjutant general of the Army of Mississippi in his adopted state. He soon became a brigadier general in that organization before he entered the Provisional Army of the Confederate States. At Camp Clark, near Corinth, on May 16, 1861, the men of the 12th Mississippi Infantry Regiment, after seven ballots, elected Griffith colonel. The regiment departed for Union City, Tennessee, to participate in an anticipated campaign by Major General Leonidas Polk to capture St. Louis. The imminence of conflict in Virginia brought about the regiment's reassignment there. It left for Virginia on July 16 but did not arrive in time to participate in the First Battle of Manassas on the 21st. On July 26 the 12th Mississippi became part of Brigadier General Richard S. Ewell's 2d Brigade of Brigadier General P. G. T. Beauregard's I Corps, Army of the Potomac.

Griffith's military association with the 12th ended quickly. When President Jefferson Davis found it impossible to create a second all-Mississippi brigade including the 12th Regiment in northern Virginia for Griffith to command, he determined to create a vacancy in the existing brigade, then commanded by Brigadier General Charles Clark. Davis had Clark reassigned to the Western theater—without his brigade. This course of action enabled Griffith's old friend to create a commission for his former adjutant as a brigadier general in the Provisional Confederate States Army on November 2, 1861, effective immediately.

On November 9 Griffith, whose brigade was stationed in Loudoun County, Virginia, received orders to report to Brigadier General Nathan C. Evans, the senior officer in that county. On November 16 Griffith's command became the 5th Brigade of the 1st Division, the latter commanded by Major General Earl Van Dorn. On December 6 Griffith's four regiments, the 13th, 17th, 18th, and 21st Mississippi, were camped near Leesburg. Three days later orders were issued for his brigade to be reconstituted with the 12th, 16th, 19th, and 21st Mississippi regiments, but apparently this order was never implemented, because his four original regiments remained under his command in mid-January of 1862, although at that time Griffith reported to Brigadier General Daniel Harvey Hill instead of to Evans.

The coming of spring brought Union Major General George B. McClellan's landing on the Peninsula. Griffith's brigade left northern Virginia on April 6 and reached Grove's Wharf, on the James River, three days later. Before the end of the month it was one of three in Brigadier General Lafayette McLaws' division. On April 30 it consisted of the 1st Louisiana Battalion, the 13th, 18th, and 21st Mississippi regiments, and five batteries, and had an effective strength of 2,774 men. On May 21 it was one of six brigades in Major General John B. Magruder's division; four of the batteries had been reassigned; and its effective strength was 2,534 men.

During their service on the Peninsula, Griffith's Mississippians engaged in considerable maneuvering and some minor skirmishing with the enemy but saw no significant action. This absence of combat continued during the engagement May 31–June 1 at Seven Pines, where, although present on the field and ready for combat, the Mississippians remained in reserve. The brigade's true baptism of fire did not come until the Seven Days' battles, which began later that month.

Continuing as part of Magruder's division, Griffith's brigade participated in the Confederate attempt to cut off and capture the Union right wing at the Battle of Gaines' Mill on June 27, only insofar as they had the attention of McClellan and prevented him from transferring troops from his left flank to reinforce his threatened flank. This relatively safe duty continued throughout the following day as well.

On June 29 General Robert E. Lee, having determined that McClellan was in full retreat for the James River, ordered his entire army to advance. When Magruder reached Fair Oaks Station in his front, he found that the enemy had already departed their fortifications and Confederate Brigadier General Joseph Kershaw's brigade of Brigadier General Lafayette McLaws' division was in possession of the works. Magruder assumed overall command and placed Kershaw's brigade to the right of the railroad, with two of Griffith's regiments extending Kershaw's line to the left of the railroad. Griffith's remaining two regiments were stationed at Kershaw's rear, close enough to provide support. No additional troops from McLaws' division appeared on the scene, but when Brigadier General Howell Cobb's brigade, which had been following Griffith's, arrived, Magruder extended his line farther to his left.

The Federals now ascertained Magruder's position and opened upon the Confederates with their long-range artillery. During what is better known as the Battle of Savage's Station, one of these Union artillery projectiles mortally wounded Griffith. He was borne from the field by two of his staff officers, Majors William H. Watt and A. M. Hawkins. Griffith died late that night or early the next morning in Richmond, Davis at his bedside at times. He was buried in Greenwood Cemetery, Jackson, Mississippi.

Lawrence L. Hewitt

Hooker, Charles E., *Mississippi*, Vol. VII in Evans, *Confederate Military History*.

Rowland, Dunbar, ed., *Mississippi: Comprising Sketches of Counties, Towns, Events, Institutions, and Persons, Arranged in Cyclopedic Form*, 1907, reprint ed. (Spartanburg, 1976).

✳ *Bryan Grimes* ✳

An outstanding previously unpublished portrait of Brigadier General Bryan Grimes, probably taken during the last half of 1864. (North Carolina Division of Archives and History, Raleigh, N.C.)

One of the best of the nonprofessional soldiers of the Confederacy, Bryan Grimes was born into a prominent family at "Grimesland," Pitt County, North Carolina, on November 2, 1828. Following an excellent early education, he graduated from the University of North Carolina in 1848 and within a year settled into the life of a planter on property given him by his father. Farming and travel occupied Grimes' attention in the antebellum years, and he was in Europe during the early stages of the sectional crisis following Lincoln's election in November 1860. Returning to the United States about the time South Carolina seceded, he visited several parts of the South to watch events unfold first-hand. Grimes supported secession as a member of the North Carolina state convention, signing the ordinance on May 20, 1861. He had "advocated the most extensive war measures" while a delegate to the convention, and readily accepted from Governor John W. Ellis a major's commission in the 4th North Carolina Infantry to rank from May 16, 1861.

Grimes and his regiment, which was commanded by Colonel George Burgwyn Anderson, arrived in Virginia too late to participate in First Manassas and spent the summer and winter of 1861–62 at drill and routine duty in northern Virginia. Transferred to the Peninsula near Yorktown as part of Winfield S. Featherston's brigade in early April 1862, the regiment saw slight action at Williamsburg on May 5. Grimes advanced to lieutenant colonel of his regiment on May 1, 1862, and experienced his first sustained combat on May 31 at Seven Pines, losing his horse (the first of seven mounts killed under him during the war) but emerging unscathed. Promoted to colonel on June 19, 1862, Grimes commanded the 4th North Carolina in a new brigade headed by Anderson in D. H. Hill's division.

Over the next two years Grimes combined great personal courage and coolness under fire to forge an enviable record as a colonel. He led an assault with great dash at Gaines' Mill on June 27, 1862, stayed in front of Richmond with the rest of D. H. Hill's division until mid-August, then rejoined the Army of Northern Virginia in time for the Maryland Campaign in September. Severely injured when a horse kicked him on September 5, Grimes nonetheless participated in the fighting at Fox's Gap on September 14. Sent to a hospital after the action on South Mountain, he missed the Battle of Antietam, in which his regiment suffered heavy casualties and George B. Anderson received a mortal wound. Grimes took temporary command of the brigade after Sharpsburg, led it during the Fredericksburg Campaign and much of the winter of 1862–63, and returned to his regiment when Stephen Dodson Ramseur replaced him in January 1863.

As a colonel under Ramseur, Grimes distinguished himself at Chancellorsville on May 3, 1863 (receiving a wound in the foot), and took part in the successful assault along Oak Ridge on July 1 at Gettysburg. Maneuvering during the Bristoe and Mine Run campaigns in the fall of 1863 and brief action in the Wilderness on May 6, 1864, preceded a memorable performance in the "Mule Shoe" at Spotsylvania on May 12, 1864. There Grimes directed his regiment in savage combat along the west side of Lee's exposed salient, taking charge of the brigade for a time when Ramseur went down with a wound. Another fine day at the Harris Farm on May 19 capped a week of superb leadership: "You have saved Ewell's Corps," Rodes told Grimes on the 19th, "and shall be promoted, and your commission shall bear date from this day." Rodes' prediction proved accurate, as Grimes learned on June 5 that the President had appointed him on June 1, to rank from May 19, succeeding Junius Daniel (who had been mortally wounded on May 12) in command of a brigade of North Carolinians.

Grimes' brigade accompanied Jubal Early and the II Corps to Lynchburg in mid-June, shortly after which Grimes went on sick furlough until early August. He rejoined Early's force on August 10 for the climactic phase of the 1864 Shenandoah Valley Campaign. At Third Winchester on September 19 he fought all day and helped cover the southern retreat; at Fisher's Hill on September 22 he warned Ramseur of the Federal flanking movement; and at Cedar Creek on October 19 he risked his life to stem the Confederate rout. Ramseur's mortal wounding late in the day at Cedar Creek left Grimes in command of the division (formerly D. H. Hill's and Rodes'), a position he retained until the end of the war. Grimes and his division left the Shenandoah Valley for Richmond on December 14, 1864, and took up a position near Petersburg four days later. As a divisional leader Grimes merited appointment to major general, a promotion he received on February 23, 1865, effective February 15. The final officer to advance to this grade in Lee's army, he accepted the honor with a "hope I shall never bring discredit upon myself."

During the last grim spring of the war, Grimes' troops defended a portion of the trenches outside Petersburg. Grimes played an important role in the Confederate surprise attack March 25 against Fort Stedman, where he was mistakenly reported killed, as well as during the retreat to Appomattox. His men fired some of the final shots of the Army of Northern Virginia. Grimes himself bitterly opposed the decision to surrender but decided against an effort to take his troops to North Carolina when told that such an action would disgrace his name and dishonor General Lee.

After the surrender Grimes returned to Grimesland and the life of a planter. He lived quietly for fifteen years, improving his property, serving as a trustee of the University of North Carolina, and rearing a large family. He was murdered on August 14, 1880, by an assassin in the employ of a pair of unsavory brothers he had sought to drive from Pitt County. His remains were buried at Grimesland.

Gary W. Gallagher

Cowper, Pulaski, *Extracts of Letters of Major-General Bryan Grimes, to His Wife, Written While in Active Service in the Army of Northern Virginia* (Raleigh, 1883).

Grimes' buttons indicate that this was taken after his February 1865 promotion to major general. His collar stars in this and the previous image both lack the regulation wreath. (U.S. Army Military History Institute, Carlisle, Pa.)

☆ *Johnson Hagood* ☆

The only known uniformed image of General Hagood, made sometime during or after the summer of 1862, this image also shows his kepi in his lap. (Museum of the Confederacy, Richmond, Va.)

Unlike many who became Confederate generals, Johnson Hagood maintained an almost life-long association with things military going back to early youth. Born February 21, 1829, in Barnwell County, South Carolina, he entered the South Carolina Military Academy—now the Citadel—in 1843, graduating four years later. Immediately he began reading law, and commenced a practice in 1850 but continued his association with the state militia, rising to the rank of brigadier general by the time South Carolina seceded in 1860.

Not surprisingly, when volunteers began to gather at Charleston to meet the threat presumably posed by Fort Sumter, Hagood won easy election to the colonelcy of the 1st South Carolina Infantry. He was with it, though chiefly as a spectator, during the bombardment and fall of Sumter, and soon afterward was ordered to Virginia to meet the threat along the Manassas–Bull Run line. Hagood was not with his regiment in the battle to come July 21, 1861, however. Instead Hagood acted as a "volunteer private" with Colonel Joseph B. Kershaw's 2d South Carolina and helped in turning around Federal cannon taken on Henry Hill to fire upon the retreating enemy.

Hagood went back to South Carolina that fall, once more with his regiment, and there participated in the defense of Charleston, including the action at Secessionville on June 16, 1862. In the fight there he actually led a brigade of two regiments and two battalions and won sufficient notice that two days later he was given command of much of James Island, and a month later of the Second Military District of South Carolina. He was also promoted to brigadier general on July 21, or effective July 21, but all records of his appointment, confirmation, acceptance, and effective date have disappeared. The earliest actual extant notice of his appointment is a letter from Adjutant General Samuel Cooper on August 4 announcing that "Colonel Hagood has been appointed brigadier general." Since the appointment was to be sent that same day, it is probable that President Davis actually made the appointment August 4 or a day earlier, and that it was to be effective from July 21.

Hagood spent almost the next two years in South Carolina's coastal defenses. He fought in engagements at Grimball's Landing on James Island, July 16, 1863, and in the late-summer operations on Morris Island, including the defense against Major General Quincy Gillmore's bombardments of Sumter and the siege of Battery Wagner. He turned over command of Wagner and Fort Gregg on July 23 but then resumed it in late August. When the celebrated attack by the 54th Massachusetts Colored Regiment was made on July 18, Hagood was in overall command of the forces in Wagner that repulsed the assault.

By early 1864 Hagood was once more in command on James Island, but on February 20 he was placed in charge of the Seventh Military District of the Department of South Carolina, Georgia, and Florida, commanded by General P. G. T. Beauregard. He remained with his headquarters on James Island until Beauregard was summoned north to the defense of Richmond. Hagood and his brigade were taken along, reaching Petersburg on May 6 just in time to meet the threat posed by Major General Benjamin F. Butler's advance toward Bermuda Hundred. Hagood now commanded the 21st, 25th, and 27th South Carolina and used them skillfully in stopping Butler's advance on May 7. Soon the 11th and 7th South Carolina battalions joined him, and again he battled Butler, fighting so effectively that Beauregard paid tribute to them. "General Hagood and his command became the heroes of the day, and were justly looked upon as the saviours of Petersburg." Hagood fought again at Drewry's Bluff on May 16, then moved on to join with General Lee in resisting General Grant's overland drive at Cold Harbor in early June.

When Grant stole a march around Lee and approached Petersburg from below, Hagood's was among the first brigades rushed to Beauregard to man the thin defenses of the city while Lee rushed to arrive with the van of the army. Thereafter Hagood and his brigade did hard duty in the trenches until December,

including participating in the August fighting for the Weldon Railroad, in which he led two hundred men from his depleted brigade in a charge that saw them briefly surrounded. When a Yankee officer seized the flag of the 11th South Carolina, Hagood shot him from the saddle, recovered the colors, then mounted the Federal's horse and led his men back to their own lines.

The threat to the North Carolina bastion at Fort Fisher led to Hagood's reassignment to his old department at the end of 1864, and after the fort's fall he joined the remnant of the Army of Tennessee under General Joseph E. Johnston as it vainly tried to resist Major General William T. Sherman's march through the Carolinas. Hagood fought at Kinston and Bentonville in March 1865, and finally was surrendered on April 26 with the rest of the army, though he was in South Carolina at the time and may never have given his parole personally.

Following the war Hagood remained prominent in South Carolina affairs. He helped elect Wade Hampton governor in 1876, and himself won the office of comptroller-general. He won reelection two years later, and then took the governorship in 1880, running an efficient and fiscally sound administration. He died at his home in Barnwell on January 4, 1898, and was buried in Barnwell's Episcopal Church graveyard.

William C. Davis

Capers, Ellison, *South Carolina*, Vol. V in Evans, *Confederate Military History*.

Hagood, Johnson, *Memoirs of the War of Secession* (Columbia, 1910).

✷ *Wade Hampton* ✷

A wonderful late-war portrait of Wade Hampton as a major or lieutenant general, previously unpublished. (William A. Turner Collection)

Born in Charleston, South Carolina, on March 28, 1818, Wade Hampton was the scion of one of the South's wealthiest families. He was graduated from South Carolina College in 1836, subsequently overseeing his family's vast landholdings and slaves, and serving in both houses of the state legislature from 1852 to 1861. A supporter of secession, Hampton embraced the Confederate cause, continuing his family's military heritage—his grandfather and father, both also named Wade, had served in the revolutionary war and the War of 1812, respectively.

With the outbreak of the Civil War, Hampton organized the Hampton Legion, purchasing most of the equipment with his own money. His wealth and personal reputation for courage—he had hunted and fought bears with a knife—secured his colonelcy and command of the legion, many of whose members came from South Carolina's leading families. The legion consisted of six companies of infantry, four of cavalry, and a battery of artillery.

The Hampton Legion arrived in Virginia in time to participate in the First Battle of Manassas, July 21, 1861. Assigned to the brigade of Theophilus H. Holmes, the legion fought near the Robinson House and the Henry House, suffering 121 casualties, including Hampton, who was grazed in the head by a bullet. In January 1862 Confederate authorities assigned Hampton to command of a brigade in the division of William H. C. Whiting. The unit consisted of the legion, 14th and 19th Georgia, and the 16th North Carolina. Hampton led his men in their first significant action at Eltham's Landing on the Virginia Peninsula on May 7. Whiting cited Virginia for "conspicuous gallantry" in the engagement, and Joseph Johnston, army commander, described him as an officer of "high merit" and requested his promotion. Hampton secured his brigadiership appointment on May 23, to rank immediately.

Eight days later, on May 31, Hampton led his brigade in an attack at Seven Pines. During the combat a bullet struck Hampton in the foot, but he stayed on horseback and later retained command even while a surgeon removed the bullet. Gustavus Smith praised Hampton in his report, writing: "General Hampton, on this as on many previous occasions, was remarkable for coolness, promptness, and decided practical ability as a leader of men in difficult and dangerous circumstances. In these high characteristics of a general he has few equals and perhaps no superior."

In the reorganization of the army after Seven Pines, Hampton's regiments were parceled out to other brigades. Hampton, however, assumed command of Samuel V. Fulkerson's brigade when that officer fell mortally wounded at Gaines' Mill on June 27. Hampton led the unit through the remaining engagements of the Seven Days' Campaign but saw limited action.

Further changes in the army of Robert E. Lee occurred after the Seven Days'. On July 28 Lee reorganized the cavalry, creating a two-brigade division for J. E. B. Stuart. Fitzhugh Lee received one brigade and Hampton the other. Hampton's new command consisted initially of the 1st North Carolina; 10th Virginia; and the Hampton, Cobb, and Jeff Davis legions. For Hampton, his assignment to Stuart and the cavalry shaped the remainder of his Confederate career.

During the fall of 1862 Hampton participated in raids undertaken by Stuart against Union supply lines and cavalry forces. On three occasions Hampton directed the operations in northern Virginia. By year's end Robert E. Lee had commended Hampton as "an officer of standing and gallantry," and offered him an infantry brigade of South Carolinians. Hampton declined, choosing to remain in the cavalry.

Although Hampton served under Stuart for nearly two years, the pair never became close friends. Nearly fifteen years Stuart's senior in age, Hampton was too consciously a South Carolinian and groused about the numbers of and favoritism shown to Virginians in the cavalry's officer corps. He even went around Stuart, complaining to Lee about the situation. Both Stuart and Hampton possessed inordinate egos, which contributed to their relationship.

Hampton demonstrated his growing prowess as a cavalry officer throughout the heavy fighting of 1863.

Hampton early in the war, probably as colonel and commander of the Hampton Legion in 1861. (Cook Collection, Valentine Museum, Richmond, Va.)

Hampton is presumably a brigadier in this well-known image made in 1862 or 1863. (New-York Historical Society, New York, N.Y.)

At Brandy Station, on June 9, his brigade was in the center of the combat, delivering a counterattack that swept the Federal horsemen off Fleetwood Hill. Hampton suffered a slight wound, while his brother, Frank, commanding the 2d South Carolina, fell mortally wounded. Twelve days later, at Upperville, the brigade routed Judson Kilpatrick's Union command. A Confederate trooper who saw Hampton lead the charge described him as "a veritable god of war." One of Stuart's staff officers, writing of Upperville, argued that "this success was mainly due to that personal influence which...has marked Hampton as a leader of men."

At Gettysburg on July 3, Hampton again led his cavalrymen into the ranks of the Union horsemen. His men fought valiantly, with Hampton suffering two saber slashes to the head and a shrapnel wound to the body. After the campaign Stuart described his subordinate as a "brave and distinguished officer," and Lee recommended Hampton for promotion, "both for his service and his gallantry." He received his major-generalcy on September 3, to rank from August 3, 1863.

Hampton rejoined the army in November and assumed command of one of Stuart's two divisions. When Stuart fell mortally wounded on May 11, 1864, Lee did not immediately name a successor. During the next three months, however, Hampton performed brilliantly and secured the command of the cavalry corps. June 11–12 at Trevilian Station, his troopers stopped the advance westward of Philip H. Sheridan's raiding Federals in a furious engagement. Two weeks later Hampton again defeated a Union force at Samaria Church, north of the James River. Finally, on August 11 Lee named Hampton as Stuart's successor. Hampton soon proposed the creation of a Bureau of Cavalry, an idea Lee endorsed.

Hampton's direction of the beleaguered Confederate cavalry during the Petersburg Campaign was brilliant. He believed in the superiority of force and often achieved that edge in combat, despite his numerical weakness. His horsemen fought well at Reams' Station August 24–25; raided behind Union lines on September 16, securing 2,468 head of cattle for Lee's hungry troops; and defeated a Union force on October 27 at Burgess' Mill. In this latter engagement, his son, Frank Preston, was mortally wounded; and another son, Wade IV, fell wounded.

In January 1865 Lee sent Hampton with part of the cavalry to the Carolinas to arouse the morale of the civilians and assist Joseph Johnston's forces. Promoted to lieutenant general on February 15, 1865, to rank from February 14, Hampton was present when Johnston surrendered to William Sherman in April 1865.

Hampton returned to his ruined plantations but quickly restored them. An outspoken opponent of Radical Reconstruction, he was elected governor of the state in 1876 and 1878. He then served two terms in the United States Senate, 1879–91, before becoming commissioner of the Pacific Railway. Hampton died in Columbia, South Carolina, on April 11, 1902, and was buried there.

Wade Hampton, Richard Taylor, and Nathan Bedford Forrest were the only three civilians without formal military training who attained the rank of lieutenant general in the Confederacy. Although Hampton lacked Stuart's flamboyance and eye for reconnaissance, he proved a worthy successor to the Virginian. His men believed Hampton was a "born soldier" with an unconquerable spirit. During the war's final year Hampton proved to be one of Lee's best officers. Perhaps one of his troopers summarized Hampton's career best when the cavalryman wrote: "Under Stuart stampedes were frequent, with Hampton they were unknown."

Jeffry D. Wert

Freeman, Douglas Southall, *Lee's Lieutenants: A Study in Command* (New York, 1942–44).

Longacre, Edward G., *The Cavalry at Gettysburg* (New York, 1986).

Thomas, Emory M., *Bold Dragoon: The Life of J. E. B. Stuart* (New York, 1986).

Brigadier General Hampton, posing resplendently for the camera in or around 1863. (Museum of the Confederacy, Richmond, Va.)

A previously unpublished portrait of Colonel Roger W. Hanson, who was killed less than three weeks after promotion to brigadier, and thus probably never posed for the camera at his highest rank. (William A. Turner Collection)

⋆ *Roger Weightman Hanson* ⋆

A commander of the famed Orphan Brigade, Hanson was born in Winchester, Clark County, Kentucky, on August 27, 1827. After attending local schools, he volunteered for the Mexican War. As a 1st lieutenant in Captain John S. "Cerro Gordo" Williams' company, Hanson earned a reputation for reckless bravery. Soon after returning home he was left after a duel with a permanent limp and "Bench-leg" as a nickname.

Hanson read law and opened a practice in Winchester. After a gold-rush trip to California he moved to Lexington and became known for his success in criminal cases. He lost a close race for the state house of representatives to John Williams in 1851 but won elections in 1853 and 1855. First a Whig, he changed to Know-Nothing as the Whig party broke up. In 1857 he was defeated by James B. Clay, a son of Henry Clay.

In 1860 Hanson campaigned for John Bell and the Constitutional Union party. A Unionist, he supported Kentucky's neutrality until he became convinced that a Union victory would jeopardize the rights of the states. On August 19, 1861, Hanson was commissioned a colonel in the Confederate army. Then thirty-four years old, he was physically active despite the bad leg and a tendency toward stoutness. Intelligent, perceptive, and witty, he believed in discipline and drill more than many of the men he commanded. A sense of humor helped save him from becoming a martinet.

The 2d Kentucky Regiment, organized at Camp Boone, Tennessee, was mustered into service on July 16, 1861. Hanson became its colonel on September 3 following the resignation of Colonel James M. Hawes. He also commanded the brigade that was being assembled until November 16 when John C. Breckinridge assumed command of the 1st Kentucky Brigade.

Lacking military training, Hanson worked diligently to master his duties. Much time and labor were expended in building extensive fortifications at Bowling Green, where the main Federal advance was expected. On January 20, 1862, the 2d Kentucky and Rice Graves' battery were detached and sent to Fort Donelson. On February 11 Hanson was placed on the extreme right of the Confederate line that protected the fort. Many Kentuckians experienced enemy fire for the first time on February 13 when they beat off Union attacks. Two days later, when orders were not forthcoming, Hanson showed initiative by going to help Nathan B. Forrest take a troublesome battery. They were appalled by an order to return to their positions. When Federals overran Hanson's original line, he rallied his men and established another position.

In early morning February 16, Hanson led the 2d Kentucky to a position from which it could help open an escape route through the Union trap. But there was a muddled command situation; the attack did not occur; and when Simon B. Buckner surrendered, Hanson and his men became prisoners of war.

Hanson was sent to Camp Chase, Ohio, and then to Camp Warren, near Boston. Confederate Congressman E. M. Bruce, who worked to secure an exchange, called Hanson "the best colonel in our service," and after several delays, Hanson was exchanged in August 1862. He met the 2d Kentucky in Chattanooga, where the men had been sent. They joined the brigade in Knoxville, where Breckinridge was preparing to join Braxton Bragg and Kirby Smith in Kentucky. But the Confederates left Kentucky after the inconclusive battle at Perryville on October 8, and the Kentuckians were denied a visit to their state.

When Breckinridge, now commanding the division, reorganized the brigade on October 26, 1862, Hanson was given the command. He had the 2d, 4th, 6th, and 9th Kentucky regiments, and the 41st Alabama was soon added. The batteries of Robert Cobb and Rice Graves were attached to the 1st Brigade. During two relatively peaceful months in the vicinity of Murfreesboro Hanson tried with limited success to restore discipline and improve proficiency. Ed Thompson, the brigade's early historian, wrote that "Hanson went every-where, saw every-thing, knew every-body upon whom any responsibility rested," but the Kentuckians were never a good camp outfit, and Hanson was not totally pleased with the results.

In early December the 1st Brigade cooperated with John Hunt Morgan in the destruction of a Federal force at Hartsville, Tennessee. Hanson remained with two regiments held in reserve while the 2d and 9th regiments and Cobb's battery participated in the successful assault. On December 20, 1862, President Jefferson Davis, then on a western tour, announced Hanson's promotion to brigadier general, effective December 13.

The peaceful interlude ended in late December when William S. Rosecrans finally advanced his Union army. The Battle of Stone's River was fought from December 31, 1862 to January 2, 1863. Breckinridge's division was on Bragg's extreme right, on the east side of the stream; Hanson was posted on the left of the division's front, next to the river. Most of the savage fighting was west of the river until January 2 when Bragg ordered Breckinridge to take a Union-occupied hill several hundred yards in front of his position. His brigade commanders agreed with Breckinridge that massed Union artillery across the river made the mission impossible; a furious Hanson had to be restrained from going to kill Bragg. The 1st Brigade was on the left in the first line when the attack began at 4:00 P.M. Moving in good order, the Confederates seized the hill, but as the Federals cleared the position, their guns opened a devastating fire. In the early moments a fuse from a case shot severed the artery in Hanson's left knee. Nursed by his wife, he died on Sunday morning, January 4, 1863. Buried temporarily in Nashville, he was reinterred in the Lexington cemetery on November 11, 1866. In 1895 the survivors of the Orphan Brigade dedicated a monument to his memory.

During his brief military career Hanson was a dependable subordinate who could be counted on to have his men ready to fight and to carry out orders. Breckinridge wrote in his battle report: "Endeared to his friends by his private virtue, and to his command by the vigilance with which he guarded its interests and honor, he was, by the universal testimony of his military associates, one of the finest officers that adorned the service of the Confederate states." The senate confirmed his generalcy posthumously, on April 22, 1863.

Lowell H. Harrison

Cooling, Benjamin Franklin, *Forts Henry and Donelson* (Knoxville, 1987).

Cozzens, Peter, *No Better Place to Die* (Urbana, 1990).

Davis, William C., *The Orphan Brigade* (Garden City, 1980).

Thompson, Ed Porter, *History of the Orphan Brigade* (Louisville, 1898).

The better-known variant of Hanson, also as a colonel, and probably taken prior to his capture at Fort Donelson. (William A. Turner Collection)

✯ *William Joseph Hardee* ✯

While many variants of this outstanding portrait of Hardee exist, none show as much as this carte-de-visite hidden away in his service record at the National Archives. (National Archives)

One of the best-known American military figures of the mid-nineteenth century, William J. Hardee was born at "Rural Felicity" Plantation, Camden County, Georgia, on October 12, 1815, into a locally prominent family. His early education came from private tutors. He entered the United States Military Academy in 1834 and graduated four years later, standing twenty-sixth in a class of forty-five.

Hardee served in the United States Army for the next twenty-three years, slowly rising through the officer grades and eventually gaining fame because of his publications. From his graduation until December 1849 he was a 2d lieutenant in the 2d Dragoons. From 1839 until 1844 he was a 1st lieutenant in the same regiment. In 1844 he was promoted to captain, and in 1855 to major. This last promotion was accompanied by a transfer to the 2d. U.S. Cavalry Regiment. In June 1860 he became the lieutenant colonel of the 1st U.S. Cavalry Regiment. On January 31, 1861, he resigned to go with Georgia into the Confederacy.

Hardee was selected to go to France from 1840 to 1842 to study at that country's cavalry school at Saumur—a designation that he owed to influential political connections. Early in the Mexican War (1846) he was involved in a controversial surrender, but a court of inquiry ruled that he had behaved properly. Later in that conflict he won acclaim, for which he was honored by the legislature of Georgia.

In 1853–1854 Hardee was busy on a project of rewriting the army's manual *Rifle and Light Infantry Tactics*. The revised work, published in 1855, was intended to update the drill and tactics of the army in light of the changes that technology was bringing to the battlefield. The new version of the manual emphasized speed and flexibility of drill and maneuver. Acceptance of the work assured Hardee's fame, and over the next ten years many an officer spent long hours studying *Hardee's Tactics* and instructing his men in the drill prescribed therein. Hardee's work on the manual was followed by a stint (1856–1860) as commandant of cadets at the Military Academy.

After his 1861 resignation, Hardee served briefly with the Georgia state forces and was appointed a Confederate brigadier general on June 17. Confederate President Jefferson Davis, who had been U.S. secretary of war in the mid-1850s, had a high appreciation for Hardee's abilities. Davis sent Hardee first to Fort Morgan on the Gulf Coast at Mobile and then to raise, organize, and train troops in Alabama.

In September 1861 Hardee was ordered to take many of his Arkansas troops to Bowling Green, Kentucky, where he and they became part of what was eventually to become the Army of Tennessee—the Confederacy's main force in the crucial area between the Mississippi River and the Appalachian Mountains. For almost all of the remainder of the war Hardee would be associated with that army. He would play a key role in many of its battles and in its internal politics.

On October 7, 1861, Hardee was promoted to major general, effective immediately. In 1862 he and Leonidas Polk emerged as the two chief subordinates in the Army of Tennessee. As that army evolved toward a two-corps organization, they naturally became the corps commanders. On October 11, 1862, Hardee was promoted to lieutenant general, to rank from October 10.

On the battlefield Hardee usually proved a steady, reliable—but never brilliant—corps commander. Perhaps his best performance came at Murfreesboro, Tennessee, on December 31, 1862, when he attacked and rolled up the right of the Federal line.

In 1862 and 1863 Hardee also emerged as a leader of a group of officers who were opposed to General Braxton Bragg, commander of the Army of Tennessee. The intramural squabbling to which this feud gave rise poisoned relations among the army's generals, hampered military operations, demoralized the troops, and played a major role in the Confederacy's loss of the West.

In July 1863 Hardee was ordered to Mississippi to help organize and command troops there. Three months later he returned to the Army of Tennessee to resume command of a corps. When Braxton Bragg resigned from command of the army in November

Though heavily retouched, this is definitely a photograph of Hardee. He appears to be in old Army uniform, but since he may have worn that outfit into his Confederate service, as did so many others, it is impossible to state categorically that this is not a Confederate era image. (*Civil War Times Illustrated* Collection, Harrisburg, Pa.)

The same is the case with this standing portrait. (Chicago Historical Society)

after the debacle at Missionary Ridge, Hardee, as senior officer present, assumed command. Hardee, however, made it clear that he did not want the job permanently, and when Joseph E. Johnston was placed at the head of the army in late 1863, Hardee returned to his corps.

In the Atlanta Campaign of 1864 Hardee found himself eclipsed by the much younger but far more flamboyant Lieutenant General John Bell Hood. In July, when Hood was jumped over Hardee's head to replace Johnston, Hardee was very displeased and asked to be transferred. President Davis denied his plea. In the July and August battles around Atlanta Hardee did not give Hood his full cooperation, and the two soon fell to bickering about the responsibility for lost battles.

After Atlanta fell, Davis, Hood, and Hardee were in agreement that Hardee should be sent elsewhere. He was, therefore, sent to command the troops at Savannah, Georgia. When that city had to be evacuated in December 1864 Hardee moved with his troops into the Carolinas. He and his command were included in the surrender of Rebel forces in North Carolina in late April 1865.

Hardee married twice. His first wife, whom he married in 1840, was Elizabeth Dummett. She died in 1853. Ten years later Hardee married Mary Foreman Lewis. His four children were by his first wife. His only son, William Joseph ("Willie") was mortally wounded at the battle of Bentonville, North Carolina, on March 21, 1865, while serving in his father's command.

For several months immediately after the war Hardee lived on and managed two of his wife's plantations in western Alabama. He also derived income from property in Georgia and Florida. In 1866 he and his family moved to Selma, Alabama, where Hardee was active in several facets of the town's economic life—warehousing, insurance, and railroads among them.

Hardee died November 6, 1873, in Wytheville, Virginia, as he was returning to Alabama. He was buried in Live Oak Cemetery in Selma.

Richard M. McMurry

Connelly, Thomas Lawrence, *Army of the Heartland: The Army of Tennessee, 1861–1862* and *Autumn of Glory: The Army of Tennessee, 1862–1865* (Baton Rouge, 1967, 1971).

Hughes, Nathaniel Cheairs, Jr., *General William J. Hardee: Old Reliable* (Baton Rouge, 1965).

Woodworth, Steven E., *Jefferson Davis and His Generals: The Failure of Confederate Command in the West* (Lawrence, 1990).

Taken at the same time as the full seated portrait, this variant of Hardee as a major or lieutenant general shows the toll the war years have taken on him. (Library of Congress)

✫ *William Polk Hardeman* ✫

The only known uniformed portrait of General Hardeman is this, which appears to show him as a brigadier. That would date the image to March 1865 or later. (William C. Davis Collection)

William Polk "Gotch" Hardeman was born November 4, 1816, in Williamson County, Tennessee. He moved to Texas in 1835 and settled with his father in Matagorda County. He took part in the Texas revolution and fought in many Indian campaigns during the 1830s and 1840s. During the Mexican War he served under Ben McCulloch; following the war he headed an exploring party into west Texas and New Mexico. He was a delegate to the Texas secession convention from January 28 until February 4, 1861, representing Guadalupe County. Hardeman listed his occupation as planter and his place of residence as Plum Creek.

When the Civil War began, he was elected captain in the 4th Texas Cavalry, which was mustered into Confederate service by September 20, 1861. Hardeman took part in Brigadier General Henry H. Sibley's invasion of New Mexico, and participated in the Battle of Valverde as a captain under Lieutenant Colonel William R. Scurry. Hardeman led "the last brilliant and successful charge, which decided the fortunes of that day." He was subsequently promoted to lieutenant colonel and then colonel of the 4th Texas. The brigade took part in the recapture of Galveston on January 1, 1863, and then went to Louisiana under Sibley but eventually came under the command of Brigadier General Thomas Green.

Hardeman fought in the battles at Fort Bisland, La Fource, Fordoche, and Bayou Bourbeau. On December 31, 1863, Colonel Hardeman was listed in Tom Green's cavalry division as commander of Green's old brigade, which included the 4th, 5th, and 7th Texas Cavalries, as well as Waller's 13th Texas Battalion. The troops remained in Louisiana until December 1863 when the Texans headed home because of a threat of Union invasion along the coast.

Early in 1864 they returned to Louisiana and took part in the Red River Campaign. Hardeman led his regiment at Mansfield on April 8, and Pleasant Hill on April 9, 1864. When Tom Green was killed at Blair's Landing on April 12, 1864, Hardeman briefly succeeded to command of the cavalry. On October 28, 1864, Lieutenant General Edmund Kirby Smith recommended him for promotion, and noted that he now commanded the 3d Texas Cavalry Brigade. A promotion, wrote Smith, "is deserved and will give satisfaction." Hardeman was one of three whom Kirby Smith claimed "are pronounced superior cavalry officers—the best brigade commanders in Trans-Mississippi."

In November 1864 Hardeman's brigade was sent to southern Arkansas. In March 1865 Hardeman's brigade was part of Major General John A. Wharton's cavalry corps. Hardeman also commanded a brigade in Brigadier General Hamilton P. Bee's division. He was finally promoted to brigadier general on March 18, 1865, to rank from the previous day.

When the war ended, Hardeman went to Mexico, where he worked as a land surveyor in Durango and Metlakanka. Sometime in the late 1860s he returned to Texas and engaged in farming until 1874. After this date he served as assistant sergeant-at-arms of the Texas House of Representatives, then as state inspector of railroads, and finally as superintendent of public buildings and grounds in Austin. This last position included his supervising the Texas Confederate Soldiers' Home. He died at Austin on April 8, 1898, and was buried in the Texas State Cemetery.

Anne Bailey

Oates, Stephen B., *Confederate Cavalry West of the River* (Austin, 1964).

Roberts, O. M., *Texas*, Vol. XI in Evans, *Confederate Military History*.

Nathaniel Harris has three stars on his lapel, presumably meaning that he was a colonel in this pre-1864 image. (U.S. Army Military History Institute, Carlisle, Pa.)

⋆ Nathaniel Harrison Harris ⋆

Born in Natchez, Mississippi on August 22, 1834, this Vicksburg lawyer became captain of the Warren Rifle Company April 25, 1861. After a month's duty in the Mississippi State Army his company entered Confederate service on May 14, 1861. Ordered to Richmond May 18, the Rifles became Company 19th Mississippi Infantry Regiment, June 11, 1861.

The 19th, the first Mississippi regiment enlisted "for the war," Joined Joseph E. Johnston at Bunker Hill, July 7. As part of his army's Fifth Brigade, it reached Manassas the morning after First Bull Run. The Mississippians served on that front until March.

Harris left them on February 9 for recruiting in Mississippi. He resumed command April 3 just as Cadmus Wilcox's Brigade, including the 19th, reached Yorktown from North Carolina. Harris served in the Warwick River trenches twenty-one days under constant shelling before the regiment went into reserve.

Wilcox's assault at Williamsburg on May 5, 1862, marked Harris' first big battle. His lieutenant-colonel, Lucius Lamar, reported that to Harris and two other officers "especial praise is due not only for their gallant bearing on the field, but for their unremitting attention to their respective commands."

Although slightly wounded May 5, Harris was present when fighting resumed May 31. His regimental superiors fared worse. Colonel Christopher Mott was killed at Williamsburg, and Lamar's vertigo disabled him. The 19th, accordingly, went into Seven Pines and the Seven Days' under Major John Mullins, with Harris as second-in-command. The regiment was slightly engaged May 31 and saw much action June 1, 27, and 30, 1862. Following Mullins' severe wounding at Gaines' Mill, Harris led the outfit until he was shot at Frayser's Farm. Ten days later Harris was back on duty.

His sturdy service on the Peninsula brought promotion to major, backdated to May 5, 1862. Because Lamar and Mullins never returned, Harris thereafter led the regiment. He was appointed lieutenant-colonel December 20, 1862, ranking from November 24. Then April 2, 1863, he became colonel, again backdated to Mott's death May 5, 1862. This extra eleven months seniority proved crucial when Harris was considered for general in 1864.

By then, he had done more fighting in a new Mississippi brigade formed June 18, 1862, under Winfield S. Featherston (under Carnot Posey after January15, 1863). Harris saw little action at Kelly's Ford August 21, but fought heavily in James Longstreet's counterattack at Second Manassas August 30. Wounded again, this time more critically, Harris could not resume command immediately but had to take leave, September 15-October 5.

He thus missed Antietam but returned for Fredericksburg, although not engaged there. He battled severely at Chancellorsville, especially May 3, 1863. Skirmishing at Franklin's Crossing, June 5; Gettysburg, July 2; and Brandy Station, August 1, completed his summer.

Enlargement of his spinal coccyx necessitated leave, August 23-October 26, 1863. On returning, he assumed command of the brigade containing the 12th, 16th, 19th, and 48th Mississippi Infantry Regiments, vice Posey, mortally wounded, October 14, 1863. Harris' troops saw slight action in the Rappahannock and Mine Run operations.

Posey's death November 13, 1863, necessitated finding a permanent brigadier. Division commander Richard H. Anderson recommended Colonel Samuel E. Baker of the 16th. R.E. Lee concurred November 26, that although Harris and two other colonels "are officers of intelligence & best disciplinarian. ...his regt. is in the best condition...." The War Department agreed, but Jefferson Davis objected to disregarding seniority.

Reexamination excluded senior colonel William Taylor and sustained Baker. Concerning Harris and the others, Lee told the President, January 11, 1864, "I know nothing against them. They ...are all gentlemen of intelligence & character. All have behaved well in battle. I do not know of any distinguishing act that would characterize one...above the others. If Anderson's and Lee's support for Baker are not sufficient to over-rule Col. Harris' priority of rank, his appt. had better be made. The brigade has been among the best in the army but was languishing without a general."

Despite such lukewarm endorsement, fellow Warren Countian, Jefferson Davis, seized Lee's line to direct Harris' promotion January 20, 1864, Harris was proposed February 5, and appointed brigadier-general and confirmed on February 17, 1864, ranking from January 20. Acceptance came March 4.

Ensuing campaigns dispelled doubts about his fitness for brigadier. He fought well at the Wilderness May 6, and Spotsylvania, May 8-10, 1864. May 12 marked Harris' highpoint in the Civil War. After demanding that Lee protect himself, his Mississippians charged into the Mule Shoe. When two other generals fell, Harris became senior brigadier present. In twenty hours of perhaps the most savage combat of the war, he contained Winfield Hancock's breakthrough and bought time to seal the breach.

Harris subsequently operated at Myers' Farm, May 14; North Anna, May 24; Turkey Hill, June 6; and Second Riddell's shop, June 13, 1864. At Petersburg, his Mississippians saw less action than some other brigades of William Mahone's Division, but they did participate at First Weldon Railroad, June 22-23; Second Deep Bottom, August 18; Globe Tavern, August 21; Burgess' Mill, October 27; Hicksford, December 7-14; and Dabney's Mill, February 6-7, 1865. Except for leave, July 5-15 and illness, August 21, 1864, Harris served throughout these operations. He commanded three of Mahone's brigades helping protect Richmond, August 17-20.

Mahone went into reserve along the Boydton Plank Road on November 9, 1864. After wintering there, that division transferred to Bermuda Hundred, March 5, 1865. Harris went to Richmond in mid-March to oppose Philip Sheridan's raiders but rejoined Mahone's right on March 20.

Five Forks forced Harris' recall to Petersburg, early on April 2, 1865. He reached his old winter quarters just after the VI Corps overran Wilcox. Again, Harris' Brigade saved the army. First in skirmishing, then in desperate stands in Forts Alexander and Gregg, his men and Wilcox's remnants repeatedly repulsed the XXIV Corps. Finally the Bluecoats overran Gregg, and Harris abandoned Alexander. His stand, however, gave Longstreet time to secure the sector and thus allowed the orderly abandonment of Petersburg overnight.

In ensuing operations, Harris formed battleline at Sayler's Creek and Cumberland Church. At Appomattox, only 372 men remained in his valiant little brigade.

Postwar, he lived in Mississippi, South Dakota, and California. Following death in England, August 23, 1900, his ashes lie in Brooklyn, New York.

This inexperienced citizen-soldier matured into a sturdy, reliable, competent regimental and brigade commander. Twice he faced and met the challenge of preventing defeat from becoming disaster.

Richard J. Sommers

Harris, Nathaniel H., " 'General Lee to the Rear' - The Incident with Harris' Mississippi Brigade" and "Defense of Battery Gregg," *Southern Historical Society Papers*, Vol. VIII: 105-110 and 475-488, 1880.

Harris, William M., *Movements of the Confederate Army in Virginia and the Part Taken Therein by the Nineteenth Mississippi: From the Diary of Gen. Nat. H. Harris* (Duncansby, Mississippi, 1901).

Krick, Robert K., "General Nat Harris' Diary: The Rarest Army of Northern Virginia Book?," *Blue & Gray* Magazine, Vol. VIII: 30-31, August, 1991.

"Nineteenth Mississippi Regiment," *Confederate Veteran*, Vol. VI: 70-71, 1898.

This portrait of Nathaniel Harris was taken in 1864 or 1865, showing him at the peak of his career. (Museum of the Confederacy, Richmond, Va.)

✷ *James Edward Harrison* ✷

No uniformed image of General Harrison has been found. This is probably post-war. (Miller, *Photographic History*)

James E. Harrison was born in Greenville District, South Carolina, on April 24, 1815. His family moved to Alabama, where in 1823 his brother, future Brigadier General Thomas Harrison, was born. From there the family moved to Monroe County, Mississippi, and James Harrison served two terms in the Mississippi Senate. His brother Thomas had moved to Texas in 1843, and James followed him in 1857, settling in central Texas near Waco. Because he could speak the language of both the Choctaw and Creek Indians, he served as an Indian commissioner. In February 1861 he was appointed by the state of Texas as one of the commissioners to the Choctaw, Chickasaw, Creek, Seminole, and Cherokee tribes in the Indian Territory.

When the Civil War began, Harrison helped raise the 15th Texas Infantry, which was organized in 1862 by the expansion of J. W. Speight's 1st Texas Infantry Battalion. The regiment was attached to Colonel W. R. Bradfute's brigade with the 20th, 22d, and 24th Texas cavalry regiments (dismounted). On April 9, 1863, Harrison reported to Fort Smith, Arkansas, where Brigadier General William Steele reported that the brigade was badly organized, without discipline, and almost destitute of clothing and supplies. Many of the men were unarmed and the weather was very cold, forcing them to suffer great hardships. A detachment from the brigade had been captured at Charleston, Arkansas, and at that time all the command's transportation was destroyed.

In May 1863 Lieutenant Colonel Harrison, commanding Speight's brigade, was ordered to Alexandria, Louisiana. He served under Brigadier General Thomas Green in Louisiana and participated in the battles in the southern part of the state. At the action on the Fordoche he led his command "most gallantly to the attack," and Tom Green reported that "all honor is due...." Major General Richard Taylor said of his conduct that Harrison was "especially deserving of mention." He participated in the Red River Campaign in April 1864, and in October Lieutenant General Edmund Kirby Smith recommended Harrison for promotion. Smith believed he should take command of an infantry brigade, commenting that Harrison was "best meriting promotion" and he was "especially recommended" for higher rank. Although there was not a command to give him, Smith observed that he needed a place as he was "doubtless a deserving officer." In December Adjutant General Samuel Cooper wrote that Jefferson Davis had recommended the promotion of Harrison, Hardeman, and Lane. Harrison was promoted to brigadier general January 6, 1865, to rank from December 22, 1864.

In March 1865 Harrison was instructed to proceed to Texas to Huntsville, Nacogdoches, or wherever William H. King's brigade was located; take command of it; and move to Houston. This force numbered an aggregate present of 1,363 and included the 15th Texas Infantry, 17th and 31st Texas Dismounted Cavalry, and Colonel George W. Merrick's battalion. In April his command changed slightly and he was ordered to concentrate his brigade near Harrisburg outside Houston. On June 2, 1865, Harrison was ordered to proceed to Galveston to take part in the official proceedings of the surrender and to perform the duties of commissioner as commanding officer of the District of Texas.

When the war ended, he returned to Waco and served as a trustee of Baylor University from 1861 to 1874. Harrison died on February 23, 1875, and was buried in the First Street Cemetery in Waco.

Anne Bailey

Oates, Stephen B., *Confederate Cavalry West of the River* (Austin, 1964).

Roberts, O. M., *Texas*, Vol. XI in Evans, *Confederate Military History*.

⋆ *Thomas Harrison* ⋆

No uniformed view of Thomas Harrison has come to light. This is probably postwar. (Albert G. Shaw Collection, Virginia Historical Society, Richmond, Va.)

Harrison was born on May 1, 1823, in Jefferson County, Alabama. Like Thomas, his older brother, James Edward, would also serve as a brigadier general in the Confederate army. The Harrisons moved to Monroe County, Mississippi, while Thomas was still a child. In 1843 he moved to Brazoria County, Texas, and studied law. By 1846 Harrison had returned to Mississippi, where he practiced law at Aberdeen. He enlisted in Colonel Jefferson Davis' 1st Mississippi Rifles when the Mexican War began and fought at Monterrey and Buena Vista. Harrison moved to Houston, Texas, after the war. He was elected to the Texas legislature as representative from Harris County in 1850 but resigned the next year when he moved to Maclin. Then in 1855 Harrison established his permanent home in Waco.

Harrison became captain of a militia company when the Civil War began, and in February 1861 his men moved into west Texas to help force United States troops to evacuate Fort (or Camp) Cooper. The company was mustered in on September 9 as Company A of Colonel Benjamin F. Terry's Texas Rangers cavalry regiment. Terry's men traveled via New Orleans and Nashville to Bowling Green, Kentucky, to join General Albert Sidney Johnston's army. There the unit was formally organized in November as the 8th Texas Cavalry Regiment. Harrison was elected major of the regiment.

He commanded the unit during a skirmish with Union cavalry at Tompkinsville on November 14. The rangers helped cover the retreat of Johnston's army to Nashville and then to Corinth. They fought in the Battle of Shiloh, April 6–7, 1862. As a result of a wound received during the first day's fighting, Colonel John A. Wharton turned command of the regiment over to Harrison on April 8. Harrison led the men in an action that day near Monterey under the command of Colonel Nathan Bedford Forrest. The regiment became part of Forrest's brigade when it was organized at Chattanooga on June 19 and accompanied the brigade on its raid into middle Tennessee during July and August. On July 13, the rangers participated in the capture of the Union garrison at Murfreesboro. Forrest wrote later that during this action Harrison had acted with his "usual daring and bravery."

Forrest's brigade joined General Braxton Bragg's army in Kentucky in early September. On the last day of that month Forrest turned over command of his brigade to Wharton; and Harrison, as lieutenant colonel, assumed direction of the regiment. The rangers saw skirmishing near Bardstown during the Union army's advance from Louisville and fought in the Battle of Perryville on October 8. Wharton's promotion to brigadier general on November 18 resulted in Harrison becoming colonel of the 8th Texas. The regiment fought at the Battle of Murfreesboro, December 31, 1862–January 3, 1863. His men had given Harrison the nickname "Old Iron Sides" by this time, because he had escaped injury in all the regiment's engagements. However, during the second day of fighting at Murfreesboro, he received a flesh wound in the hip, an injury so slight that he did not have to relinquish command.

Wharton's brigade accompanied Major General Joseph Wheeler on his raid against Union supply lines on the Tennessee River in February 1863 and participated in the unsuccessful attack on Fort Donelson on February 3. Wharton soon was given command of a division under Wheeler, and Harrison became commander of the brigade. Harrison's men did picket and outpost duty in Middle Tennessee, September 30–October 17, to disrupt the Union army's supply lines. On October 5 the brigade captured a small Union force at Christiana Station, burned the stockade and warehouse there, and destroyed some of the railroad.

Harrison and his men were detached in November and assigned to a division commanded by Brigadier General Frank C. Armstrong. They took part in the Knoxville Campaign, November 4–December 23, 1863. During the retreat from Knoxville to Russellville the brigade engaged in several skirmishes with the enemy. Harrison and his men remained in East Tennessee during the early months of 1864 and fought in several minor actions against Union cavalry forces. By April 30 the brigade had joined the Army of Tennessee at Dalton, Georgia, and was assigned to a division under Brigadier General William Y. C. Humes.

The men fought in engagements at Rocky Face Ridge, May 5–9, and Resaca, May 14–15. In the battles at Big Shanty and New Hope Church, Harrison's brigade fought dismounted and did its share of digging

entrenchments. During the Federal cavalry raids near Atlanta in July, Harrison's brigade helped pursue the column commanded by Brigadier General Edward M. McCook. The Confederates surrounded McCook's men at Newman on July 30 and routed them. Harrison accompanied Wheeler on his raid against the Union supply lines in northern Georgia and Middle Tennessee, August 10–September 10. The brigade assisted in defeating a small enemy force near Nashville during this raid. Wheeler's cavalry rested at Tuscumbia and rejoined the Army of Tennessee near Rome, Georgia, on October 8.

After small skirmishes in northern Georgia, Wheeler's men were sent to oppose Major General William T. Sherman's March to the Sea. Harrison's men fought in skirmishes near Griswoldville, November 20–21; at Waynesborough, November 26; and at Millen's Grove, December 1. When Wheeler's cavalry was reorganized in early January 1865, Harrison retained command of his brigade in Humes' division. He was promoted to brigadier general on February 18, to rank from January 14. The brigade participated in all of the marches of the Carolinas Campaign, February–April 1865. Harrison was wounded in an engagement at Monroe's Cross Roads, North Carolina, on March 10 and went to Greensboro to recover. He was paroled there at the end of the war.

A historian of Terry's Texas Rangers has written that Harrison "possessed rare, sound judgment" and concluded, "He may have been a bit cautious in venturing upon dubious enterprises, but when he did initiate one, he was in it body and soul. He was a well of inspiration to his men."

After the war, Harrison returned to Waco and resumed his law practice. He served as district judge from 1866 to 1877 and served as a presidential elector for the Democratic party in 1872. Harrison died in Waco on July 14, 1891, and was buried in the First Street Cemetery.

Arthur W. Bergeron, Jr.

Blackburn, James K. P., *Reminiscences of the Terry Rangers* (Austin, 1919).

Jeffries, C. C., "The Character of Terry's Texas Rangers," *Southwestern Historical Quarterly*, LXIV (April 1961).

Roberts, O. M., *Texas*, Vol. XI in Evans, *Confederate Military History*.

☆ *Robert Hopkins Hatton* ☆

No uniformed portrait of General Hatton has been found. This previously unpublished prewar image probably dates from the late 1850s. (Alabama Department of Archives and History, Montgomery, Ala.)

Born in Youngstown, Ohio, November 2, 1826, Hatton was the son of an itinerant Methodist minister. In 1835 the Hatton family moved to Tennessee, first to Nashville and then to rural Sumner County, where Robert received most of his formal schooling. He graduated from Cumberland University in Lebanon, Tennessee, in 1847. He then taught school for a year but reentered Cumberland University as a student in its nascent law department. Although he dropped out of law school, he continued to study jurisprudence on his own and was admitted to the Tennessee bar in 1850.

Shortly after opening a law practice in Lebanon, Tennessee, Hatton became actively involved in state politics. At first a staunch Whig, he shifted to the Know-Nothing (or American) party as the Whig party began to die in the mid-1850s. He was elected to the state legislature in 1855, as a Whig-American, and authored legislation promoting teacher training and railroad expansion. Quickly establishing a reputation as a forceful and articulate public speaker, Hatton was nominated by his party in 1857 to run for governor against Democrat Isham G. Harris. After a heated campaign, including an outbreak of fisticuffs between the two candidates, Hatton lost the election. Two years later, however, he won election to Congress as a member of the "Opposition" ticket.

Entering Washington as the nation drifted toward civil war, Congressman Hatton established himself as a strong Unionist, regularly debating both southern radicals and northern congressmen with abolitionist leanings. When the states of the lower South began to withdraw from the Union, Hatton worked with the Crittenden Compromise to prevent further disruption of the country. He actively supported the pro-Union elements in his district, and personally pleaded against secession. At one point, he was threatened by an angry crowd of secessionists in his home town and was burned in effigy.

When President Lincoln called for volunteers after the firing on Fort Sumter, however, Hatton lost all faith in the Union and soon pledged his loyalty to the South. Raising a company of volunteers, he was elected colonel of the 7th Tennessee Infantry in May 1861. In July Hatton's regiment was brigaded with the 1st and 14th Tennessee, under the command of Brigadier General Sam Anderson. Soon thereafter, the Tennesseans were ordered to Virginia, where they participated in the Cheat Mountain campaign. Throughout the fall and winter the Tennessee brigade served successively under Robert E. Lee and "Stonewall" Jackson in western Virginia. Constantly bothered by sickness, harsh weather, and fruitless marches, Hatton and his Tennesseans lobbied hard but unsuccessfully to be returned to their native state. Instead, in late February the brigade was transferred to a part of Joseph E. Johnston's army at Fredericksburg. In April the Tennesseans marched with Johnston's army to the Peninsula to participate in the month-long siege at Yorktown. With the Tennessee brigade serving in the Confederate rear guard on the retreat to Richmond, Hatton assumed command of the unit upon the resignation of General Anderson. Hatton received his commission as brigadier general on May 23, 1862, to rank immediately.

Assigned to Whiting's division, the Tennessee brigade arrived on the battlefield of Seven Pines late on the afternoon of May 31. With Hatton in front on horseback, the brigade entered a dense, entangled woods where it plowed into a division of fresh Federal troops. Hatton's horse was shot from under him, and as he moved forward a few yards on foot, he was killed instantly by a Minié bullet. With merciless fire continuing to pour into their ranks, the Tennesseans fell back, bearing the body of their commander.

Hatton was buried in Richmond, but his body was returned to Lebanon, Tennessee, in 1866. At the time of his reburial, the Louisville *Journal* noted: "…few public men, indeed, had a brighter future than Robert Hatton. He was one of the purest, noblest, and best men whose public life and services have ever adorned the annals of Tennessee."

Charles F. Bryan, Jr.

This portrait of Hatton is so indistinct and apparently retouched in places that it is impossible to say with certainty that it is, or is not, a genuine uniformed view. If it is, it shows him as colonel of the 7th Tennessee. (Museum of the Confederacy, Richmond, Va.)

Bryan, Jr., Charles F., "Robert Hatton of Tennessee," M.A. thesis (University of Georgia, 1973).

Drake, James Vaulx, *Life of General Robert Hatton* (Nashville, 1866).

⋆ *James Morrison Hawes* ⋆

James M. Hawes grew up in the charmed circle of the Lexington, Kentucky, home of the Clays and Breckinridges, the Morgans and the Dukes. He was born there January 7, 1824, and later easily secured an appointment to the U.S. Military Academy, which he entered on July 1, 1841. The end of four years saw him emerge with an undistinguished record, twenty-ninth out of forty-one in the class of 1845. Still, when he received his brevet commission as a 2d lieutenant, he was assigned to the dragoons instead of the infantry, the customary assignment for men in the bottom half of their class.

Almost immediately the army sent him to Texas, putting him right on the scene for the opening of the war with Mexico. Hawes saw repeated action, including the fights at Vera Cruz, Contreras, Churubusco, Molino del Rey, and the final occupation of Mexico City. His performance earned him a brevet to 1st lieutenant, and when the war ended, he returned to West Point for a series of academic postings. He was an assistant professor of infantry tactics, mathematics, and cavalry tactics prior to 1850, when he went on a prized two-year assignment to observe French cavalry tactics and receive instruction at the cavalry school at Saumur.

Returning to the United States in 1852, Hawes finally sought frontier postings to see more action. He went to Texas, served briefly in Washington, then took part under Colonel Albert Sidney Johnston in the 1857 Mormon expedition, and finally wound up in Kansas as the army tried to act as buffer between pro- and antislavery forces contesting control of the territory's organization for statehood.

When the secession crisis came, Hawes did not wait to see what his native Kentucky would do. On May 9, 1861,

he resigned his commission as captain of the 2d Dragoons and promptly offered his allegiance to the new Confederacy. At first he was made a captain, there being no higher positions available for officers from states that did not actually have units in the Southern service. On June 16 he was promoted to major and less than two weeks later was made a full colonel to command the newly raised 2d Kentucky Cavalry, the 1st Kentucky having just reported for duty under fellow Kentuckian Benjamin Hardin Helm. Both regiments were raised out of Kentuckians who slipped out of the Bluegrass—which was still officially neutral—to Camp Boone in Tennessee, where they organized and trained.

Hawes commanded his regiment through the fall of 1861, making at least one raid into Kentucky to the Green River to burn bridges, but then did something that to many seemed inexplicable. He gave up his commission as a colonel and instead accepted one as a major in the infant Confederate Regular service. Perhaps it was a sign of his certainty of Southern independence that he preferred a commission in such an organization, assuming that all volunteer commissions would be retired at the end of the war.

However, when Albert Sidney Johnston, now a full general in the Confederate service, took command in Department No. 2, he quickly sought out his old companion-in-arms from Texas and Mormon expedition days. As early as October 27 he recommended to

This portrait of General Hawes was taken in Blessing & Patrick's Gallery in Houston, Texas. The absense of his collar insignia rank dates the photograph to the end of the war, most certainly 1865. (Lawrence T. Jones Collection)

Richmond that "there is no one available who, in my opinion, has higher qualifications for [brigadier general] than Major Hawes." Despite such high praise, it would not be until March 14, 1862, that the President gave Hawes the appointment, to rank from March 5. In his final pre-Shiloh organization of his army on March 29, Johnston assigned General Hawes command of all cavalry in the army not specifically attached to the infantry corps. In this position Hawes led the advance into Tennessee, though he played no actual role in the subsequent battle itself. After the battle April 6–7, and Johnston's death, his successor, General P. G. T. Beauregard, put Hawes in command of a brigade in Major General John C. Breckinridge's division, consisting of the 31st Alabama, the 4th and 9th Kentucky, an Alabama battalion, and Byrne's Kentucky battery.

When Beauregard left the army that June, General Braxton Bragg took over, and very quickly he protested a want of confidence in Hawes "as, in my judgment, unsuited for [his] responsible position." The basis of this attitude is unknown, but just a month later Hawes was reassigned to the Trans-Mississippi command of Major General Theophilus H. Holmes and given command of a cavalry brigade posted along the White River in Arkansas.

Hawes would spend the rest of the war in the Trans-Mississippi Department, shifting back and forth from cavalry to infantry, and again to cavalry. In June 1863 during the effort to relieve the siege of Vicksburg, he commanded the 8th, 18th, and 22d Texas infantries during the attack at Young's Point on June 7, though he was not actively engaged. His division commander, Major General John G. Walker, did not expressly criticize Hawes' performance in not following orders to attack, but certainly implied a measure of displeasure with him. The following February Hawes was reassigned to Major General John B. Magruder's District of Texas, even though Lieutenant General Richard Taylor thought highly enough of Hawes to ask that he be allowed to keep him in his command.

But Hawes went to Texas, where he took over a cavalry brigade of three small Texas regiments. By the summer Magruder had placed him in command of the Sub-district of Galveston, with a small garrison of fewer than three thousand present for duty. Magruder seems to have been less than pleased with Hawes, having to remind him to carry out orders for defense. Then Hawes became high-handed with the civil officials

of Galveston, accusing many in the city of "treason of the darkest dye." In April 1864 he actually proposed to arrest the mayor and city council and evict them from the city.

Hawes also held a nominal field command in General Kirby Smith's organization of the Army of the Trans-Mississippi, his Galveston garrison of the 2d and 29th Texas, the 1st Texas Heavy Artillery, and an unnumbered Texas regiment comprising his brigade. But he saw no action of any note, and even though by March 1865 he commanded a "division," including a cavalry brigade of sorts, he led barely three thousand men. And Magruder was still not happy with him. With the war all but over, Magruder relieved him of command on April 14, 1865.

Hawes returned to Kentucky at the end of the conflict to open a hardware business in Covington, and in this he prospered for more than twenty years, finally dying November 22, 1889, to be buried in Covington's Highland Cemetery.

Based upon his prewar experience, there should have been much to expect from Hawes, but he seems rarely to have measured up to the needs and expectations of his superiors, an example of the fact that the best in military training and opportunity for experience do not necessarily guarantee leadership ability, as so many in the Civil War demonstrated.

William C. Davis

Johnston, J. Stoddard, *Kentucky*, Vol. IX in Evans, *Confederate Military History*.

Kerby, Robert, *Kirby Smith's Confederacy* (New York, 1969).

✶ *Alexander Travis Hawthorne* ✶

No uniformed portrait of Hawthorne is known. This is probably a postwar image. (Albert G. Shaw Collection, Virginia Historical Society, Richmond, Va.)

Alexander Travis Hawthorne was born on January 10, 1825, in Conecuh County, Alabama. He attended school at Evergreen Academy and Mercer University in Macon, Georgia. In 1846 and 1847 he studied at Yale University, then moved to Arkansas, where he took up the practice of law.

When the Civil War began, he joined the 6th Arkansas Infantry and was elected lieutenant colonel; in 1862 he became colonel. In October 1861 William J. Hardee reported four regiments of Arkansas infantry under him, and one of these was commanded by Hawthorne. At the Battle of Shiloh Hawthorne's 6th Arkansas was part of Thomas C. Hindman's 1st Brigade, Hardee's III Corps, Army of the Mississippi. At the unit's reorganization on May 14, 1862, he was defeated for reelection, but in June 1862 Hawthorne was listed as commander of the 5th Brigade in Hardee's III Corps. This brigade consisted of the 33d Alabama, 17th, 21st, and 23d Tennessee as well as Austin's Battery, and in August it was reported on the railroad between Atlanta and Chattanooga.

By December 1862, Hawthorne was back in Arkansas and in command of an Arkansas regiment assigned to James Fagan's Brigade, Shoup's Second Division, Hindman's Corps, Army of the Trans-Mississippi. He took part in the Battle of Helena on July 4, 1863, where he temporarily commanded an Arkansas infantry brigade. During the battle he was under Fagan's direction and fought at Graveyard Hill. Hawthorne reported that he had begun the skirmishing as his command was positioned in the front, stating: "Without waiting for the other regiments of the brigade to form, I gave the order to charge, which was responded to by loud shouts along my entire line."

He drove the Federals back to their fourth line of defense by 7:00 A.M. But his men became tired and discouraged when no reinforcements came from Major

General Sterling Price, Brigadier General John S. Marmaduke, or Brigadier General Lucius M. Walker. Although Brigadier General Mosby M. Parsons and Brigadier General Dandridge McRae stormed across Graveyard Hill, they could not take the fort on Hindman's Hill; the attack was unsuccessful, and at 10:30 Fagan ordered a withdrawal. Hawthorne, who offered to cover the retreat in person with nine volunteers, kept up the fire for twenty more minutes, allowing the Confederates to escape. He did not pull back until the little group ran out of ammunition; three of their number died protecting the army's retreat. Fagan reported: "Colonel Hawthorne was constantly to the front, cheering his men on from one success to another. When orders came from Lieutenant-General Holmes to abandon the field, Colonel Hawthorne remained with a small number of his men engaging the enemy until the last of the army had left the field and retired behind the high hills which lay between them and danger."

Hawthorne was promoted to brigadier general February 23, to rank from February 18, 1864. In April 1864 he took part in the Camden Expedition, where Brigadier General Thomas J. Churchill reported he "gallantly" came to the rescue of Brigadier General James Tappan at Jenkin's Ferry. Churchill wrote after the battle that he wanted to thank Hawthorne for the "promptitude" with which he executed all his orders, and for the "skillful and masterly manner" in which he handled his brigade. Hawthorne was seen in the "thickest of the fight cheering" on his men to victory.

In September 1864 Hawthorne's brigade was part of Churchill's 1st Division, II Corps, Army of the Trans-Mississippi. It was composed of the 34th, 35th, and 37th Arkansas as well as Colonel Cadwallader Polk's Arkansas regiment. Hawthorne's brigade was stationed at Monticello in southern Arkansas.

When the war ended, Hawthorne moved to Brazil, where he stayed until 1874. Upon returning to the United States, he moved to Atlanta and in 1880 became a Baptist minister. He returned to Texas, where he died in Dallas on May 31, 1899, and was buried at Marshall, Texas.

Anne Bailey

Harrell, John M., *Arkansas*, Vol. X in Evans, *Confederate Military History*.

✫ *Harry Thompson Hays* ✫

A previously unpublished image of Harry T. Hays as a brigadier probably late in the war. (Southeastern Louisiana University, Hammond, La.)

Harry Thompson Hays, born in Wilson County, Tennessee, on April 14, 1820, was raised by an uncle in Wilkinson County, Mississippi, after being orphaned. Upon graduating from Baltimore's St. Mary's College, he opened a law practice in New Orleans and engaged in local politics. Hays served with distinction in the Mexican War, became a prominent Whig in the 1850s, and was a Whig presidential elector in 1852, supporting Winfield Scott.

After Louisiana seceded in 1861, Hays was elected colonel of the 7th Louisiana Volunteers and was known to be an officer who drank hard and fought harder. One soldier said he was highly respected and treated his officers well. Upon the conclusion of business, Hays often would invite an officer into his tent where he would "always find a black bottle filled with the best that can be procured in times like these." Hays also had a sense of humor, and upon his suggestion the Army of Northern Virginia began using the tune "Yankee Doodle" to drum disgraced soldiers out of service rather than the "Rogue's March." As Hays put it, more rogues marched to the "Yankee Doodle" on any given day than to the latter tune.

As part of Jubal Early's brigade in Virginia, Hays' regiment saw action at Blackburn's Ford on July 18, 1861, and participated in Early's flank attack against Irvin McDowell's forces at First Manassas. After becoming part of the 1st Louisiana Brigade under Richard Taylor, Hays' regiment then swept through the Shenandoah Valley in 1862 with "Stonewall" Jackson. Hays led his men in action at Middletown, Winchester, and Port Republic. At Port Republic the 5th and 27th Virginia regiments were also put under his command. Faced by a superior force in an open field, Hays attempted to throw the enemy off balance by attacking. Charles Winder wrote, "Hays moved his command forward in gallant style with a cheer." This attack failed to dislodge the Yankees, however, and Hays was badly wounded.

Hays was out of action for several months but was not forgotten. When Taylor was promoted and sent west, he recommended Hays be given command of the brigade of Louisiana Tigers. Hays received his brigadier's star on July 25, 1862, effective immediately, but because of his

Hays' best-known likeness, probably made earlier in the war when he had a full beard. (Cook Collection, Valentine Museum, Richmond, Va.)

wound was unable to rejoin the brigade until days before the Battle of Antietam. At Antietam, Hays' brigade was in support of Jackson's front line near the famous cornfield. After enduring fierce artillery fire, he was finally ordered into action. Running headlong into the enemy in the cornfield, the brigade engaged in a vicious fight before retreating to the Dunkard Church. In thirty minutes Hays lost 336 men, over sixty per cent of his small brigade.

Hays was only lightly engaged at Fredericksburg in December 1862, but supply shortages and his Tigers' preying on neighboring farms made for a miserable winter. Early, in whose division the brigade served, complained so much to Hays about his men's thievery that Hays briefly tried to get his brigade transferred. His relationship with Early improved, however, in time for the Chancellorsville Campaign in spring 1863. When Lee headed for the Wilderness to intercept Joseph Hooker, Early's division was left to confront the Union force near Fredericksburg. After several days of skirmishing and marching, Hays led his men in a spectacular charge against the Yankees at Salem Church on May 3, 1863. Attacking across rugged hills, the brigade smashed through two Union lines. "Hays seemed to be everywhere," wrote one soldier, who remembered the general riding up and down the line urging the men onward. Watching from atop a nearby hill with Lee, Early reportedly exclaimed, "Those Louisiana fellows may steal as much as they please now!" as he watched Hays surge forward. Unfortunately, a third Federal line stopped the assault, and many of the Tigers were captured, being too exhausted to escape. In the six days spent around Fredericksburg, Hays' casualties were 669.

In the Gettysburg Campaign Hays' star continued to rise. On June 14, 1863, he led the assault that captured the main fort protecting Winchester, prompting Early to write, "The charge of Hays' brigade upon the enemy's works was a most brilliant achievement." General Richard S. Ewell told one officer that next to God, he was most indebted to Hays' brigade for the victory at the Second Battle of Winchester. At Gettysburg on July 1 Hays joined John B. Gordon in smashing the Federal right flank. Cutting off the Yankees from Gettysburg, Hays captured more prisoners than he had men, and one of his officers put the total number of prisoners at three thousand. When Ewell hesitated to continue the attack against Cemetery Hill, Hays reportedly urged him to order the assault. Ewell only laughed and teased if the Tigers had not had enough fighting for one day. Hays bristled and snapped that he was only trying to save lives later. At sunset on July 2 Hays

was finally sent against the hill with his and Robert Hoke's North Carolina brigade. In a daring twilight attack Hays fought his way up the hill and captured two batteries before being forced out by Federal reinforcements. Nonetheless, Ewell said that the effort "was worthy of the highest praise." In the three days at Gettysburg Hays lost another 313 men.

In November 1863 tragedy struck Hays' brigade at Rappahannock Station. The Louisiana brigade and part of Hoke's brigade were surprised and overwhelmed by the Yankees while guarding a pontoon bridge across the river. In a surprise attack the Federals poured into the works and surrounded Hays. Before he could surrender, however, his horse bolted and carried him safely back across the bridge through a hail of gunfire. Seven hundred of his men were not so lucky and ended up in prison camps. Later that month Hays temporarily took command of Early's division during the Mine Run Campaign, when Early took the II Corps from an ill Ewell.

Hard service followed in 1864. In the Wilderness Hays was posted on the left of Ewell's line and attacked the Yankees with vigor on May 5, but fell back with a loss of 250 men—over one-third of his command. Due to heavy losses, the 1st Louisiana Brigade was then consolidated with the 2d Louisiana Brigade and put in Edward Johnson's division. The new consolidated brigade was placed under Hays' command, but this position was shortlived when he was seriously wounded on May 9 in the trenches at Spotsylvania.

Upon recovering from his wound Hays was transferred in autumn 1864 to Louisiana, where he tried to assemble absentee soldiers. On May 10, 1865, he was appointed major general by Kirby Smith but was never nominated by Davis or confirmed by the Senate due to the collapse of the Confederacy. After the war Hays returned to New Orleans and was appointed sheriff for Orleans Parish in 1866. Philip Sheridan removed him, however, after he was suspected of using deputies to attack carpetbagger supporters during a New Orleans riot. Hays continued to practice law and was affiliated with the White League before dying of Bright's disease on August 21, 1876. He was buried in the Washington Avenue Cemetery in New Orleans.

Terry L. Jones

Jones, Terry L., *Lee's Tigers: The Louisiana Infantry in the Army of Northern Virginia* (Baton Rouge, 1987).

A slight variant of previous image and probably made at the same sitting. (Museum of the Confederacy, Richmond, Va.)

✴ *Louis Hébert* ✴

No uniformed image of Hébert has been found. This is a prewar image. (Museum of the Confederacy, Richmond, Va.)

Louis Hébert, a first cousin of Confederate Brigadier General Paul Octave Hébert and brother-in-law of Brigadier General Walter H. Stevens, was born in Iberville Parish, Louisiana, on March 13, 1820. A member of a wealthy planter family, Hébert received his education from private tutors and at Jefferson College in St. James Parish. He then graduated third in the West Point class of 1845. Taking a commission in the engineering corps, Hébert served only one year as an assistant engineer for construction at Fort Livingston, Louisiana. He resigned his commission in 1846 when family illness forced him to take over his father's sugar plantation in Iberville Parish. From 1847 to 1861, he continued his military career in the state militia, holding the ranks of major and colonel. Hébert also served in the state senate (1853–55), as Louisiana's chief engineer (1855–59), and on the Board of Public Works (1860–61).

At the outbreak of war, Hébert was elected colonel of the 3d Louisiana Infantry, a regiment comprised mostly of north Louisiana men. He was a strict disciplinarian and at first was resented by the regiment, but later the men came to regard him as a first-rate officer. Placed in Ben McCulloch's command, Hébert's regiment saw hard fighting at Wilson's Creek, Missouri, on August 10, 1861. When the Yankees attacked the Confederate camp from two directions, Hébert's regiment was quickly sent into action against Franz Sigel's force in the rear. Sometimes the regiment fought in fragments, but Hébert was in the thick of the battle and his men took five cannon. One officer wrote that the Confederates were preparing a second attack, "but the Louisianians under Colonel Hébert had fully satisfied Colonel Sigel, and he retreated without giving us another chance at him." McCulloch also praised the "coolness and bravery" of Hébert and his other colonels.

After Wilson's Creek Hébert was given the 2d Brigade in Sterling Price's command. On March 7, 1862, Hébert aided in the attack on Samuel Curtis'

Federal force at Pea Ridge, Arkansas. On March 8 while leading an attack against the Yankee line, Hébert and some of his men became separated from the main force and were overwhelmed and captured. His superiors at first reported him killed in action and praised his leadership during the fight.

After being exchanged, Hébert was promoted to brigadier general on May 26, 1862, to rank from that date. Returning to the 2d Brigade in Henry Little's division, Hébert again fought well. When Union Major General William S. Rosecrans attacked Price's force at Iuka, Mississippi, on September 19, 1862, Hébert's brigade helped defend a vital crossroads in the rear. When Little was killed, Hébert took command of the division and was said to have "kept up the fight with vigor." Price withdrew during the night, and Hébert continued to command Little's division until the Confederate attack on Corinth. During that engagement October 3–4, Hébert was ill and relinquished command to Brigadier General Martin Green.

After Corinth Hébert returned to his brigade of mostly Mississippi infantry and was placed under John C. Pemberton at Vicksburg when Price was sent to the Trans-Mississippi Department. Hébert's brigade defended Snyder's Bluff near Vicksburg during the winter of 1862–63 and held the trenches just north of the railroad during the siege. As part of John Forney's division, Hébert's men saw heavy action during the siege, particularly during the Federal attacks of May 18 and May 22. He and his men were surrendered with the rest of the garrison on July 4, 1863.

After being exchanged a second time, Hébert was assigned to the Army of Tennessee and was finally sent to assume command of the heavy artillery in and around Fort Fisher on the North Carolina coast. For the remainder of the war he served in both this capacity and as the chief engineer for the Department of North Carolina.

After the war Hébert worked as a newspaper editor and teacher in both Iberville and St. Martin parishes. He died in St. Martin Parish on January 7, 1901, and was buried in Breaux Bridge.

Terry L. Jones

Dimitry, John, *Louisiana*, Vol. X in Evans, *Confederate Military History*.

Tunnard, William H., *A Southern Record: The Story of the Third Louisiana Infantry* (Baton Rouge, 1866).

✶ *Paul Octave Hébert* ✶

The only known image of Hébert in uniform, probably as colonel of the 1st Louisiana in 1861. (Museum of the Confederacy, Richmond, Va.)

Born on December 12, 1818, at Acadia Plantation in Iberville Parish, Louisiana, Paul Octave Hébert was a first cousin of Confederate Brigadier General Louis Hébert. Like his cousin, Hébert was part of a wealthy family and had private tutors, graduating first in both the 1836 class at Jefferson College and the 1840 class of West Point. His high class ranking won Hébert a 2d lieutenant 's commission in the engineers and an appointment as acting assistant professor of engineering at the academy. In July 1842 he was sent to south Louisiana to superintend work on the Mississippi River defenses. Hébert resigned from the army in 1845 to become survey general of Louisiana and worked on the construction of the western passes to New Orleans. He also developed a passion for hunting and horse racing, and became president of the Metairie Jockey Club.

In 1847, during the Mexican War, Hébert resigned his state engineer's position to become General Isaac Johnson's aide-de-camp, but soon afterwards he was appointed lieutenant colonel of Franklin Pierce's 14th U.S. Infantry. Serving in numerous battles, Hébert was brevetted colonel for gallantry at Molino del Rey. He was often mentioned in reports by Pierce as the gallant young Creole colonel.

In 1848 Hébert returned to his plantation near Bayou Goula. Although he was defeated for the state senate in 1849, he was a delegate to the 1852 state constitution convention and was elected governor the same year. A Democrat, Hébert was said to have been the youngest governor ever elected in Louisiana. As governor he supported railroad construction, public education, and the improvement of navigable waterways. After leaving office, Hébert helped get his former West Point classmate, William T. Sherman, appointed superintendent of the Louisiana Seminary of Learning and Military Academy.

During the secession crisis of December 1860, Hébert was appointed to the military board responsible for preparing Louisiana's defenses. When the Civil War came, he was first commissioned colonel of the 1st Louisiana Artillery but soon afterwards was appointed brigadier general of state troops. Then on August 17, 1861, he was commissioned a brigadier general in the Virginia army, effective immediately, and was given command of the Department of Texas. Hébert concentrated his efforts on the defense of Galveston but was hampered by a lack of arms and munitions. At times he was so desperate for funds that he had to ask the Galveston civilians for monetary donations. Furthermore, his men and guns were often stripped from him for service in Arkansas. Such frustrations pained Hébert. Soon after arriving at Galveston, he wrote Judah P. Benjamin, "I much fear that I have brought my little military reputation to an early end." Not surprisingly, Hébert's weak force could not stop the Federals from taking Galveston in October 1862.

After the fall of Galveston, Hébert worked to raise more troops in Texas, train them, and secure supplies from Mexico. Again his forces were taken away, this time for the defense of Vicksburg, and he was constantly plagued by deserters, Texas Unionists, and unethical Mexican traders. Exasperated, Hébert requested to be given command of the Texas troops in any future campaign. Instead, he was given command of north Louisiana and spent much of 1863 guarding railroads and rivers, scouting Union forces, and smuggling supplies into besieged Vicksburg. Some sources claim he saw action in the battle at Milliken's Bend, Louisiana, on June 7, 1863, but it does not appear that he actually saw combat there. In July Yankee raiders forced him to evacuate the city of Monroe and burn five thousand bales of cotton stored there. One postwar source gives Hébert credit for developing a plan to force U.S. Grant from Vicksburg by attacking the Union supplied upriver from the city, but states that Hébert's superiors never accepted it.

In August 1864 Hébert replaced Major General John B. Magruder as commander of the District of Texas. Within a month, however, he was relieved by Major General James G. Walker and took over the Eastern Sub-district of Texas. Hébert held this post until May 1865. After Robert E. Lee surrendered in April, Edmund Kirby Smith turned the Trans-Mississippi Department over to Magruder, who immediately gave it to Hébert. Both Kirby Smith and Magruder then left for Mexico. On May 26, 1865, the day after assuming command of the department, Hébert surrendered it to Union Major General Gordon Granger. Although officially a brigadier general, Hébert was considered by many a major general by virtue of his having commanded a military department both early and late in the war. Supposedly a major general's commission was made out for him, but Jefferson Davis never signed it.

After the surrender Hébert returned to his Home Place Plantation. He took the oath of allegiance and through an endorsement by Sherman received a presidential pardon from Andrew Johnson. He became a Liberal Republican during Reconstruction, thus angering many Louisianans, and supported the carpetbagger governor Henry Clay Warmouth. In the 1872 presidential election Hébert campaigned for Horace Greeley, but then later supported Grant's bid for a third term. Grant appointed him to various engineering boards, and Hébert worked both as a state and federal engineer in postwar Louisiana. Stricken with paralysis in 1879, he died from cancer on August 29, 1880, in New Orleans, and was buried in the Catholic Cemetery at Bayou Goula.

Terry L. Jones

Dupont, Albert Leonce, "The Career of Paul Octave Hébert, Governor of Louisiana, 1853–1856," *Louisiana Historical Quarterly*, XXXI, (1948).

✶ *Benjamin Hardin Helm* ✶

A brother-in-law of Abraham Lincoln, Benjamin H. Helm was born in Bardstown, Kentucky, on June 2, 1831. After early education at Elizabethtown Seminary and Kentucky Military Institute, he entered West Point in 1847. Helm graduated in 1851, ninth in his class of forty-two. Commissioned a 2d lieutenant the 2d U.S. Cavalry, he served on the Texas frontier for six months before returning home because of poor health. Helm resigned his commission on October 9, 1852, studied law at the University of Louisville and Harvard Law School, then practiced with his father in Elizabethtown until 1856. Elected to the state house of representatives in 1855 as a Whig, he served one term. From 1856 to 1858 Helm was the commonwealth's attorney for the Third District. At the end of his term he moved to Louisville, where he practiced law with a brother-in-law.

In 1860 Helm was appointed assistant inspector general of the state guard. A well-proportioned six-footer with blue eyes, brown hair, and a genial countenance, he was not a staunch Southern supporter as the crisis developed. He probably supported Bell and the Constitutional Union party in 1860, but he gradually became suspicious of the intentions of the Lincoln administration, and he refused the President's offer of a major's commission as army paymaster. Finally committed to the Confederate cause, Helm began raising the companies that made up the 1st Kentucky Cavalry. The regiment joined the Confederate army that entered the state in September, and Helm was commissioned its colonel on October 19, 1861. When Albert Sidney Johnston organized the Army of Central Kentucky in late October, he attached Helm's command to the 1st Kentucky Brigade. Helm engaged in scouting and outpost duties in south central Kentucky until the Confederates withdrew from Bowling Green in mid-February 1862. Just prior to Shiloh, where Helm helped guard the Confederate flanks, he was promoted to brigadier general on March 18, to rank from March 14. On April 28 he left the cavalry to command the 3d Brigade in John C. Breckinridge's division.

After medical leave for an operation, Helm rejoined the army in the Vicksburg area. On July 8, 1862, he was shifted to command of the 2d Brigade. During Breckinridge's futile attempt to take Baton Rouge Helm was seriously injured when his horse fell and crushed his right thigh during a wild encounter. When he was able to resume duty in September, Helm was given command of the post at Chattanooga. From there he was sent to command the Eastern District, District of the Gulf, with headquarters at Pollard, Alabama. After the death of Roger W. Hanson at Stone's River, Tennessee, the 1st Kentucky Brigade had several temporary commanders, but on February 14, 1863, Helm became its head.

Although he believed in drill and discipline as much as had Hanson, Helm had a kinder, gentler attitude that endeared him to the men. He was the best-loved commander that brigade ever had. He cemented the brigade's reputation for drill. In regimental competition the Orphans defeated a crack Louisiana brigade during the spring of 1863, and a presidential aide who inspected them reported, "Their performance was rapid, yet precise, their appearance tough and active, and they will compare

A curious image, somewhat retouched, that has been tentatively identified as Helm. While the identification is questionable, there are sufficient superficial similarities to warrant including it here. (Erick Davis Collection)

for efficiency with any brigade in the Confederate Army." During the absence of Breckinridge, Helm commanded the division.

In late spring and early summer Helm was involved in the futile effort of Joseph E. Johnston to break the siege of Vicksburg. He wrote his wife that the campaign was the most trying and disagreeable of his military experience. After a welcome respite near Morton, Mississippi, the division was ordered to join Braxton Bragg at Chattanooga as he sought to halt the advance of William S. Rosecrans at Chickamauga Creek. The Confederates turned and attacked on September 18. Breckinridge's division, on the extreme left of Bragg's line, saw little action September 18–19. Then it was shifted to the right end of the line, and Breckinridge and Brigadier General Patrick Cleburne were ordered to attack at 9:30 A.M. on September 20.

Cleburne was delayed, and Breckinridge moved out without waiting for him. Located on the left of the divisional line, Helm's left flank was open because of Cleburne's delay. Breckinridge's division overlapped the Union left, and Helm's brigade was split when it hit that point. Part of his brigade hit the Union flank and rear and made progress, but Helm was with the regiments that ran headlong into strong positions and determined opposition. Casualties mounted as they made three attacks on their stubborn foes. Sometime during the melee Helm was struck in the right side by a rifle ball that knocked him from his horse.

There was no hope of recovery, but Helm lingered for several hours. As the sounds of battle diminished, he inquired how the day had gone. He was pleased with the answer, and the last word he was heard to murmur was "victory." Helm died that night, and on September 23 was buried in the Atlanta cemetery. On September 19, 1884, his remains were reinterred in the family burial grounds near Elizabethtown, Kentucky.

Breckinridge wrote Helm's widow, "Your husband commanded them [The Orphans] like a thorough soldier. He loved them, they loved him, and he died at their head, a patriot and a hero." In his battle report General Daniel H. Hill declared that Helm's "gallantry and loveliness of character endeared him to everyone."

Lowell H. Harrison

Ben Hardin Helm, probably as colonel of the 1st Kentucky Cavalry late in 1861 or early 1862. (Albert G. Shaw Collection, Virginia Historical Society, Richmond, Va.)

Davis, William C., *The Orphan Brigade* (Garden City, 1980).

McMurty, R. Gerald, *Confederate General Ben Hardin Helm: Kentucky Brother-in-Law of Abraham Lincoln* (Madison, 1958).

Thompson, Ed Porter, *History of the Orphan Brigade* (Louisville, 1898).

☆ *Henry Heth* ☆

Henry Heth as colonel of the 45th Virginia in 1861. (Medford Historical Society, Medford, Mass.)

Henry Heth was born in Chesterfield County, Virginia, on December 16, 1825. He attended several preparatory institutions, among them Georgetown College in Washington, and later secured one of the prized appointments to the United States Military Academy, matriculating with A. P. Hill and others in 1843. At West Point the young Virginian displayed a carefree attitude, amassing numerous demerits and repelling all challengers to his post of thirty-eighth in a graduating class of that very number in 1847.

Heth emerged from the academy as a ripe prospect for the Mexican War and was soon serving in the 1st United States Infantry. Later, while with the 6th Infantry, Heth was the third member of a soon-to-be-famous mess that included Lewis A. Armistead and Winfield S. Hancock. The green graduate never had an opportunity to employ his military education during the Mexican War; his first serious action was not until 1851 while stationed on the plains. He spent his entire antebellum career on the frontier, vigorously chasing buffalo, Indians, and Mormons as a member of the 19th United States Infantry.

The highlight of Henry Heth's Old Army career was his work with various systems of marksmanship. He prepared a manual that served as a synopsis of the various methods then in use, relying heavily on French texts of his own translation. The result appeared in 1858—officially sanctioned by the War Department—and was the standard manual of the army for many years thereafter.

In April 1861 Heth made the painful decision to forsake his career for the defense of the South. He tendered his professional services to Jefferson Davis, who endorsed Heth's application with a note praising the Virginian as "a first rate soldier and of the caste of men most needed." Heth was appointed major of infantry to rank from March 16, 1861, but quickly rose to the rank of lieutenant colonel and served as Acting Quartermaster General of Virginia State Forces until May 31, 1861. Soon afterward his stretch of ill luck commenced. Heth joined General John B. Floyd for the purpose of organizing and training that politician's forces in anticipation of action in western Virginia. The result was, according to eyewitness Heth, "one of the most farcical and ridiculous campaigns that occurred…in any war…." In addition to aiding Floyd, Heth organized the 45th Virginia Infantry and served as its colonel through 1861.

A December 1861 plan to promote Heth to major general and hustle him to the Trans-Mississippi as a troubleshooter went awry. Instead he was appointed brigadier general on January 6, 1862, to rank immediately, and sent to Lewisburg in western Virginia. The peculiarities of mountain campaigning proved too great for Heth, and his forces were roundly thrashed at the battle of Lewisburg on May 23, 1862. Some of the Lewisburg locals had been "much struck with General Heth's resemblance to Napoleon, but after this affair we heard no more of this fancied resemblance. General Heth was [now] short, rotund, and square-faced."

Henry Heth next served in E. Kirby Smith's column as it invaded Kentucky, joining that army on July 1, 1862. He played a minor role in the campaign, and hence by the end of 1862 Heth actually had seen very little fighting. The Senate rejected his nomination for major general in October 1862, and, weary of his isolation, he applied for service with the Army of Northern Virginia in November. Heth's friendship with Robert E. Lee and President Davis perhaps aided him, as he transferred to Virginia on January 17, 1863.

Once in his home state, Heth inherited seasoned troops, a veteran brigade from the Northern Neck of Virginia whose allegiance he soon captured. But he was serving under the notoriously difficult "Stonewall" Jackson and had not been the first choice of that hero. Furthermore, Heth was the senior brigadier in A. P. Hill's division, to the unhappiness of the division's battle-tested brigadiers. His first challenge came at Chancellorsville. When Jackson fell, the ensuing shake-up left Heth commanding the division on May 3, at which time he received his first battle wound. When the post-Chancellorsville reorganization commenced, the relatively obscure Heth obtained his own division. He was commissioned major general on May 23, 1863, to rank from the following day.

Henry Heth's considerable anonymity in Virginia lasted no longer than a few months, for it was he who precipitated the Battle of Gettysburg on July 1, 1863. In the course of the punishing fighting that followed, the general "fell senseless" after being walloped on the head by a Minié bullet that penetrated his padded hat, cracked his skull, and incapacitated him for further duty during the three-day battle. He spent the remainder of his life attempting to justify his activities of July 1, with limited success.

A woeful defeat awaited Heth on July 14. His division comprised the rear guard during the Confederate withdrawal across the Potomac River at Falling

Waters. Someone in the division made an awful blunder, allowing hundreds of men from the Virginia brigade to be encircled and made prisoners. To his discredit, Heth maintained that only stragglers were captured. His role in the defeat is not certain, but his juggling of the facts reflected poorly on him.

For the remainder of the war Heth commanded his division in the II Corps competently, reliably, and without dash or brilliance. At the Wilderness he fought his old friend Hancock to a standstill on May 5, 1864, but failed to consolidate his position overnight and was routed on May 6. At Spotsylvania he had his horse killed under him. As the armies drifted southward, Heth continued to perform solidly. He particularly distinguished himself in the defense of the vital positions south of Petersburg, and won praise for personally carrying some colors into the Union breastworks at Reams' Station on August 25. One observer described Heth during this period as a "most courteous, handsome man," and indeed he was always recognized for grace and social polish.

Heth surrendered the fragments of his division at Appomattox. His postwar life was a struggle to stay afloat. He tried his hand at mining, life insurance, and railroading, all without appreciable success. After a stint with the Bureau of Indian Affairs, his health declined in the 1880s and 1890s. Shortly before his death from Bright's disease, Heth wrote his memoirs. He died on September 27, 1899, having been paralyzed for several months, and found his final resting place among his comrades in Hollywood Cemetery, Richmond, Virginia. Thus ended the career of the only officer in the Army of Northern Virginia whom—according to legend—General Lee addressed by his given name.

Robert E. L. Krick

Heth, Henry, *A System of Target Practice For the Use of Troops when Armed with the Musket,...* (Washington, 1858).

Morrison, James L., ed., *The Memoirs of Henry Heth* (Westport, 1974).

Major General Heth taken sometime after May 1863. (Cook Collection, Valentine Museum, Richmond, Va.)

☆ *Edward Higgins* ☆

An outstanding, previously unpublished image of General Higgins made sometime after October 1863, and the only known uniformed image of him. (Alabama Department of Archives and History, Montgomery, Ala.)

Higgins was born in 1821 in Norfolk, Virginia. As a youth he went to live with an uncle in Iberville Parish, Louisiana. In 1836 Higgins received an appointment in the United States Navy with the rank of midshipman. He remained in that service until 1854, resigning in that year as a lieutenant. His last two years in the navy saw him commanding a merchant marine ocean steamer carrying mail between New Orleans and New York, and he continued to command such a vessel until 1858.

Higgins received a commission as captain of Company I, 1st Louisiana Heavy Artillery Regiment, on April 12, 1861. This company did not finish its organization, and Major General David E. Twiggs made Higgins an aide-de-camp on June 12, shortly after he assumed command at New Orleans. Higgins helped to fit out several steamers as gunboats. In July Twiggs wrote to the secretary of war regarding Higgins: "Indeed, I have so high an opinion of his experience and skill, that I would gladly see him placed in charge of the naval defenses of this coast."

In September the War Department authorized Twiggs to assign Higgins to ordnance duty. Twiggs ordered Higgins to organize the 1st Confederate Light Battery on October 9, and he became its captain when it was mustered in twenty days later. Higgins continued drilling the battery after Major General Mansfield Lovell replaced Twiggs.

Higgins resigned his commission on January 2, 1862, to help state authorities fit out vessels as warships. Several weeks later Lovell seized these steamers under orders from the War Department and turned them over to the naval commander at New Orleans. This deprived Higgins of a possible command, but apparently he assisted the navy in converting the vessels.

Higgins received an appointment as lieutenant colonel of the 22d Louisiana Infantry Regiment on February 13, 1862, although the unit did not complete its organization until March 28. Lovell sent him to repair a raft between Fort Jackson and Fort St. Philip that had given way. Higgins could not make the necessary repairs but did attempt to construct a second raft. Brigadier General Johnson K. Duncan, who commanded the coastal defenses of Lovell's department, placed Higgins in charge of the two forts, a duty he assumed on March 17. The promotion of Martin L. Smith made Higgins colonel of the 22d Louisiana effective April 11, but he did not know of his advancement for some months.

During the Union naval bombardment and campaign against the forts, which began on April 18, Higgins exercised supervision of the batteries of Fort Jackson. Duncan, who had gone to the forts to assume immediate command of their defense, praised Higgins "for his indefatigable labors in preparing his heavy batteries" and "for the quiet, skillful, and judicious manner in which he caused them to be fought." One report stated that at one point Higgins did not leave the ramparts of the fort for forty-eight hours and that the heavy bombardment never disconcerted him. The passage of the forts by the Federal squadron caused the garrisons to mutiny, so Higgins surrendered them on April 28. Higgins was exchanged on August 13 and made his way to Jackson, Mississippi, so that he could rejoin the remnants of his regiment, which was then serving at Vicksburg as heavy artillerists.

The 22d Louisiana was assigned to man batteries at Snyder's Bluff on the Yazoo River north of Vicksburg in late November. Shortly after the unit arrived there, a controversy broke out over who its field officers were. Lovell had reorganized the regiment in May, and a new set of field officers was elected. This reorganization was soon overturned, but the ousted officers did not give up their claims to their new ranks.

During Union operations against Chickasaw Bayou, the ironclad *Benton* steamed up to engage the Snyder's Bluff batteries. On December 27 Higgins' men heavily damaged the ironclad with accurate cannon fire and forced her to retreat. This action brought Higgins praise from Lieutenant General John C. Pemberton. The War Department appears to have decided the field-officer controversy against Higgins and his lieutenant colonel and major in January 1863. This result led Pemberton to place Higgins in charge of the river batteries at Vicksburg, where he had assumed command by February 8. He exercised his duties through the siege of Vicksburg, May 22–July 4. Pemberton again praised Higgins for directing his batteries in the sinking of the ironclad *Cincinnati* on May 27.

Again a prisoner of war after the surrender of Vicksburg on July 4, Higgins placed his troops in a parole camp at Enterprise, Mississippi. When Major General Dabney H. Maury learned in early October that Higgins had been declared exchanged, he asked Jefferson Davis to promote Higgins to brigadier general and order him to Mobile to command both the lower bay and harbor defenses. Maury thought Higgins' service had given him skill in defending fortifications against ships. On Maury's recommendation Davis made the necessary appointment on November 2, and Higgins received his promotion to rank from October 29, 1863. Higgins arrived in Mobile and assumed command in early November. He became ill in early February 1864 and went on sick leave to Tuskegee, Alabama, for several months. Some of Higgins' subordinates were happy to see him go; one lieutenant called him "irascible."

Higgins returned to Mobile from sick leave in early June and assumed command of the city works and bay batteries, also known as the artillery brigade. He temporarily commanded the District of the Gulf during Maury's absence from late July until mid-August. Maury's confidence in Higgins had eroded, however. He wrote that "while he is well qualified to fight ships, he is possessed of such an infirmity of temper as sets the whole community, including the officers under him, against him."

Higgins left his command without orders in September when he thought the enemy would attack Mobile, and Maury removed him from duty. When Higgins applied for reinstatement, Maury informed his superiors of Higgins' conduct and asked that they not allow him to return to Mobile. Higgins never held another command during the war, and there is no indication that he received a parole at the end of the conflict.

He made his home in Norfolk after the war and went into the import and insurance businesses while residing there. In 1872 he moved to San Francisco to work as an agent for the Pacific Mail Steamship Company. He died on January 31, 1875, in that city and was buried in Holy Cross Cemetery.

Arthur W. Bergeron, Jr.

Bergeron, Jr., Arthur W., "'They Bore Themselves With Distinguished Gallantry': The Twenty-Second Louisiana Infantry," *Louisiana History*, XIII (1972), 253–82.

Dimitry, John, *Louisiana*, Vol. X in Evans, *Confederate Military History*.

Higgins' uniform is difficult to distinguish in this portrait. Since he left the U.S. Navy at 33 and looks older than that here, this is quite possibly an 1861 or 1862 image of him as an officer in one of his Louisiana units. (Museum of the Confederacy, Richmond, Va.)

✶ *Ambrose Powell Hill* ✶

A little-known portrait of A.P. Hill that, like many others, shows a colonel's insignia on his collar, though it was almost certainly taken after his promotion to one of his several grades of general. (William A. Turner Collection)

A product of Piedmont Virginia aristocracy, "Powell" Hill was born November 9, 1825, on the family estate west of Culpeper. He received a private education and entered the U.S. Military Academy at the age of sixteen. Illness at West Point forced Hill to drop back a year. He graduated in the upper third of the class of 1847.

The new artillery lieutenant arrived in Mexico too late to see but limited action in the field. Seven years of duty assignments followed in Mexico, Texas, and Florida. In 1855 Hill transferred to Washington and joined the staff of the U.S. Coastal Survey service. His 1859 marriage to Kitty Morgan McClung, the widowed sister of Kentuckian John Hunt Morgan, ultimately produced four daughters. Two reached maturity.

By March 1861, Hill considered civil war inevitable. The ardent Southerner resigned from the army six weeks prior to Fort Sumter. With the April formation of Virginia's military forces, Hill became colonel of the 13th Virginia Infantry.

He was always an easily recognizable figure. Five feet, nine inches tall, he weighed but 145 pounds and was called "Little Powell." Hill rarely wore a uniform or insignia. He commanded in shirt sleeves (preferring a bright red shirt for battle) and was never without a revolver, sword, field glasses, and a pipe, which he smoked regularly.

Extraordinary talents in organization, drill, and discipline led to Hill's February 26, 1862, promotion to brigadier general, to rank immediately. Hill's first Civil War battle came May 5 at Williamsburg in the early stage of McClellan's Peninsular Campaign against Richmond. Troops under Hill swept away a Union attack so convincingly that Hill emerged from the engagement as the most conspicuous brigade commander on the field.

On May 26, only four months after his first promotion, Hill received appointment as major general, again effective immediately. He took command of the largest division (six brigades) the Confederate armies ever had. Hill was in the forefront of the Seven Days' fighting. He impetuously opened the counteroffensive by Lee with an unauthorized attack at Mechanicsville. His "Light Division" also took heavy losses at Gaines' Mill and Frayser's Farm. Hill had quickly won a reputation as one of Lee's most aggressive generals.

Late in July 1862, Lee sent Hill's division to reinforce "Stonewall" Jackson's command facing the advance of General John Pope's army in north central Virginia. The arrival of Hill and his troops at a critical point in the August 9 battle of Cedar Mountain helped turn the engagement in the South's favor. For two days at Second Manassas, Hill maintained his position against repeated attacks.

A personal estrangement had meanwhile developed between Jackson and Hill. Shortly after Lee crossed the Potomac into Maryland, Jackson placed Hill under arrest. Hill obtained reinstatement to command a week later. The timely arrival of Hill's division at Antietam Creek (September 17) saved Lee's army from almost certain destruction. In the December 13 battle at Fredericksburg, a portion of Hill's front line was inexplicably left unmanned and resulted in unnecessarily high casualties.

Hill was slightly wounded at Chancellorsville (May 1–4, 1863) in the same accidental fire that crippled Jackson. Following the death of the latter, Lee reshuffled his command structure. Hill's fighting prowess was the key factor in his May 23, 1863, promotion to lieutenant general, to date from the following day, and command of the newly formed III Corps. This assignment proved a mistake. Although Hill was in Lee's opinion the best division leader in the army, Hill was unable to broaden his perceptions to the larger corps level.

The attack by Hill's Corps opened the July 1–3 Battle of Gettysburg. Illness played some part in hampering Hill's performance in that engagement. He was well enough on July 14 to deliver a smashing repulse to Federals at Falling Waters, Maryland. Then came the lowest point in Hill's war career. On October 14 he launched a precipitate assault on Federals at Bristoe Station, Virginia. Two Confederate brigades charged into two entrenched Federal corps and suffered fifteen hundred losses in forty minutes of fighting. Hill openly admitted his mistake and silently accepted a rebuke from Lee.

Hill wears three stars again in this thoughtful pose. (U.S. Army Military History Institute, Carlisle, Pa.)

Again he wears three stars on a homespun jacket, providing more than ample evidence of Hill's careless attitude toward uniform. (Museum of the Confederacy, Richmond, Va.)

On May 5, 1864, Hill led one of two attacking columns against U. S. Grant and the Army of the Potomac. The two-day Battle of the Wilderness was a Confederate victory but dearly bought. As the two armies shifted toward Spotsylvania for more combat, Hill had to relinquish command of his corps. Neither he nor the surgeons knew that the general was suffering from a progressive kidney disease. Hill returned to duty too soon, for his leadership in the action at the North Anna River was disappointing. Yet he seemed his old self in the June 1–3 fighting around Cold Harbor.

It was in the long Siege of Petersburg that Hill's fighting ability reached its zenith. Although his corps by then was barely the size of a full division, Hill was Lee's most dependable general in the last year of the war. A high-ranking officer noted that from June 1864 to March 1865, "every Federal effort to break Lee's right was met and defeated by General Hill with promptness and without heavy loss on his part." His victories included actions at Jerusalem Plank Road, Weldon Railroad, the Crater, Reams' Station, Peebles' Farm, and Burgess' Mill.

By February 1865, Hill's health was deteriorating with the onset of uremia. Grant launched an all-out attack against Petersburg at dawn on April 2. Hill was desperately trying to reach his shattered lines when he was shot and killed by a Federal infantryman. He is buried beneath his statue in a residential area of Richmond.

Genial and approachable, a general who commanded with a pleasant touch, Powell Hill was also restless and impetuous in battle. He did not hesitate to risk heavy losses if the potential gains were substantial. Hill epitomized much that was the Southern Confederacy. Colonel Charles Venable of Lee's staff commented after the war: "The name of A. P. Hill stands recorded high on the list of those noble sons of Virginia at whose rollcall grateful memory will ever answer: " "Dead on the field of honor for the people [he] loved so well." "

James I. Robertson, Jr.

Hassler, William W., *A. P. Hill: Lee's Forgotten General* (Richmond, 1957).

Robertson, Jr., James I., *General A. P. Hill: The Story of a Confederate Warrior* (New York, 1987).

Schenck, Martin, *Up Came Hill: The Story of the Light Division and Its Leaders* (Harrisburg, 1958).

Only in this pose, presumably made after his February 1862 promotion to brigadier, does Hill give in to full uniform. (Museum of the Confederacy, Richmond, Va.)

✷ *Benjamin Jefferson Hill* ✷

Born in McMinnville, Tennessee, on June 13, 1825, Hill attended common schools in the community and later, in the early 1850s, entered the mercantile business in his hometown. Elected to the Tennessee Senate in 1855, he continued to hold that office until the Civil War began.

Hill entered military service as the appointed colonel of the 5th Infantry Regiment, Provisional Army of Tennessee. He resigned his commission to enter the Confederate service and was recommissioned colonel of his old regiment on September 11, 1861. Although initially called the 1st Tennessee Mountain Rifle Regiment by its members and officially designated the 35th Tennessee Infantry by the Confederate Adjutant and Inspector General's Office in November (another regiment had already been designated the 5th), the regiment was generally known as the 5th (Hill's) Regiment. It was not until the secretary of war finally put his foot down in late 1863 and insisted that the unit refer to itself as the 35th that the matter was finally settled.

On September 17, 1861, the regiment was ordered to Camp Trousdale, Sumner County, Tennessee, and from there to Bowling Green, Kentucky, on the 25th. At Bowling Green the regiment was assigned to Brigadier General Patrick R. Cleburne's brigade of Major General William J. Hardee's corps. Composition of the brigade changed constantly during the next five months, but the 35th remained with Cleburne throughout. In mid-February the brigade withdrew from Bowling Green to Murfreesboro, Tennessee, and from there it continued to Camp Hill, near Corinth, Mississippi.

Hill fought with distinction at Shiloh April 6–7, 1862, commanding the left wing of Cleburne's brigade during a portion of that engagement. Although its losses are unknown, the 35th entered the fight with 369 men and captured approximately one hundred Federals during the battle.

On May 28 the regiment participated in a sharp engagement at Shelton's Hill, on the Farmington Road on the outskirts of Corinth. Both Hill and his men were commended by General P. G. T. Beauregard and Cleburne. Beauregard issued a special general order the following day, which stated: "The general commanding mentions with great pleasure to the army the distinguished conduct of Col. B. J. Hill and his regiment, the Fifth Tennessee Volunteers, in an affair with the enemy on yesterday. This order is issued with the greater satisfaction that the gallant officer and his command have been before conspicuous for their action on the field."

The regiment withdrew from Corinth to Baldwin, then to Tupelo, and finally arrived at Verona on June 17. General Braxton Bragg, who had succeeded Beauregard, detached Cleburne's brigade and one other for service under Major General Edmund Kirby Smith in East Tennessee.

Under Kirby Smith, Hill led Cleburne's brigade into Kentucky in August, Cleburne being in command of a provisional division. At the Battle of Richmond, Kentucky, on August 30, Hill's men fired the opening volley and never ceased pressing the enemy. Although wounded three times, Hill remained in command of

The only uniformed portrait of Benjamin Hill shows him probably as a colonel of the 35th Tennessee prior to November 1864. (Courtesy of Mike Miner)

his brigade and was commended for his performance.

Hill returned to regimental command and the brigade rejoined Major General William J. Hardee's corps of Bragg's army on October 7. Cleburne led the brigade the following day at the Battle of Perryville, but, apparently because he was seriously wounded in the engagement, no official report of the brigade's participation in that battle has been found. The Confederate army now retreated to Knoxville.

During the Battle of Murfreesboro, December 31, 1862–January 2, 1863, the 35th Tennessee formed part of Brigadier General Lucius Polk's brigade of Major General Cleburne's division, of Lieutenant General Hardee's corps. Following that engagement, the regiment was stationed at Tullahoma and Wartrace, Tennessee, until July 1, when it joined in the army's retrograde movement to Chattanooga and then into northern Georgia.

When Bragg finally turned and attacked the enemy at Chickamauga on September 19, Hill led his regiment into battle. The division had been temporarily assigned to the corps of Lieutenant General Daniel Harvey Hill, who observed Hill during the fighting and paid him the following tribute: "The extraordinary merit of Colonel Hill of the Thirty-fifth Tennessee came under my personal observation. This noble officer has been distinguished on many a hard-fought field, and has been content with a subordinate position, provided he can serve his country."

On October 1 the 35th moved to Cooper's Mills, near Georgetown, Tennessee, where Hill soon found himself commanding the 35th/48th Consolidated Tennessee Infantry. His four hundred men busied themselves grinding wheat for the army. The Tennesseans left Georgetown on November 24 to participate in the Battle of Missionary Ridge the following day. During that engagement Hill not only held his ground but charged the enemy, an action which resulted in the capture of Federal soldiers and colors.

After participating in Cleburne's rearguard action, which earned those present the thanks of the Confederate Congress, General Joseph E. Johnston appointed Hill provost marshal of the Army of Tennessee before the end of 1863. Despite his new assignment, Hill still found time to share the hardships of the Atlanta Campaign with his regiment. Relieved from his duties as provost marshal on August 24, 1864, Hill returned to full-time field duty during the closing operations of the struggle for Atlanta, being assigned to Brigadier General Hiram Granbury's brigade.

For his outstanding service during General John Bell Hood's invasion of Tennessee that fall, Hill was promoted to brigadier general, to rank immediately on November 30, 1864. Hill had served with distinction while in charge of a cavalry command that cooperated with Major General William Bate's infantry division in the latter's attempt to destroy the railroad and blockhouses between Nashville and Murfreesboro. Their operations were part of Major General Nathan Bedford Forrest's siege of Murfreesboro.

During 1865 Hill commanded a cavalry brigade under Lieutenant General Forrest and participated in the closing operations against Union Major General James Wilson's cavalry raid through central Alabama. Hill fought at Decatur on April 23 and again at Selma, where he surrendered and was paroled.

Returning to McMinnville, Hill resumed his mercantile activities and established a law practice as well. He died on January 5, 1880, in McMinnville, where he is interred.

Lawrence L. Hewitt

Horn, Stanley, ed., *Tennesseans in the Civil War: A Military History of Confederate and Union Units with Available Rosters of Personnel* (Nashville, 1964).

Porter, James D., *Tennessee*, Vol. VIII in Evans, *Confederate Military History*.

✴ *Daniel Harvey Hill* ✴

Perhaps the best of D.H. Hill's wartime poses is this, showing a brigadier's buttons, dating it no earlier than July 1861. (Museum of the Confederacy, Richmond, Va.)

Hill was born on a plantation in the York District, South Carolina, on July 12, 1821. The death of his father when Hill was four years old left the family in difficult financial circumstances, and Hill later remarked somewhat bitterly that he had "had no youth." He entered West Point in 1838 and ranked twenty-eighth at graduation in the famous class of 1842, receiving a commission as brevet 2d lieutenant on July 1 and joining the 1st Artillery in August 1842. Transferred to the 3d Artillery on October 20, 1843, and promoted to 2d lieutenant of the 4th Artillery on October 13, 1845, Hill saw extensive service in the war with Mexico, fighting at Monterrey under Zachary Taylor and in the campaign from Vera Cruz to Mexico City under Winfield Scott. Promoted to 1st lieutenant on March 3, 1847, and awarded brevets to captain at Contreras and major at Chapultepec, he remained in the army until February 28, 1849, when he resigned to join the faculty at Washington College in Lexington, Virginia.

Hill spent the remainder of his antebellum career as an educator. After five years as professor of mathematics at Washington College (1849–54), he accepted a similar position at Davidson, a Presbyterian school in North Carolina, where he taught until 1859. Hill dominated the faculty at Davidson (one student called him the institution's "controlling spirit") and while there published an algebra textbook and two books on religious topics. In 1859 he accepted the superintendency of the newly founded North Carolina Military Institute in Charlotte, a post he held until the outbreak of war in April 1861.

A staunch advocate of Southern rights, Hill quickly offered his services to Governor John W. Ellis and on

Since all of Hill's uniformed poses show him with a brigadier's buttons, it is impossible to date them, for he may simply have left his buttons the same throughout the war. (Cook Collection, Valentine Museum, Richmond, Va.)

April 24, 1861, was given a colonelcy and command of the camp of instruction for North Carolina volunteers at Raleigh. Elected colonel of the 1st Regiment of North Carolina Volunteers on May 11, 1861, Hill led his unit in a successful skirmish with Federals at Big Bethel, Virginia, on June 10, 1861. This small victory placed Hill in the public eye and hastened his promotion to brigadier general in the Confederate army, to rank from the date of his appointment on July 10, 1861. Several months of unexceptional duty on the Peninsula of Virginia and along the coast of North Carolina preceded a stint in quasi-independent command near Leesburg, Virginia, over the winter of 1861–62 during which he impressed his superiors. Promoted to major general on March 26, 1862, to rank immediately, Hill took command of a division and joined Southern forces near Yorktown.

The next nine months witnessed Hill's greatest contributions as a Confederate officer. Five feet ten, slight, somewhat stooped from a chronic spinal affliction, and as devoutly religious as his brother-in-law, "Stonewall" Jackson, he seemed an unlikely candidate for martial success. But he fought aggressively at Williamsburg on May 5, enjoyed the best day of all Southern generals at Seven Pines on May 31, and figured prominently in the Seven Days' battles of Mechanicsville, Gaines' Mill, and Malvern Hill, where he elicited high praise from R. E. Lee and Jackson. Close association with North Carolina marked Hill as the obvious person to take charge of the Department of North Carolina when that post became vacant shortly after the Seven Days', and he left the Army of Northern Virginia on July 17, 1862. Within a month Lee informed Jefferson Davis that he considered Hill "an excellent executive officer [who] does not appear to have much administrative ability." Restored to command of his old division in late August, he rejoined the army shortly after Second Manassas.

Hill played a crucial role in the 1862 Maryland campaign (contrary to popular belief, he almost certainly was not responsible for the loss of a copy of Lee's Special Order No. 191). Often criticized for his conduct at South Mountain on September 14, he in fact mounted a reasonably strong defense of the gaps against long odds; on September 17, he displayed abundant courage in resisting Federal assaults against the Confederate center at Sharpsburg. His division saw limited action at Fredericksburg on December 13, 1862, and on January 1, 1863, Hill tendered his resignation,

citing health as the principal reason: "I have a very feeble frame & have been a great sufferer since boyhood. I have been in service more than twenty months…[never] free a single moment from pain and that too, often of the most excruciating character."

Lee expressed regret at the possible loss of "so good & faithful an officer," but in truth Hill's habitual carping probably had alienated his chief. Hill had criticized superiors and subordinates freely since the outset of the war (including Lee in his reports of the Seven Days' and the Maryland campaigns), frequently indulged in pessimistic predictions, and earned a reputation as a disputatious "croaker." No one doubted Hill's bravery. John Haskell echoed most of the army when he noted Hill's "high and well deserved reputation as a hard fighter" who always seemed "to go from choice into the most dangerous place he could find on the field." But heroism was not enough. An official in the Confederate War Department correctly labeled him "harsh, abrupt, often insulting in the effort to be sarcastic"—a man who would "offend many and conciliate none." In the end Lee recommended that Hill go back to the Department of North Carolina, an assignment made official on February 7, 1863.

Hill commanded in North Carolina until early July (in late May his department was enlarged to include Petersburg, Virginia, and the southern approaches to Richmond); on July 11 he learned from Jefferson Davis of his appointment to lieutenant general, effective that date, and soon he traveled west to lead a corps under Braxton Bragg. After participating in the Battle of Chickamauga September 19–20, 1863, Hill engaged in a violent quarrel with Bragg. Davis eventually supported Bragg and authorized Hill's removal from the Army of Tennessee. Relieved of his duties October 15, Hill went first to Richmond and then home to North Carolina, where he waited in vain for confirmation of his promotion to lieutenant general.

In effect reduced in rank to major general, Hill saw limited action through the remainder of the war. Posted to Charleston in February–March 1864, he served as a volunteer aide to P. G. T. Beauregard at Petersburg from May 5 to June 13, 1864 (briefly leading a division in the defense of that city May 18–21), and as inspector of trenches under Beauregard in early July. He assisted in the defense of Lynchburg against David Hunter's army in mid-July, then spent the balance of 1864 without assignment until ordered on December 23 to report to Beauregard in the Military

Division of the West. Hill took command of the District of Georgia in mid-January 1865, remaining until late February, when he returned to field duty with Joseph E. Johnston's forces in North Carolina. Given a division at Charlotte on March 3, he fought at Bentonville March 19–20 and surrendered with his troops at Durham Station on April 26.

Nearly a quarter-century of life remained to Hill after the war. Bitter against the North, he kept alive feelings of Southern partisanship with *The Land We Love*, a monthly magazine published between 1866 and 1869, and *The Southern Home*, a weekly newspaper in Charlotte during the 1870s. He wrote widely elsewhere about his role in the conflict, including a series of articles for the Century Company's *Battles and Leaders of the Civil War*. In 1877 he accepted the presidency of Arkansas Industrial University (later the University of Arkansas), leaving that institution in 1885 to be president of the Middle Georgia Military and Agricultural College. Ill with cancer through 1888 and 1889, he resigned in August of the latter year, died in Charlotte on September 24, and was buried in Davidson College Cemetery.

Gary W. Gallagher

Avery, A. C., *Life and Character of Lieutenant General D. H. Hill* (Raleigh, 1893).

Bridges, Hal, *Lee's Maverick General: Daniel Harvey Hill* (New York, 1961).

Shepherd, Henry E., "General D. H. Hill as a Teacher and Author," in *North Carolina Booklet* 16 (April 1917): 191–208.

A dim and faded but wonderfully direct pose, probably made late in the war when his beard had grown. (*Civil War Times Illustrated* Collection, Harrisburg, Pa.)

⋆ *Thomas Carmichael Hindman* ⋆

Several images of Hindman in uniform exist, all of them with the uniform added by an artist. This is the only genuine uniformed portrait known, and it was taken on October 22, 1865, months after the surrender. Hindman poses with his three children, and probably from his residence in exile in Mexico. (Courtesy of Robert J. Younger)

On January 28, 1828, a son was born in Knoxville, Tennessee, to Thomas Carmichael and Sallie Holt Hindman. As the family's first son, he was named for his father. In 1832 the senior Hindman, a long-time supporter of President Andrew Jackson, was named as agent for the Creek Nation and moved his family to Jacksonville, Alabama. Nine years later, in 1841, with the inauguration of a Whig administration in Washington, D.C., the father lost his position with the Federal government and headed west and purchased a large plantation in Tippah County, Mississippi. Thomas received his primary education in Jacksonville and Ripley, the latter the Tippah County seat. He also spent four years at the Classical Institute in Lawrenceville, New Jersey.

Word that American blood had been spilled on American soil electrified the eighteen-year-old Hindman. He volunteered for the war against Mexico and in the autumn of 1846 helped raise a company in Tippah County that was mustered into Federal service with Hindman as lieutenant in Company E, 2d Mississippi Infantry. His service was uneventful. Soon after his muster out in August 1848 and return to his home, Hindman was admitted to the Mississippi bar. A fiery orator and champion of Southern rights, he stumped northern Mississippi in support of Jefferson Davis' unsuccessful 1851 race against Henry S. Foote for governor. Hindman in 1854 was elected to the state legislature from Tippah County as a Democrat.

Two years later he relocated to Helena, Arkansas, where on November 11, 1856, he married Mary Watkins Biscoe of that town. Achieving rapid success as an attorney in his new Arkansas home, he faced the voters in November 1858 and was elected as a Democrat to represent the 1st District in the 36th Congress. He was reelected in 1860. In December 1860, several weeks after the election of Abraham Lincoln as sixteenth president, Hindman met Henry S. Foote at Memphis in a debate. Hindman took the stance that the time for secession had arrived.

By January 8, 1861, with the lame-duck Buchanan administration showing some backbone as the crisis precipitated by the secession of South Carolina deepened, Hindman and Senator R. W. Johnson advised the people of Arkansas to secede. Responding to President Lincoln's April 15 call for volunteers to repossess Fort Sumter and other Federal property in the seven seceded states, a state convention reassembled in Little Rock on May 6 and voted Arkansas out of the Union. Whereupon Hindman resigned his congressional seat and commenced recruiting volunteers.

He organized the 2d Arkansas Infantry, was elected its colonel, and, along with the regiment, was mustered into Confederate service at Hopefield on June 12, 1861. To arm and equip his unit, Hindman undertook extralegal actions to obtain funds. Upstream-bound steamboats were boarded, and if they were carrying sugar consigned to Northern merchants, the sugar was seized and sold. Hindman and his regiments soon reached Memphis, where they were joined by other units to constitute an ad hoc force known as Hindman's Legion.

Early in August Hindman traveled to Springfield, Missouri, to muster into Confederate service those units of the Arkansas State Guard who had participated in the Battle of Wilson's Creek August 10. He was unsuccessful, despite his best efforts and a stump speech, and the state guard returned to northwest Arkansas, where they were mustered out. On his return to Fayetteville, Hindman crossed the Mississippi River and reported to Major General William J. Hardee, commanding the Army of Central Kentucky, headquartered at Bowling Green. He learned that he had been made a brigadier general, to rank from the date of appointment, September 28. Ten weeks later at Rowlett's Station, Hindman fought his first engagement as a brigade commander.

Hindman led his brigade on the long retreat from Bowling Green to Corinth, Mississippi. On April 3, 1862, when the Army of Mississippi left its camps to attack the Union army at Pittsburg Landing, Hindman commanded a two-brigade division in Hardee's Corps. At Shiloh, on Sunday, April 6, Hindman's conduct "was marked by a courage which animated his soldiers and a skill which won their confidence." About noon, as his troops drove the Yankees from their positions along the Purdy Road, Hindman's horse was killed by a cannonball, and the general was "disabled by the concussion of the ball and the fall of his horse." Hindman, promoted major general on April 14, to rank from April 4, rejoined the army on May 10 at Corinth and assumed command of a division in Braxton Bragg's corps.

On May 26 he was relieved from duty with the Army of Mississippi and ordered to return to Arkansas, charged to organize its troops for the defense of that state. Confederate fortunes in Arkansas and the Indian Territory were bleak. Earl Van Dorn's Army of the West, the region's only effective fighting force, had been, despite protests, pulled out of the state and rushed to Corinth. Union troops held much of northern Arkansas, had thrust a column to within thirty-five miles of Little Rock, and had carried the war deep within the Cherokee Nation.

Hindman took stern but unpopular measures to meet the crisis. Martial law was declared. By rigorously enforcing the conscription and impressment laws, within ninety days he created an effective fighting force. He established shops for manufacture of needed supplies. The enemy threatening Little Rock turned back and took position at Helena, and in the west, Hindman's troops crossed the Boston Mountains and prepared to thrust into Missouri and Kansas. Hindman's harsh actions, although successful, caused states rights politicians to howl, and President Jefferson Davis listened. Major General Theophilus H. Holmes, who had failed as a leader of troops in the East, was rushed to Arkansas and on August 12 superseded Hindman as commander of the newly constituted Trans-Mississippi Department.

Hindman, then in western Arkansas organizing an army to carry the war into southwest Missouri and on to Fort Scott, Kansas, was called to Little Rock by Holmes, and while he was absent, his force, led by the inept and hard-drinking Douglas Cooper, was outmaneuvered, mauled, and scattered by Union columns. Hindman was assigned to command a corps in the department's army. On December 7, having taken the offensive, he was defeated at the Battle of Prairie Grove, and with winter at hand, retreated to Fort Smith, south of the Boston Mountains.

Disenchanted at serving under Holmes, whom he deemed a "granny," Hindman on January 30, 1863, was relieved from duty in the Trans-Mississippi. He spent the next six months on the shelf before being ordered to Braxton Bragg for assignment. Reporting for duty at Chattanooga on August 13, he was placed in command of the division in Leonidas Polk's corps formerly led by Jones Withers.

Hindman was one of the Confederate generals involved in the September 10–11 misfire at Davis' Crossroad that aroused General Bragg's ire and enabled the Federals to withdraw two divisions that had rashly pushed into McLemore's Cove. At Chickamauga on September 20 Hindman was assigned to James Longstreet's left wing and was in the onslaught that routed the elements of two Union corps and then made repeated assaults on Horseshoe Ridge. In the day's fight Hindman's division suffered the greatest loss of any of Longstreet's divisions.

Hindman was commended by General Bragg for his gallantry and good conduct and for "keeping his saddle," despite a severe contusion, "until he witnessed the success in which his command largely participated."

Hindman was on leave during the battles that drove the Army of Tennessee from the approaches to Chattanooga (November 23–25) and into northwest Georgia. The army went into camp in and around Dalton, and there on December 15 Hindman assumed command of the corps formerly led by John C. Breckinridge and retained this position until February 28, 1864, when John B. Hood reported for duty.

During the Atlanta Campaign Hindman led one of the three divisions constituting Hood's Corps. He also beginning on May 7, was in almost daily contact with the foe until July 3, when a serious eye injury he received while commanding troops on the Smyrna line incapacitated him for further service in the field. Up until that day Hindman and his troops had stood tall in the face of slashing enemy attacks at Resaca (May 14–15), held the New Hope Church rifle-pits (May 25–June 4), and were savaged by the Federals at Kolb's Farm (June 22). He closed out the war overseeing administrative commands in Arkansas and north Mississippi.

In the summer of 1865 Hindman fled the country, emigrating to Mexico to manage a coffee plantation. Mrs. Hindman was unable to adapt to her new homeland, and in 1867 they returned to their prewar home in Helena. Hindman, as might be expected, became a vocal and formidable voice against the Arkansas Republican party and congressional reconstruction. On the night of September 28, 1868, while the general sat in his parlor, he was shot to death by night riders, who fired a shotgun blast through a window. His murderers were either linked with Radical Republicans or seeking revenge for harsh actions taken by Hindman in 1862 while rallying forces to shore up the state's defenses. He was buried in Maple Hill Cemetery in Helena.

Edwin C. Bearss

Harrell, John M., *Arkansas*, Vol. X in Evans, *Confederate Military History*.

Helena, *Arkansas Gazette*, September 29, 1868.

Nash, Charles E., *Biographical Sketches of Gen. Pat Cleburne and Gen. T. C. Hindman* (Little Rock, 1898).

Thomas, D. Y., *Arkansas in War and Reconstruction* (Little Rock, 1926).

This blurred image exists in many much better prints, all of them evidencing an artist's heavy retouching. This may, however, be a genuine uniformed print. (Museum of the Confederacy, Richmond, Va.)

✶ George Baird Hodge ✶

Politics was almost always mixed with military policy in the naming of generals in the Civil War, and George Baird Hodge provides an excellent example.

He was a native of Fleming County, Kentucky, born April 8, 1828. In a move somewhat unusual for one born so far inland, he obtained an appointment to the U.S. Naval Academy at Annapolis, Maryland, graduating in 1845 with the rank of midshipman. He served six years in uniform, rising to the rank of lieutenant before he resigned in 1850 to take up the study of law. Kentucky already had a crowded and rather illustrious bar at the time, but Hodge passed his examinations and commenced what proved to be a prosperous practice at Newport.

Meanwhile he also took a hand in state politics. being an ardent Democrat. In 1852 he unsuccessfully sought the congressional seat from his district but later won a place in the commonwealth's legislature in Frankfort. When the election of 1860 came, he went to the Democratic National Convention in Charleston committed to the candidacy of fellow Kentuckian John C. Breckinridge. Like Breckinridge, Hodge decried secession, but when the clash between the sections pulled hard at his loyalties, he found that his bound him more tightly to the doctrine of states rights than to the Union.

Late in 1861 he enlisted as a private in one of the regiments then forming at Camp Boone, Tennessee, but almost immediately left the ranks to take a seat in the Confederate Congress after the Russellville, Kentucky rump convention declared that Kentucky was seceded and Richmond "admitted" the commonwealth to the Confederacy. Hodge served throughout the remaining period of the Provisional Congress and was reelected to the First Confederate Congress that met in Richmond in February 1862. Kentuckians in fact never voted at all in such elections, being behind Yankee lines. Hodge and fellow Kentucky delegates were elected instead by Kentucky Confederate soldiers in the field.

Congressman Hodge actively supported the Davis administration, and along with the rest of a prominent Kentucky lobby, pressed for an early invasion and "liberation" of their native state. Putting his life where his mouth was, Hodge not infrequently spent the recesses between sessions of Congress out in the field. Breckinridge, not a brigadier in Confederate service, appointed him a captain and adjutant on his staff, in which capacity Hodge served with distinction at Shiloh, resulting in his May 6, 1862, promotion to major. One year later to the day he had risen to colonel. Meanwhile he joined with other Kentucky representatives in pressuring Davis for General Braxton Bragg's invasion of Kentucky, and in criticism of Bragg after its failure.

Quite possibly to placate Hodge, Richmond gave him a field command, a small nine-hundred-man cavalry "brigade" in Lieutenant General Simon Buckner's Department of East Tennessee. With it Hodge participated in raids into Kentucky, chiefly leading the 1st Kentucky Mounted Rifles, and more than once finding himself a pawn in the troubled interdepartmental politics between commanders in the region. Late that fall

No uniformed image of Hodge has been found. This is almost certainly postwar. (Miller, *Photographic History*)

the War Department ordered him to Richmond, on October 15, 1863, and there Davis gave him an appointment as brigadier general on November 21, to date from the previous day.

There the politics commenced. Having been a pawn between contending military commanders, Hodge now became a ball batted back and forth between pro- and anti-Davis factions in Congress. The Senate refused to confirm his promotion. Meanwhile the War Department assigned him to command a "brigade" composed of the 27th Virginia Battalion of Cavalry, the 2d and 3d Kentucky Mounted Rifles, and Jessee's Mounted Kentucky Rifles. Reporting to Major General Joseph Wheeler, he served well throughout the winter of 1863–64, winning Wheeler's compliments for his performance.

By the summer of 1864 Davis was ready to try again for a generalship for Hodge. What kept the case constantly before him was Hodge's close relationship to Davis' most trusted aide, the Kentuckian William Preston Johnston, across whose desk in the executive office passed a steady stream of correspondence with prominent Kentuckians, all designed toward influencing the President to promote him. On August 4 Davis once more appointed Hodge a brigadier, to rank from August 2, and immediately the War Department assigned him to command a district in the Department of Alabama, Mississippi, and East Louisiana that just happened to encompass Woodville, Davis' boyhood home and still the residence of many of his kin, with whom Hodge was soon on friendly terms. Yet again, however, the Senate rejected the nomination. Meanwhile Hodge lamented from his command that "my life here is a very lonely one." By March 1865, his latest nomination having been rejected on February 8, Hodge was in Jackson, Mississippi, virtually alone. "I, a brigadier by your order," he wrote to Davis, "am without my command." Hodge finally gave up his own near-constant politicking to get his commission confirmed, and the close of the war ended the matter.

With peace, Hodge gave his parole at Meridien, Mississippi, on May 10, 1865, and went home to Kentucky. He returned to the practice of law and to politics, serving two terms in the Kentucky senate 1873–77, and attending the Democratic National Convention in 1872 as a Horace Greeley delegate. In 1877 he removed to Longwood, Florida, where he died August 1, 1892. His remains were taken back to Newport for burial.

Hodge typified the politician-cum-soldier. His appointments were achieved through sheer influence and political expedience, though he was undeniably a brave man and marginally effective within the limited sphere open to him. His best service to the Confederacy, however, was with his 1866 publication in D. H. Hill's *Land We Love* magazine of his "History of the First Kentucky Brigade," one of the earliest and best accounts of the early days of the famed "Orphan Brigade."

William C. Davis

Barrett, Mason, Collection, Tulane University Library, New Orleans.

Johnston, J. Stoddard, *Kentucky*, Vol. IX in Evans, *Confederate Military History*.

✫ *Joseph Lewis Hogg* ✫

No photo of any kind has been found of Joseph L. Hogg. This portrait is clearly an artist's representation, and probably adds a uniform to a prewar painting. (Museum of the Confederacy, Richmond, Va.)

Joseph Lewis Hogg was born on September 13, 1806, in Morgan County, Georgia, but moved with his family to near Tuscaloosa, Alabama, in 1818. There he grew up, eventually acquiring a plantation and slaves of his own. By the age of thirty-three he had already studied law, delved into politics, and served in the local militia. In 1839 Hogg moved westward and settled near Nacogdoches in east Texas. He became very active politically in the new republic and it was said his remarkable physical resemblance to Andrew Jackson only helped his career. Being a supporter of Sam Houston, Hogg was elected to the Texas congress in 1843 and was a delegate to the Convention of 1845, in which he advocated annexation by the United States. When the Mexican War erupted, Hogg resigned a seat in the state senate and joined a volunteer regiment as a private. He was defeated in the election for regimental colonel, but remained in the unit as a private and served at the battle of Monterrey.

In the 1850s Hogg lived and practiced law in Cherokee County. He quickly became a prominent lawyer and bank promoter, and represented the county in the Texas legislature. In 1861 he served as a delegate to the Texas secession convention, where he campaigned for secession. After an unsuccessful campaign for the Confederate Congress, Hogg received a colonel's commission and was sent to east Texas to raise troops for the Confederacy. He served in this capacity for months before being appointed a Confederate brigadier general on February 4, 1862, to rank immediately. Given a mixed brigade of Texas and Arkansas cavalry, infantry, and artillery, Hogg was dispatched to Corinth, Mississippi, in the spring. At the Corinth encampment he quickly was struck down with dysentery and died on May 16, 1862. Some say his Confederate service was so short that he never donned a Confederate uniform. Hogg was first buried near Mount Holly School House, but his remains were exhumed in 1918 and placed in Corinth's Confederate Cemetery. His son, James Stephen Hogg, also successful in Texas politics, served as governor 1892–96.

Terry L. Jones

Webb, Walter Prescott, ed., *The Handbook of Texas* (Austin, 1952), Vol. I.

✴ *Robert Frederick Hoke* ✴

Robert Hoke was born in Lincolnton, North Carolina, on May 27, 1837. The son of a successful businessman and politician who ran on the Democratic ticket for governor in 1844, Hoke received an education in local schools and at the Kentucky Military Institute. By the age of seventeen, he was managing his family's iron works, cotton mill, and other business interests.

Hoke entered Confederate service in the spring of 1861 as 2d lieutenant of the 1st North Carolina. In the regiment's first engagement, the Battle of Big Bethel on June 10, Hoke performed so capably that D. H. Hill, the unit's commander, praised him for "coolness, judgment and efficiency." Promotions followed—to major of the 1st and then lieutenant colonel of the 33d North Carolina.

By the spring of 1862 Hoke and the 33d North Carolina had returned to their native state, assigned to the brigade of Lawrence O'Bryan Branch. On March 14 at New Berne Hoke led five companies of the regiment in a three-hour struggle. When the regiment's colonel was captured, Hoke assumed command. Branch reported afterward that the unit "moved into action with as much promptness and steadiness as I ever saw in its ranks on dress parade, and its fire, with Enfield rifles, was terrific" and cited its field officers, including Hoke, for their conduct and duty "against an overwhelming force."

Two months later Confederate authorities transferred Branch's brigade to Virginia, where it was assigned to A. P. Hill's "Light Division." Hoke commanded the regiment throughout the Seven Days', Cedar Mountain, Second Manassas, and Sharpsburg campaigns. At Second Manassas on August 30 Hoke's veterans repulsed the Union attacks and joined in the counterattack. "The Thirty-third under

Colonel Hoke," reported James Lane, "fought well in the woods, and once gallantly advanced into the open field in front, and drove the enemy back in disorder."

Hoke was promoted to colonel and assigned to the command of the 21st North Carolina. At Fredericksburg on December 13 he assumed temporary command of Isaac Trimble's brigade, leading the regiments in a riveting counterattack that sealed a gap in Confederate lines and drove the Federals rearward. By now the tall, confident Hoke had become a marked man, and his promotion to brigadier general came on April 23, to rank from January 17, 1863. He was given permanent command of Trimble's brigade, comprised of 6th, 21st, 54th, 57th North Carolina and 1st North Carolina Battalion.

On May 4, 1863, in the fighting at Marye's Heights during the Chancellorsville Campaign, Hoke fell wounded. When he recovered, he was returned to North Carolina, where he commanded troops along the Roanoke River. On April 17, 1864, his command with the support of the ironclad *Albemarle* advanced on the Union garrison at Plymouth. The Federals, numbered 2,834, surrendered three days later. Hoke's April 23 promotion to major general, one year to the day from his last promotion, was dated April 20, 1864.

Within a month Hoke's seventy-one-hundred—man division marched to Petersburg, Virginia. During the Bermuda Hundred campaign his brigades fought well at Drewry's Bluff in mid-May. On May 12 when a strong Union force advanced on his position, he informed a superior that "I shall fight them if met from all sides." His division then in June joined the

The only known photo of Hoke as a brigadier, made during or after 1863. (Southern Historical Collection, University of North Carolina, Chapel Hill, N.C.)

Army of Northern Virginia for the Second Battle of Cold Harbor, remaining with the command through the fall of 1864 in the Petersburg operations.

Hoke once again returned to his native state in November and participated in the fighting at Fort Fisher. During the war's final weeks he commanded Braxton Bragg's division in the actions at Bentonville on March 19 and 21, 1865. When the Confederate army surrendered, Hoke told his troops to tell their children that "the proudest days in all your proud careers was that on which you enlisted as Southern soldiers."

Hoke lived for nearly half a century after the war. He engaged in "inconspicuous private pursuits" and served as a director of the North Carolina Railroad Company. He had been a superb regimental commander, an excellent brigade commander, and an above-average division commander. Hoke died in Raleigh, North Carolina, on July 3, 1912, and was buried there.

Jeffry D. Wert

Freeman, Douglas Southall, *Lee's Lieutenants: A Study in Command* (New York, 1942–44).

Robertson, William Glenn, *Back Door to Richmond: The Bermuda Hundred Campaign, April–June 1864* (New York, 1987).

Schiller, Herbert M., *The Bermuda Hundred Campaign: Operations on the South Side of the James River, Virginia—May, 1864* (Dayton, 1988).

Hoke as colonel of the 21st North Carolina, probably in 1862. (Cook Collection, Valentine Museum, Richmond, Va.)

✳ Theophilus Hunter Holmes ✳

Theophilus H. Holmes was born on November 13, 1804, in Sampson County, North Carolina. He graduated from the United States Military Academy in 1829 forty-fourth out of forty-six. Holmes was one of three of the Confederacy's poorer students (the other two were Hood and Longstreet) who attained a rank beyond major general. In the Old Army he served on the frontier and fought in the Seminole War of the 1830s, where he earned a brevet for gallantry. During the Mexican War he received a second brevet.

On January 5, 1861, he was the superintendent of recruiting services at Fort Columbus on Governor's Island, New York, and received instructions to detach two hundred men to send to Fort Sumter on the *Star of the West*. When the Civil War began, he resigned, effective April 22. He had achieved the Regular rank of major in the 8th Infantry and was one of fifteen field-grade officers from the Old Army to join the Confederacy.

Holmes, a West Point classmate of Jefferson Davis, was appointed a brigadier general on June 5, 1861, to rank immediately, and ordered to assume command of the troops at Fredericksburg, Virginia. He was at the First Battle of Manassas but took no part in the action. On October 7, 1861, effective immediately, he was promoted to major general and on October 22 was ordered to take command of the Aquia District in the Department of Northern Virginia. On March 23, 1862, he was relieved from the Aquia District, assigned to temporary duty with Robert E. Lee, and instructed to report to the adjutant and inspector general's office for further orders. At the same time he received instructions to proceed to Goldsboro and take over operations in the Department of North

Carolina. He commanded a division during the Seven Days' and fought at Malvern Hill, where he failed to distinguish himself; his actions provoked severe criticism from D. H. Hill. At one time during the battle the nearly deaf Holmes was heard to inquire, "I thought I heard firing?"

On July 16, 1862, Holmes was ordered to the Trans-Mississippi Department, and assumed command on July 30, replacing the energetic but controversial Thomas C. Hindman. Holmes, who arrived at Little Rock in August, was an unfortunate choice. He was not easy to get along with and could sometimes prove extremely discourteous. Subordinates recalled that he would "cuss and roar," and frequently "bawl out" his staff. Moreover, he tended to think in terms of what best served his own department rather than what might be best for the Confederacy as a whole.

Holmes was promoted to lieutenant general, to rank immediately, on October 13, 1862. When asked to provide reinforcements for Vicksburg, he procrastinated and used his personal friendship with President Davis to prevent the movement of troops out of his department. He wrote Richmond that any such decision would have serious consequences. "Solemnly, under the circumstances," pointed out Holmes, "I regard the movement ordered as equivalent to abandoning Arkansas." Not only did he effectively get out of providing real assistance to Vicksburg, but he was also responsible for not adequately defending his own borders; in

The only known uniformed portrait of Holmes from the war is this one. Though his collar insignia is that of a colonel, he was commissioned directly as a brigadier, so this portrait could date from any time during the war. (Library of Congress)

December the Confederates lost at Prairie Grove in northwest Arkansas, and in early January 1863 Arkansas Post in the southeast surrendered. Although there were already serious problems in the Trans-Mississippi when Holmes arrived, he did little to improve the situation. Richard Taylor, soon after he took over the District of Louisiana, had complained that Holmes gave little attention to any area except Arkansas. This feeling of abandonment created serious morale problems not only in Louisiana but all throughout the Trans-Mississippi. Taylor observed that the people were "apathetic if not hostile from disaster and neglect...Such was the military destitution that a regiment of cavalry could have ridden over the State."

Holmes, in fact, recognized that he was not administering his entire geographic area adequately. He wrote to Richmond in October 1862 requesting to be relieved. By January the Confederate government was ready to comply. Secretary of War James A. Seddon reported in March 1863 that the most deplorable accounts had reached the department of "the disorder, confusion, and demoralization everywhere prevalent, both with the armies and people of that State." Holmes, he thought, had "lost the confidence and attachment of all," and the result was "fearful." Since Holmes was a personal friend of Davis, the change in department commanders was made ostensibly to lighten the general's load of "multifarious duties." Richmond agreed, and on January 14, 1863, assigned Lieutenant General Edmund Kirby Smith to the command of the Southwestern Army, embracing the Departments of West Louisiana and Texas. Holmes thanked Davis personally for sending help to Louisiana and Texas: "I was," he wrote, "unable to do anything here."

On February 9 the command was extended to cover the entire Trans-Mississippi Department. On March 18 Holmes was officially relieved from the command of the department and assigned to command of the District of Arkansas, including the Indian Territory and Missouri. A Texas captain wrote of Holmes removal: "This will indeed be gratifying news as every body soldier and citizen are tired of the Old *Granny Genl.* as General Holmes is universally styled. Nobody expects any thing of him. Nobody cares any thing for him & nobody has any respect for him and hence for the sake of the country and the efficiency of the army we hail the advent of such a Genl as Kirby Smith and the retirement of Genl H."

As head of the District of Arkansas Holmes continued to show little interest in doing anything directly to aid Vicksburg but did authorize John S. Marmaduke to take Confederates on a raid into Missouri in the spring. On July 4, 1863, he assaulted the Federal stronghold at Helena, but his mismanaged attack failed miserably. Because of illness Holmes relinquished command of the district from late July until late September and did not direct the army during the fall of Little Rock. He resumed command on September 25, 1863.

In early 1864 Holmes learned that Kirby Smith, Arkansas Senator R. W. Johnson, Governor Thomas Reynolds of Missouri, and Governor Harris Flanagin of Arkansas, as well as the Arkansas congressional delegation, were all petitioning President Davis for his removal. Rather than face a discharge, Holmes decided to resign and did so March 16, 1864. Holmes was ordered to North Carolina, where he took command of the reserves on April 18, 1864, and remained there until April 1865. This position was largely administrative, and Holmes was able to make a contribution to the Confederacy that equalled his moderate talents.

After the war he farmed near Fayetteville in Cumberland County, North Carolina. He died on June 21, 1880, and was buried in Fayetteville. Without a doubt Holmes was ineffective as both a department and district commander. His physical health was poor, and some suspected that he had "softening of the brain." He was criticized as "weak, vacillating, and totally devoid of energy." Holmes was described as "simple in his tastes, brave, true, and just...a splendid example of an unpretentious North Carolina patriot and gentleman." One historian observed: "A soldier Holmes was, but not in the full sense of the word a general. As his performance in Arkansas ultimately revealed, he was unfit for a high command involving combat operations."

Anne Bailey

Freeman, Douglas Southall, *Lee's Lieutenants* (New York, 1942–48).

Kerby, Robert L., *Kirby Smith's Confederacy* (New York, 1969).

⋆ *James Thadeus Holtzclaw* ⋆

Holtzclaw was born December 17, 1833, at McDonough, Georgia. His parents soon returned to their home in Chambers County, Alabama, where he grew up. He attended the Presbyterian high school at Lafayette, Alabama, and the East Alabama Institute. Holtzclaw received an appointment to West Point in 1853 but declined it. He studied law in Montgomery and was admitted to the bar in 1855.

Holtzclaw served as a lieutenant in a militia company called the Montgomery True Blues and, when the Civil War began, went with that unit to assist in the capture of the Pensacola Navy Yard. He was appointed major of the 18th Alabama Infantry in August 1861, and the regiment was organized at Auburn on September 4. The 18th Alabama received orders to report for duty at Mobile as a part of Brigadier General Leroy P. Walker's brigade. Holtzclaw was promoted lieutenant colonel in December while the regiment was at Mobile.

In March 1862 the regiment went to Corinth, Mississippi, and joined Brigadier General John K. Jackson's brigade. At the Battle of Shiloh April 6, Holtzclaw was dangerously wounded when a Union bullet passed through his right lung. He was next to the colors of his regiment, which attracted the enemy fire. It was thought at first that this was a mortal wound, but he recovered and rejoined his regiment in about ninety days.

The 18th Alabama was detached from General Braxton Bragg's army on July 23 and assigned to the garrison at Mobile. There the unit recruited and performed mostly guard duty. On October 8 a brigade

was formed of four Alabama regiments and called the 1st Brigade, Army of Mobile. Holtzclaw was now colonel of his regiment and as senior colonel assumed command of the brigade. He held this position for only about two weeks, when Brigadier General Alfred Cumming reported for duty at Mobile and was placed in charge of the brigade.

In March 1863 Cumming's brigade moved to Pollard, Alabama, to do outpost duty. Late the next month Cumming received orders to take his men to Tullahoma, Tennessee, and join the Army of Tennessee. There the regiment was assigned to the brigade of Brigadier General Henry D. Clayton. The 18th Alabama participated in the various marches of the army during the Tullahoma Campaign and the retreat into northern Georgia. Holtzclaw led his men in the Battle of Chickamauga September 19–20. During the fighting on the afternoon of September 19 he was thrown from his horse and injured. He turned over command to his lieutenant colonel that evening but returned the next morning. The brigade was heavily engaged about noon and forced to retreat. Holtzclaw rallied a portion of his regiment, but soon his injuries forced him to leave the field again. He did not resume command for two days. The 18th Alabama lost 322 officers and men out of the 536 present when the battle started.

Clayton had also been wounded at Chickamauga, and Holtzclaw led the brigade during the Chattanooga Campaign. During the afternoon of the Battle of

Holtzclaw seems not to have left behind a genuine uniformed photo. This engraving is all that can be found. (Miller, *Photographic History*)

Lookout Mountain November 24, the brigade reinforced troops near the Craven House and held back the enemy advance until midnight. The men were only lightly engaged the next day in the Battle of Missionary Ridge, and they retreated with the army to Dalton. In February 1864 when Union forces made a reconnaissance toward Dalton, Clayton's brigade saw some action at Rocky Face Ridge, or Crow's Valley. The men defeated an attack by a Union brigade twice their strength on February 25 in an engagement lasting about half an hour.

During the opening stages of the Atlanta Campaign, the brigade fought at Rocky Face Ridge, May 7–12; Resaca, May 14–15; Cassville, May 18; and New Hope Church, May 25–27. Holtzclaw was promoted brigadier general on July 8, to rank from July 7, to succeed Clayton, who had been promoted and given command of the division. Reports indicate that Holtzclaw's senior colonel commanded the brigade during the Battles of Atlanta (July 22) and Jonesborough (August 31–September 1), while he was present at the Battle of Ezra Church on July 28. These reports do not give any reasons for Holtzclaw's absence. He was away sick in mid-September and may have been ill during the two battles mentioned.

The brigade went with the army on its march through northern Georgia into Alabama preparatory to the Nashville campaign. November 28–29 Holtzclaw and his men participated in the feint attacks made south of Columbia, Tennessee, to hold the enemy's attention while most of the army marched toward Spring Hill to get behind the Union army. The division reached the battlefield at Franklin too late to participate in the fighting there on November 30. Holtzclaw's brigade was not heavily engaged in the first day's battle at Nashville on December 15. His troops repulsed several enemy attacks the next day. Two of Holtzclaw's regiments threw back an assault by a brigade of black troops and captured one regiment's flag. The men withdrew from the field with the rest of the division after the Union onslaught crushed the army's left and center. During the retreat back to the Tennessee River, Holtzclaw and his men sometimes acted as the army's rear guard.

On January 20, 1865, Holtzclaw's brigade was detached from the Army of Tennessee and ordered to Mobile. There the men received the assignment of guarding earthwork entrenchments being constructed at Blakely and Spanish Fort. The brigade made up a part of the garrison at Fort Blakely when the Union army began its campaign against Mobile in March.

After seeing some minor skirmishing in that vicinity, the brigade was transferred on March 31 to Spanish Fort. There Brigadier General Randall L. Gibson assigned Holtzclaw to command of the left wing of the defenses, consisting of his own and Colonel J. A. Andrews' Texas brigade. Holtzclaw performed valuable service in this capacity until the post was evacuated on the night of April 8. He and his brigade were paroled at Meridian, Mississippi, in May when Lieutenant General Richard Taylor surrendered the Department of Alabama, Mississippi, and East Louisiana.

Holtzclaw resumed his law practice at Montgomery after the war. He was a delegate to the Democratic convention in 1868 and served as a Democratic party elector in 1876 and 1888. The governor of Alabama appointed Holtzclaw to the state railroad commission in early 1893. He died shortly afterward on July 19 in Montgomery and was buried there.

Arthur W. Bergeron, Jr.

Memorial Record of Alabama (Madison, 1893), Vol. II.

Owen, Thomas M., *History of Alabama and Dictionary of Alabama Biography* (Spartanburg, 1978), Vol. III.

Wheeler, Joseph, *Alabama*, Vol. VII in Evans, *Confederate Military History*.

The most photographed of the Confederacy's lieutenant generals, except for Forrest, Hood appears here sometime after October 1862. His young and vigorous look suggests that it predates his severe 1863 wounds. (William A. Turner Collection)

✶ John Bell Hood ✶

Last and youngest of the Confederacy's full generals, John Bell Hood was born in Owingsville, Kentucky, on June 29, 1831. His father was a medical doctor and his mother a member of a prominent family. Hood received his basic education from private tutors or local schools. In 1849 he was appointed to the United States Military Academy by an uncle then serving in Congress.

Hood did not distinguish himself at the academy, graduating in 1853 forty-fourth among the fifty-two in his class. In his first year he picked up eighteen demerits for violating the school's regulations; in the last year, he received 196. Upon graduation he joined the 4th Infantry Regiment in California.

Transferred to the 2d Cavalry in 1855, Hood went with that regiment to Texas. In 1857 he won praise for his conduct of an engagement with Indians near Devil's River, and in 1858 he was promoted from 2d lieutenant to 1st lieutenant. On April 16, 1861, he resigned to join the Confederacy.

Hood was named colonel of the 4th Texas Infantry Regiment—one of three Lone Star State units serving in Virginia. Hood proved a fine regimental commander. On March 6, 1862, he was appointed brigadier general, to rank from March 3, to command what came to be called "Hood's Texas Brigade."

On June 27, 1862, Hood took the brigade into the Battle of Gaines' Mill, where his personal leadership played a crucial role in the Confederate victory. When the division commander went on sick leave, Hood as senior officer present assumed command of the division.

At the Second Battle of Manassas in August and at the Battle of Antietam in September, Hood fought with great distinction. In both engagements his division played a key role, and for his conduct that summer Hood won wide praise. On October 11 he was promoted to major general, to rank from October 10, and given command of a division in the I (Longstreet's) Corps of the Army of Northern Virginia.

At Gettysburg on July 2, 1863, just as his division entered the battle, Hood was severely wounded. Shell fragments struck his left arm, damaging the nerves and muscles. For the rest of his life he had no use of his left hand.

Two months later Hood's troops were among reinforcements sent to Georgia. Hood, not recovered fully from his Gettysburg wound, accompanied his men. On September 20 in the Battle of Chickamauga, he was wounded in the right leg so seriously that the limb was amputated at the hip.

Hood spent the winter of 1863–64 in Richmond, recuperating from his wounds, preparing to rejoin the army, and pursuing Sally Buchanan Campbell Preston, a South Carolina belle who spent most of the war in Richmond flirting with Confederate officers. Hood's battlefield success won him promotion to lieutenant general. (The promotion was decided in October 1863, but it was not made until February 11, 1864, and was backdated to rank from September 20.) When he left Richmond for his new post as a corps commander in the Army of Tennessee, Hood was engaged to Sally Preston.

In the first part of the Georgia Campaign of 1864 Hood commanded his corps without distinction. Meanwhile he became increasingly disillusioned with his army commander, Joseph E. Johnston, as that general fell back to Atlanta. Hood along with others criticized Johnston's conduct of the campaign. (Hood's criticisms went beyond those of most others, and some believe that he was seeking to undermine Johnston to obtain command of the army for himself.) On July 17 President Jefferson Davis named Hood—temporarily promoted to full general the following day—to replace Johnston as commander of the army.

In July and August Hood fought four battles in an effort to preserve Atlanta from the Union army of Major General William T. Sherman. Forced out of Atlanta after Sherman cut the railroads supplying the city, Hood marched northward, hoping to draw Sherman after him and, perhaps, to find an opportunity to fight on advantageous terms.

Frustrated in north Georgia, Hood drifted into Alabama, at a loss as to his next step. Eventually he

121

Hood's collar insignia "says" colonel, while his buttons and sleeve braid proclaim brigadier. The latter is probably the case, making this a spring or summer 1862 image. (Cook Collection, Valentine Museum, Richmond, Va.)

The same is the case with this companion portrait, made certainly at the same sitting. (Cook Collection, Valentine Museum, Richmond, Va.)

Hood is at least a major general by the time this image was shot. His arm does not look withered by the wound of Gettysburg yet, so it may be from early 1863. (Museum of the Confederacy, Richmond, Va.)

Hood has aged in this image and the companion that follows. Other images
not in uniform but apparently taken at the same time show him with a crutch,
so this is presumably taken after the loss of his leg at Chickamauga. (William A.
Turner Collection)

A variant portrait made at the same sitting. (Museum of the Confederacy, Richmond, Va.)

decided to move into Tennessee. If he could defeat the Yankee army there, he might yet redeem the Confederacy's fast-sinking fortunes.

Confused by problems of logistics and administration, Hood floundered for weeks in northern Alabama. Not until November 20 did he commence his march into Tennessee. He probably intended to get around the Federal force in his front to reach Nashville or possibly the Ohio River.

At Spring Hill on November 29 the command system of Hood's army fell apart in a fiasco of poor administration, murky orders, mental confusion, and physical exhaustion. After getting into position on the flank of a retreating Federal army, Hood's men simply halted for the night, allowing the enemy to escape. Meanwhile Hood slept in a nearby house, too exhausted to understand what was happening.

The next day a frustrated, angry Hood started north in pursuit. Overtaking the Yankees at Franklin, he threw his men into a costly assault on the enemy's position. After the Federals withdrew, Hood followed them to Nashville. There on December 15–16 his army was routed by the Unionists. The Rebels fled to northern Mississippi, and Hood was soon relieved from command. Never again did he hold a position of authority in the Confederacy. On May 31, 1865, in Natchez, Mississippi, he surrendered to Federal officers.

Hood lived for fourteen more years. For most of that time he was in New Orleans, engaged in the insurance business or as a cotton factor. In 1868 he married Anna Marie Hennen. (The engagement to Sally Preston had broken up in 1865.) On August 30, 1879, Hood died of yellow fever. For several years prior to his death Hood had worked on his memoirs, and they were posthumously published as *Advance and Retreat*.

As a combat commander Hood had no superior and few equals. His ability to lead and inspire men in battle contributed much to the Confederates' 1862 successes in Virginia. He never grew beyond that role, however, and he was unable to adjust to the higher commands in which he found himself after 1863. He is often cited as an example of the "Peter Principle"—one promoted beyond the level of his or her competency.

Richard M. McMurry

Connelly, Thomas Lawrence, *Autumn of Glory: The Army of Tennessee, 1862–1865* (Baton Rouge, 1971).

McMurry, Richard M., *John Bell Hood and the War for Southern Independence* (Lexington, 1982).

Woodworth, Steven E., *Jefferson Davis and His Generals: The Failure of Confederate Command in the West* (Lawrence, 1990).

✴ *Benjamin Huger* ✴

There is no way of saying with certainty when this portrait of General Huger was made, because even though the buttons are those of a brigadier, he may not have changed them after his promotion to major general. (Museum of the Confederacy, Richmond, Va.)

Benjamin Huger was born at Charleston, South Carolina, on November 22, 1805, a descendant of French Huguenots. He graduated from the United States Military Academy in 1825 eighth in a class of thirty-seven. He studied in Europe before transferring to ordnance, and his service in the Old Army included commanding at arsenals, membership on the Ordnance Board, and serving as chief of ordnance under General Winfield Scott in the Mexican War. For his services in Mexico he received brevets to major, lieutenant colonel, and colonel. During the war he commanded 2d Lieutenant Josiah Gorgas (future head of the Confederate department in which Huger would serve) and had a minor misunderstanding with him over supplies. Gorgas wrote: "So keenly do I feel this *slur* so publicly made, that I cannot regard Capt. H. with those kindly feelings which I would wish to maintain towards an officer under whom I am to serve; and I shall immediately on my arrival in the Capitol [Mexico City] frankly tell him so, & shall strenuously object to serving under his orders." Despite Huger's attempts to straighten out their difficulties, Gorgas did not forgive him.

On November 20, 1860, Brevet Colonel Huger took command of the Charleston Arsenal by order of the War Department, and while in Charleston promised the governor that no arms would be removed. Robert Anderson wrote that Huger was "more hopeful of a settlement of impending difficulties without bloodshed than I am. Hoping in God that he may be right in his opinion." By December 15, 1860, Huger had returned to his former duty at the Pikesville Arsenal.

In March Gorgas was ordered to report to the United States Inspector of Ordnance, who happened to be Colonel Huger. Gorgas was furious; this was one of the reasons behind his decision to resign from the army effective April 3. Unfortunately for Gorgas, Huger also resigned, on April 22, 1861. On May 23 Huger was listed as a brigadier general of volunteer forces of Virginia assigned to the troops around Norfolk. On June 17, 1861, he was appointed a brigadier general, effective immediately, and on October 7 he was made a major general, again effective immediately.

At the outset of the Peninsula Campaign (March–August 1862) he evacuated Norfolk, believing he was unable to hold it, blew up the CSS *Virginia,* and set fire to the Navy Yard before joining the army around Richmond. He led a division at Seven Pines, Gaines' Mill, Glendale, and Malvern Hill. His action in the Seven Days' battles was criticized and led to a harsh series of letters. Joseph E. Johnston claimed that Huger was not ready on time, and had his command "gone into action even at 4 o'clock the victory would have been much more complete." Huger wrote Jefferson Davis on September 21 that he wanted Johnston to prefer charges against him for the "negligence he attributes to me, and we then be examined by a court-martial. If this cannot be done, I ask a court of inquiry to examine the facts. I am entitled to this protection to my reputation and this justice to the troops I command." On August 6 Richard Taylor commented that as a result of the incident Huger had been removed from command; moreover, "Magruder is charged with incompetency and loss of head, and much blame attached to both his and Huger's slowness."

On August 26 Huger was appointed inspector of artillery and ordnance for the army; his orders would be issued through Gorgas at the Office of the Chief of Ordnance. The duties of the position sounded impressive, since it was necessary that this not appear as a demotion for General Huger. Gorgas, beyond remaining respectfully civil to him, paid little attention to Huger's new designation. Perhaps influenced by past bitterness, Gorgas wrote: "Gen. Huger's orders are intended to cover all Ord Establishments. He will do no harm, if he can do no good." Gorgas had already decided that he would ignore Huger's job, as he considered it an unnecessary position. Huger was ordered to inspect and examine all of the establishments of the Ordnance Department and the works of all contractors for the department, including all foundries and mines for iron, lead, copper, and niter working under permanent contract. He was also instructed to inspect all forts and batteries and to give orders and instructions that would increase their efficiency. Commanders of such facilities were ordered to give him all the assistance he required. Huger wrote that "when I see what had been done, and the limited means we have had to work with, I think we have cause of congratulation that we have got on so well."

On February 23, 1863, he was ordered to proceed to the Department of South Carolina and Georgia to make a thorough inspection of the artillery and ordnance at Charleston and Savannah. When Gorgas decided to decentralize his department, it gave him the chance to send Huger to the west by appointing him to the Trans-Mississippi Department. This would get him out of the way, while still giving him a position of importance. Therefore, while at Charleston, on March 23, 1863, he was ordered to proceed to the Trans-Mississippi to inspect artillery and ordnance; his instructions ordered him to report to Edmund Kirby Smith at Alexandria. Huger's arrival unbalanced some of Smith's plans, as he had just assigned Major Thomas G. Rhett as his chief of ordnance and artillery. Huger reported that in the early part of 1863 he was ordered to report to Smith to "give such advice and assistance as my enlarged experience enabled me to do...." Smith directed that all the returns and reports previously made to Richmond would be made to Huger. He made a tour of inspection through the country, visiting the different establishments for manufacturing ordnance supplies, and on his return, with the approval of General Smith, established the office of the bureau. He impressed others as a "competent officer" endeavoring to do his duty, and was probably responsible for starting the arsenal at Tyler, Texas.

After the war he lived in Fauquier County, Virginia, but returned to Charleston, South Carolina, shortly before he died on December 7, 1877. He was buried in Green Mount Cemetery in Baltimore.

Anne Bailey

Capers, Ellison, *South Carolina,* Vol. V in Evans, *Confederate Military History.*

A slight variant, made at the same sitting. (*Civil War Times Illustrated* Collection, Harrisburg, Pa.)

⋆ *William Young Conn Humes* ⋆

General Humes has not left behind a uniformed image. This portrait is postwar. (Miller, *Photographic History*)

Humes was born May 1, 1830, at Abingdon, Virginia. Although having to borrow money to obtain an education, he graduated second in his class at the Virginia Military Institute in 1851. Humes taught school for a time and then moved to Knoxville, Tennessee, to study law. After he was admitted to the bar, he practiced there for a time but moved to Memphis in 1858 to open a law office.

Humes enlisted in Confederate service in June 1861 as a lieutenant in Captain William Keiter's Company No. 10 of Colonel John P. McCown's Artillery Corps of Tennessee. The company was stationed initially at New Madrid but later moved to Columbus, Kentucky. Humes became captain of his company when Keiter was killed on November 8. After the evacuation of Columbus, Humes' company returned to New Madrid and was assigned to man a heavy artillery battery on Island No. 10. Humes commanded the artillery on the island and exercised immediate control of two batteries of ten guns during the operations against the place, March 3–April 7, 1862, and he became a prisoner of war when the Confederate forces surrendered. Major General John P. McCown, in his report for the campaign, said Humes "deserves commendation for his energy and proper bearing at times."

Humes was exchanged in September and reported at Jackson, Mississippi. Brigadier General Gideon J. Pillow asked for Humes and his company to be assigned to his command at Oxford, Mississippi, for refitting as a light artillery battery, but this request was apparently denied. In October Humes was commanding a "consolidated battalion" of exchanged prisoners who were being reorganized for assignment to Major General Sterling Price's Army of the West. The battalion seems to have served as infantry and was for a time in Brigadier General Dabney H. Maury's division of Price's army.

By January 1863 Humes and his unit, referred to as Company C, Tennessee Light Artillery, had been ordered to join the garrison at Mobile, Alabama. Humes commanded what were known as the Bay Batteries (earthworks on various islands at the head of Mobile Bay) for at least a month. Later his company formed a part of Brigadier General James E. Slaughter's brigade at Mobile. Major General Joseph Wheeler asked for Humes as his chief of artillery, and the War Department assigned him as such with the rank of major, effective March 15.

Humes remained on Wheeler's staff through the summer and fall of that year. During Wheeler's raid into Middle Tennessee, September 30–October 17, Humes was wounded in an engagement at Farmington, and his superior praised him for his "great gallantry" in that fight. Upon Wheeler's recommendation Humes was promoted to brigadier general November 17, effective November 16. He was given command of a brigade of five Tennessee regiments in Brigadier General Frank C. Armstrong's division, then serving under to rank Lieutenant General James Longstreet in East Tennessee. The brigade was soon transferred to the division of Brigadier General John H. Kelly.

By late April 1864, Humes and his brigade had rejoined the Army of Tennessee at Dalton, Georgia. There he was given command of a division of three brigades, although these units were greatly understrength. On April 29 a Union cavalry force advanced from Ringgold and drove in Humes' pickets near Tunnel Hill. Humes reestablished his picket line after the Federals withdrew. Humes' division contested the advance of Major General William T. Sherman's troops in May and was engaged at Varnell's Station, Rocky Face Ridge, and Cass Station. On May 15 Humes led some of his men in an attack that drove Brigadier General Judson Kilpatrick's Federal cavalry away from Confederate hospitals near Resaca. The division fought dismounted at New Hope Church on May 27 and helped repulse enemy attacks on the army's right flank.

Humes continued to operate on the army's flanks during the month of June, and his men participated in a raid led by Brigadier General William H. Jackson against the Union line of communications. With one of his brigades Humes moved to Jonesborough to protect it from

Brigadier General George Stoneman's raid, July 26–31. Humes' division participated in Wheeler's Raid into northern Georgia and Middle Tennessee in August and September and helped destroy several miles of railroad near Dalton. Wheeler complimented Humes for "gallantry and good conduct through the entire expedition."

General John Bell Hood sent Wheeler's cavalry to oppose Sherman's March to the Sea, and Humes' men were frequently engaged in skirmishes with the Union cavalry. They helped overrun a Federal force at Waynesborough, Georgia, on November 26 and drove Brigadier General Judson Kilpatrick's force from Millen's Grove on December 1. Humes had a horse killed under him during one of these engagements.

When Wheeler's Cavalry Corps was reorganized on January 2, 1865, Humes retained command of his division. Wheeler wrote General Braxton Bragg that Humes had been doing his duty well and recommended him for promotion to major general. He repeated that recommendation several days later, calling Humes a "brave subordinate and withal [a] good disciplinarian." The War Department may have considered the promotion, and some sources state that Humes received his commission on March 10, 1865, but there is no verifiable record.

The division fought in a small skirmish at Pocotaligo, South Carolina, on January 26 and was driven back from McBride's Bridge over the Coosawattee River on February 1. He led his men at the Battle of Aiken, South Carolina, on February 11. Humes received a wound, said to be his second during the campaign, when Wheeler's cavalry overran Kilpatrick's cavalry at Monroe's Cross Roads on March 10. It is unclear whether or when Humes returned to duty. A report dated April 3 shows his senior brigade commander leading the division, but some sources state that Humes participated in the Battle of Bentonville on March 19.

Humes was paroled as a part of General Joseph E. Johnston's army when it surrendered to Sherman. He returned to his Memphis law practice after the war. He died on September 11, 1882, in Huntsville, Alabama, and was buried in Memphis.

Arthur W. Bergeron, Jr.

Horn, Stanley, ed., *Tennesseans in the Civil War* (Nashville, 1964).
Porter, James D., *Tennessee*, Vol. VIII in Evans, *Confederate Military History*.

⋆ *Benjamin Grubb Humphreys* ⋆

Born on August 24 or 26, 1808, in Claiborne County, Mississippi, Humphreys was grandson of a revolutionary war veteran and son of a planter. He went to school in Kentucky and New Jersey before entering the U. S. Military Academy at West Point in 1825. Humphreys, however, did not graduate: He was among the cadets dismissed from the academy after an outburst known as the Eggnog Riot on Christmas Eve 1826. He returned home to plantation life, studied law, and in 1832 married Mildred Hickman, daughter of James H. Maury. Humphreys became active in politics, serving terms as both state legislator and senator, while making his living as a planter.

The outbreak of civil war found Humphreys living in Sunflower County, Mississippi. Like many Whigs, he opposed secession but threw his energies into helping his state's cause. At the age of fifty-two, Humphreys in May 1861 organized the Sunflower Guards—Company I of what was then the 1st Battalion Mississippi Infantry but quickly became the 21st Regiment. He entered Confederate service as the company's captain on July 2, 1861. His leadership and straightforward bearing apparently caught the eye of superiors. Humphreys catapulted to colonel of the 21st Mississippi on September 11, 1861, serving under Brigadier General William Barksdale in the division of Major General Lafayette McLaws.

Humphreys led the 21st Mississippi through many of the sternest trials of the Army of Northern Virginia. His courage, integrity, and ability often elicited praise from superior officers.

His first major engagement came at Seven Pines, May 31–June 1, 1862. He missed action at Second Manassas and Maryland Heights, but from then on his combat career became increasingly one of arriving at crucial spots at opportune moments. He stepped onto the battlefield at Sharpsburg on September 17, 1862, in time to inspire troops driving the enemy from the West Woods. Barksdale noted that the presence of Humphreys and another officer "not only cheered and animated their own regiments, but the entire brigade." He closed the year at Fredericksburg, serving with those Mississippians who had distinguished themselves in contesting the Federal crossing of the Rappahannock on December 11.

As Lee took the bulk of the army to meet Major General Joseph Hooker at Chancellorsville in May 1863, Humphreys' 21st Mississippi performed picket duty along the Rappahannock. In postwar reminiscences Humphreys recalled his and Barksdale's concern in covering a three-mile front with so few troops. Less than reassuring was the departing comrade who quipped that the next time he would hear of Humphreys, the colonel would be in a Federal prison camp. However, Humphreys avoided capture as Federals pushed his regiment from the town and from its subsequent position at Marye's Heights. A day later the Confederates regained the positions they had lost.

At Gettysburg, July 1–3, 1863, Humphreys engaged in bitter fighting in the Peach Orchard during the afternoon of the second day. Apparently known "for excelling in the soundfulness of the word of command," Humphreys' call for attention seemed especially

This crude image, possibly not even a photograph, is all that can be found showing Humphreys in uniform. (Miller, *Photographic History*)

charged that day as he brought the men up "like an electric shock" to hear the address of Barksdale before the charge. The 21st Mississippi formed on the right of the brigade and exerted a momentum that carried it through waves of Union soldiers until reaching the swale at Plum Run. Long after the war Lieutenant General James Longstreet remembered Humphreys as an example of the fighting spirit displayed that day. He wrote that Humphreys withdrew from the charge first in disbelief and then only under protest. The Mississippians had taken severe casualties, including the death of Barksdale. As the senior colonel, Humphreys had assumed command and was subsequently promoted brigadier general on August 14, to rank from August 12, 1863. Douglas Southall Freeman proclaimed the promotion "was logical as it had been long delayed."

The new brigadier had little time to savor his promotion. Humphreys' brigade—consisting of the 13th, 17th, 18th, and 21st Mississippi—headed west with Longstreet's I Corps, arriving at Chickamauga in time to be part of the attack on September 20, 1863. Humphreys' performance received mention in Longstreet's report of the battle. The Mississippians spent the fall and winter weathering terrible conditions and grueling campaigning with little to show. Humphreys' brigade was one of three attacking Fort Sanders at Knoxville, Tennessee, on November 29, 1863. A treacherous ditch and the icy slopes of the fort's parapet scuttled the attempt and resulted in charges brought against McLaws by Longstreet. Humphreys served as a witness and member of the court-martial board. Yet McLaws remained kind to Humphreys, acknowledging the Mississippian's "zeal, courage, and coolness in conducting that assault" and even recommending him for promotion.

When the I Corps returned to Virginia in the spring of 1864, Humphreys and his brigade continued to be thrust into crucial battles. Having marched more than thirty miles in twenty-four hours, the brigade helped restore order to Confederate lines and check the Federals in the Wilderness on May 6. It also arrived at Spotsylvania Court House on May 8 in time to relieve the Confederate cavalry and prevent the V Corps of the Army of the Potomac from seizing the crossroads. After escaping injury in such major contests, Humphreys was wounded at a small engagement at Berryville, Virginia, on September 3, 1864. He received gunshot wounds in "both breasts," which kept him hospitalized in Charlottesville, Virginia, until September 26 and on wounded furlough until February 28, 1865. Although

the brigade retained his name, Humphreys finished the war assigned by Jefferson Davis to command a military district encompassing his native portion of Mississippi.

After the war Humphreys received a pardon from President Andrew Johnson and in October 1865 became governor of Mississippi. He eventually was ejected from the post by federal military authorities on June 15, 1868. Under him the infamous black codes were enacted, but like many former Whigs, Humphreys advocated reconciliation of the two sections. Although he differed politically with Longstreet, who joined the Republicans after the war, Humphreys defended his former chief in the controversy concerning Day 2 at Gettysburg. Humphreys considered the dispute over Longstreet's alleged delays at Gettysburg to be the fabrication of Virginians looking for a scapegoat for defeat.

Humphreys spent the remainder of his life first as an insurance agent and then in comparative quiet on his plantation in Leflore County, dying on December 20, 1882.

William Alan Blair

Everett, Jr., Frank E., "Delayed Report of an Important Eyewitness to Gettysburg—Benjamin G. Humphreys," *The Journal of Mississippi History* XLVI (November, 1984: 305–21).

Hooker, Charles E., *Mississippi,* Vol. VII in Evans, *Confederate Military History.*

Humphreys, Benjamin, "Recollections of Fredericksburg," in *Southern Historical Society Papers,* 14: 415–28.

☆ *Eppa Hunton* ☆

Eppa Hunton's only known uniformed wartime portrait, taken subsequent to August 1863. (Cook Collection, Valentine Museum, Richmond, Va.)

Eppa Hunton is one of a half-dozen or so Confederate generals who always will be remembered more vividly for a book he wrote than for what he did on the South's battlefields. His autobiographical memoir, printed in one hundred copies in 1933, is perhaps the most desirable and expensive rare book associated with the Army of Northern Virginia.

Hunton was born in Fauquier County, Virginia, on September 22, 1822. He attended new Baltimore Academy in his native county but never received any formal higher education. After teaching school for three years in Fauquier and Prince William counties, Hunton passed the Virginia bar and began a legal career that spanned six decades. The young lawyer opened a practice at Brentsville in 1843. Five years later he became commonwealth's attorney for Prince William County, and held that post until the beginning of the Civil War.

Although the only smidgen of military experience that Eppa Hunton had before 1861 was as a peacetime militia officer, he received a commission as colonel of the 8th Virginia Infantry on May 8, 1861. The appointment came as a result of political influence. Hunton had not held important office before 1861, but he served in the state's secession convention among the rather small minority of original secessionists. The 8th Virginia had not completed its organization by the time of the First Battle of Manassas July 21, 1861, but Colonel Hunton led the eight companies that he did have into battle near the climactic stages on Henry House Hill.

Soon after that first battle Hunton succumbed to one of the bouts of ill health that repeatedly kept him out of the field and that even more often limited his ability to do hard duty. During the fall of 1861 he was incapacitated for a time by severe hemorrhage of the throat. Beginning then and continuing throughout the war, Hunton suffered from hemorrhoids and fistula so severe that he frequently could not ride. In October 1861 the colonel came out of a sickbed at his nearby home to lead the 8th Virginia at the Battle of Ball's Bluff with real distinction.

Colonel Hunton remained absent sick for most of the period between November 24, 1861, and March 20, 1862. During March he laboriously relocated his family to Lynchburg, as the Federals moved into Prince William and Fauquier. Soon after their arrival Northern troops destroyed Hunton's house and all of his property. The colonel missed Seven Pines because of health problems but led the 8th Virginia—and the whole brigade as its senior colonel, after General Pickett was wounded—at Gaines' Mill June 27. The brigade participated in the final successful charge across Boatswain's Swamp in that battle, which Hunton later reckoned to be the "hardest" fight he saw other than Gettysburg.

As soon as the Seven Days' Campaign ended, Hunton went back on sick leave. He returned in time to command the regiment at Second Manassas, where he took part in Longstreet's final assault. Colonel Hunton was present at Sharpsburg in September and also at First Fredericksburg in December, though not much engaged. He and the 8th Virginia served in the campaign around Suffolk under Longstreet. In his memoir Hunton accused General Pickett of timid behavior at Suffolk and elsewhere. A typical phrase describing the general's demeanor is this one about him at Sayler's Creek: "galloped ingloriously to the rear."

Virtually all of Hunton's war service was under Pickett's command. The most famous event of the war for both was the charge at Gettysburg on July 3, 1863, often identified by Pickett's name. The colonel began the charge on horseback, but "early in the charge" and somewhat to the Confederate left of the Codori barn, he was "shot through the right leg just below the knee. No bones were broken, but the wound bled profusely." Hunton later wrote that he had 105 men present for duty in the 8th Virginia that afternoon. The preliminary artillery duel killed five of them. Only ten men were left to answer to roll call after the charge. Their colonel wrote of them after the war: "All appreciated the danger and felt it was probably the last charge to most of them. All seemed willing to die to achieve a victory there, which it was believed would be the crowning victory and the end of the war." Hunton's postwar writing about Gettysburg generally included the firm statement that Pickett and his staff had not participated to any considerable degree in the charge.

By the time Eppa Hunton returned to duty about six weeks after his wounding, he had received promotion to the rank of brigadier general on August 12, to date from August 9, 1863. Beginning in the late summer of 1863, the new brigadier quietly garrisoned the Confederate position at Chaffin's Farm near Richmond for many months with his command. A few days after the Battle of Spotsylvania in May 1864 Hunton and his brigade rejoined Pickett's division and the Army of Northern Virginia. They were hotly engaged at Cold Harbor, where the chief of staff to the general fell victim to a Federal bullet.

The siege of Richmond and Petersburg included very little action for Hunton and his men, who were positioned on the quiet Howlett line near the James River. They fought hard, though, in the battles of late March and early April 1865 until Hunton and much of his command were captured at Sayler's Creek on April 6. The general endured more than three months of captivity at Fort Warren in Boston harbor, where he and six fellow generals made up a high-ranking mess. The most prominent of Hunton's companions was Lieutenant General Richard S. Ewell, whose poltroonish behavior in seeking to curry Federal favor brought caustic comment in Hunton's memoir.

Immediately after taking the oath and leaving Fort Warren on July 24, 1865, Benton hurried home and found his family in dire straits. He quickly rebuilt his law practice and his fortune in Warrenton, also practicing in Loudoun County, from whence most of his 8th Virginia Regiment had come. Late in the century Hunton also practiced in Washington, D.C. Meanwhile he had won election to the United States House of Representatives in 1872, where he stayed until 1881. Congressman Hunton's most famous moments during his tenure in the House came when he served as the only Southern representative on the 1877 commission that oversaw the theft of the presidential election.

Eppa Hunton maintained his primary residence in Warrenton throughout his postwar career. He died in Richmond on October 11, 1908, and was buried there in that vast city of Confederate dead, Hollywood Cemetery.

Robert K. Krick

Daniel, John Warwick, Papers (Duke University, Durham, North Carolina).

Hotchkiss, Jedediah, *Virginia*, Vol. III in Evans, *Confederate Military History*.

Hunton, Eppa, *Autobiography* (Richmond, 1933).

An 1863 or later portrait of Imboden, showing his tunic buttons in the sweeping curve favored by a number of the generals. (U.S. Army Military History Institute, Carlisle, Pa.)

⭐ *John Daniel Imboden* ⭐

John D. Imboden was born near Staunton, Virginia, on February 16, 1823. After spending two terms at Washington College, Imboden taught school, studied law, and then opened a practice in his hometown. He prospered, acquired a reputation, and twice was elected to the state's legislature. An avowed secessionist, he organized and partially equipped with his own money the Staunton Artillery and was selected its captain before Virginia left the Union.

Imboden and the battery reported to Brigadier General Joseph Johnston's command at Harpers Ferry, remaining in the lower Shenandoah Valley until Johnston joined the Confederate forces at First Manassas. During the battle, July 21, 1861, the Staunton Artillery was attached to Brigadier General Barnard Bee's brigade and fought on Henry House Hill. For half an hour, Imboden's gunners fought alone as Confederate infantry rallied. The battery remained on the field until it exhausted its ammunition.

In the wake of the Confederate victory, Imboden and two other officers served on a board of investigation that examined the reasons for the Confederate failure to pursue the routed federals after Manassas. The board concluded that the Southerners lacked adequate provisions and transportation. By the spring of 1862, Imboden had returned to his native area and begun the organization of the 1st Virginia Partisan Rangers. During the Battle of Cross Keys in June, he guarded a bridge at Mount Crawford, and the next day, June 9, participated in the Battle of Port Republic.

During the summer of 1862 Imboden, now commissioned a colonel, completed the organization of his companies, which were designated the 62d Virginia Mounted Infantry. His regiment, some cavalry companies, and an artillery battery cooperated with Brigadier General Albert Jenkins' forces during a raid into western Virginia during August and September 1862. By year's end Imboden had organized additional units, and in January 1863 Robert E. Lee wrote to him: "I hope you will meet with speedy success in filling up

your command to a brigade, when I shall take great pleasure in recommending your promotion."

On April 13, 1863 Imboden was promoted to brigadier general, to rank from January 28. His brigade consisted of his former regiment and that unit's mounted companies, which were organized into the 18th Virginia Cavalry under the command of his brother, George, and a battery of artillery. Assigned to duty in the Shenandoah Valley and northwestern Virginia, he reported directly to Lee.

On April 20 Imboden and Brigadier General William E. "Grumble" Jones' commands advanced into West Virginia. The raid lasted until mid-May as the Confederates destroyed sections of the Baltimore and Ohio Railroad, gathered supplies, and advanced to within fifty miles of Pittsburgh, causing a panic throughout that section of Pennsylvania. When the raiders returned to Virginia, Lee praised the exploit, writing that it had "rendered valuable service in the collection of stores and in making the enemy uneasy for his communications with the west."

During the June to July 1863 Gettysburg Campaign Imboden's brigade was attached to Lee's army. As the Confederate legions advanced into Maryland and Pennsylvania, Imboden's twenty-one hundred poorly armed men raided westward along the B & O Railroad toward Romney, in western Virginia. Imboden protected the army's rear as it fought the three-day battle at Gettysburg. When Lee withdrew, Imboden guarded the miles of wagons and ambulances. On July 5, at Williamsport, Maryland, pursuing Union cavalry attacked the wagon train. Imboden's men fought well until additional Confederate cavalry and infantry arrived and repulsed the Federals. Although Lee regarded Imboden's troops as "unsteady" and "inefficient," the brigadier had rendered masterful service during the retreat.

A dark-haired, darkly complexioned man, Imboden was modest, knowing his limitations. On July 28 he assumed command of the Valley District, and when friends suggested that he seek promotion to major

A portrait of Imboden made probably at about the same time and in the same tunic. (Evans, *Confederate Military History*)

Another variant, probably from the same sitting. (Courtesy of George & Katherine Davis Collection, Howard-Tilton Memorial Library, Tulane University, New Orleans, La.)

Imboden has changed his tunic for this and the following images.
(U.S. Army Military History Institute, Carlisle, Pa.)

Quite probably made at the same sitting as the
portrait above, this portrait shows the resolute,
though not especially inspired face of an average
commander. (Warner, *Generals in Gray*)

general, he responded: "I do not desire it…I really feel that I have as high a military rank as I am qualified for."

Imboden had limitations as a disciplinarian. During his command of the district, discipline problems plagued him. Two hundred men deserted from a battalion when lieutenant refused to allow them to seize horses for private use. Lee found it necessary to criticize him for accepting deserters into his command. Finally, in February 1864 Major General Jubal Early, who now commanded in the region, reported that Imboden's command was "in a very bad state of discipline." Imboden requested a court of inquiry, but Lee refused.

The brigadier did render some valuable service during this period. In October 1863, when Lee advanced northward east of the Blue Ridge, Imboden marched down the Shenandoah Valley and captured a Union garrison at Charlestown, near Harpers Ferry. Months later he fought at New Market, on May 15, 1864, but his feeble effort to cross a flooded creek allowed the defeated Federals to elude a possible trap.

His brigade then served throughout the Shenandoah Valley Campaign of 1864. It fought at Piedmont on June 5, resisted the advance of Major General David Hunter's Union army on Lynchburg, and participated in Jubal Early's raid against Washington, D.C. in July. His understrength command also suffered through the string of Southern defeats—Third Winchester, Fisher's Hill, and Cedar Creek—during September and October. During the fall Imboden was incapacitated by typhoid fever. At war's end he was serving on prison duty at Aiken, South Carolina.

Imboden moved to Richmond after the war, practicing law for a period of time before entering the mining business. He founded the town of Damascus in Washington County, where he located a large vein of bituminous coal that was named the "Imboden seam." This mediocre Confederate brigadier, whose finest moments came on a raid into West Virginia and during the difficult retreat from Gettysburg, died in Damascus on August 15, 1895. He had been married five times, and was buried in Richmond.

Jeffry D. Wert

A glum-looking Brigadier General Imboden addresses the camera in this rare portrait probably taken in 1864 or 1865. (Museum of the Confederacy, Richmond, Va.)

Brice, Marshall Moore, *Conquest of a Valley* (Charlottesville, 1965).

Davis, William C., *The Battle of New Market* (New York, 1975).

Hotchkiss, Jedediah, *Virginia*, Vol. III in Evans, *Confederate Military History*.

✳ *Alfred Iverson, Jr.* ✳

No uniformed photo of Iverson has been found. This is a postwar image. (Miller, *Photographic History*)

Alfred Iverson, Jr., was born in Clinton, Georgia, on February 14, 1829. His distinguished father represented Georgia in the U.S. Senate at the time of the secession. The younger Iverson was reared in Columbus, Georgia, and in Washington, D.C. He dropped out of a military school in Tuskegee, Alabama, to serve in the Mexican War. On August 20, 1847, at the age of seventeen, he secured a commission as a 2d lieutenant in Seymour's Battalion of Georgia Volunteers, a unit Iverson's father helped to equip.

Mustered out on July 11, 1848, Iverson returned from Mexico and began reading law, a subject he found personally distasteful, in his father's office at Columbus, Georgia. He soon abandoned this profession and began contracting work for the railroads throughout Georgia. He changed professions again on March 3, 1855, when he was commissioned directly into the newly formed 1st U.S. Cavalry as a 1st lieutenant. Iverson even recruited a company for the regiment, which consisted mainly of volunteers from Georgia and Kentucky. Reporting for duty to Colonel E. V. Sumner at Jefferson Barracks, Missouri, Iverson was sent to "Bleeding Kansas" in 1856. He left Fort Leavenworth in 1857 for Carlisle Barracks, Pennsylvania, where he married the daughter of a Georgia judge. He participated in the expedition against the Mormons in 1857 and was based out of Fort Washita, Indian Territory, during the Indian Wars of 1858–59 against the Comanches and Kiowas.

Iverson resigned from the U.S. Army on March 21, 1861, to become a captain in the Provisional Army of the Confederate States. Initially ordered to Wilmington, North Carolina, Iverson was placed in charge of the companies guarding the mouth of the Cape Fear River. Iverson almost singlehandedly recruited enough additional companies to have his command organized into a regiment, and on August 20, 1861, he was commissioned colonel of the newly formed 20th North Carolina Infantry.

His regiment was transferred in June 1862 to Virginia, where the performance of his men during the Seven Days' battles reflected Iverson's ability to train raw recruits. During the fighting at Gaines' Mill, his regiment captured a Federal battery whose fire had been enfilading the brigades of Brigadier Generals Samuel Garland and George B. Anderson. Although wounded before the Seven Days' fighting ended, Iverson recovered in time to participate in General Robert E. Lee's first invasion of the North in September.

At the Battles of South Mountain and Antietam in September 1862 Iverson commanded the brigade of Brigadier General Samuel Garland, who was killed in the latter engagement.

Promoted to brigadier general on November 1, to rank immediately, Iverson's brigade was hardly engaged at Fredericksburg the following month, but he led his enlarged command with competency at Chancellorsville the following May. However, on July 1, 1863, the opening day of the Battle of Gettysburg, Iverson's brigade was devastated by the Union I Corps northwest of the town. The responsibility for this disaster was at least partially the fault of Iverson. After seeing his brigade literally shot to pieces, Iverson, according to one historian, "went to pieces and became unfit for further command." Iverson regained his composure in time to perform creditably during the Confederate withdrawal from Pennsylvania, especially at Hagerstown, Maryland, on July 6. Nevertheless, his record was tarnished, and Lee wanted nothing more to do with him.

Iverson was exiled to his native Georgia, where he relieved Major General Henry R. Jackson as commander of state forces at Rome, Georgia. For the next several months Iverson busied himself organizing state troops, but the man rejected by Lee was given a chance to redeem his reputation as a military commander. The withdrawal of the Army of Tennessee following its defeat at Missionary Ridge and the replacement of General Braxton Bragg by General Joseph E. Johnston as its commander resulted in Iverson's assignment on February 29, 1864, to command

of a Georgia brigade in Major General William T. Martin's division of Major General Joseph Wheeler's cavalry corps.

Having reached the outskirts of Atlanta in July, Union Major General William T. Sherman determined to send his cavalry out from both flanks in an attempt to cut the final railroad that supplied Atlanta at Lovejoy Station. On July 27 Major General George Stoneman moved east with sixty-five hundred troopers, while Brigadier General Edward M. McCook led thirty-five hundred men westward. At Stoneman's request, Sherman had granted him permission to proceed southward to free some thirty thousand Union prisoners of war being held at Macon and Andersonville, but only after cutting the railroad.

Stoneman promptly forgot about cutting the railroad after leaving Sherman and headed directly for Macon after detaching one of his divisions to cover his raid. Because of this action, Wheeler's ten thousand cavalrymen successfully dealt with the three Union columns in succession. Near Macon on July 29 Iverson, with thirteen hundred men, defeated Stoneman's force of about twenty-three hundred troopers, two hundred of whom were taken prisoner. Pursuing the fleeing enemy, Iverson captured Stoneman and five hundred additional Federals at Sunshine Church. This engagement was one of the greatest cavalry victories of the war and did much to revive the sagging spirits of the defenders of Atlanta.

Iverson continued to command a cavalry brigade until he learned of Lee's surrender at Appomattox Court House, Virginia. He then surrendered himself and received a parole. Initially engaged in business in Macon, Georgia, following the war, Iverson moved to Orange County, Florida, in 1877 to manage orange groves near Kissimmee. After farming there he relocated to Osceola County, Florida, where he continued to engage in the production of oranges. While on a visit to his native state, he died in Atlanta on March 31, 1911, and was buried there in Oakland Cemetery.

Lawrence L. Hewitt

Derry, Joseph T., *Georgia*, Vol. VI in Evans, *Confederate Military History*.

Faust, Patricia L., ed., *Historical Times Illustrated Encyclopedia of the Civil War* (New York, 1986).

✻ Alfred Eugene Jackson ✻

Born in Davidson County, Tennessee, on January 11, 1807, young Jackson was educated at Washington and Greenville colleges. He farmed on East Tennessee's Nolichucky River, and subsequently became a merchant and wholesaler. An energetic, hard-driving businessman, he expanded his merchandising activities, employing wagons and steamboats as a means of boosting his ventures, which by the 1850s included stores, gristmills, and sawmills, and farms scattered across Tennessee from the Great Smoky Mountains to the Mississippi River.

On September 11, 1861, Jackson was commissioned a major in the Confederate army and entered on duty at Knoxville as quartermaster on the staff of Brigadier General Felix K. Zollicoffer's brigade. An able entrepreneur, he proved his worth by collecting and transporting supplies for Zollicoffer's troops as they marched and camped through the rugged countryside bounded on the north by the Rockcastle and Cumberland Rivers and on the south by the Clinch River. He resigned his commission January 6, 1862.

Jackson served as paymaster at Knoxville through the winter of 1862–63. In response to petitions from hundreds of East Tennessee voters and pressure from the state's congressmen, he was called to Richmond and on April 22 made a brigadier general, to rank from February 9, and assigned command of a brigade stationed in the Department of East Tennessee. Jackson established his headquarters at Strawberry Plains and posted his unit, consisting of three cavalry battalions, three infantry regiments, a detachment of sappers and miners, and an artillery company, at Bristol, Greeneville, Haynesville, and Watauga Bridge with the missions of guarding the strategic East

Tennessee and Virginia Railroad linking Chattanooga with Richmond and of overawing local Unionists. In mid-April Jackson relocated his headquarters to Jonesboro and saw his effective, as well as numerical, strength slashed when his brigade was reorganized and reduced to one cavalry battalion, two infantry regiments, the detachment of sappers and miners, and two artillery companies.

In late April Confederate authorities, learning that Union troops led by Major General Ambrose E. Burnside were massing in the Kentucky bluegrass country preparatory for a campaign to recover East Tennessee, alerted General Jackson to call in his detachments and be prepared to take the field. On May 20 Major General Simon B. Buckner, recently placed in command of the Department of East Tennessee, redefined Jackson's mission: His twelve thousand effectives were to be "distributed at the various defenses of the bridges, in minimum garrisons, with the cavalry and Indians of the brigade for scouts and police of roads." Buckner also noted that most of Jackson's soldiers had been raised for local defense.

In mid-June Jackson called out his command when Union cavalry led by Colonel William P. Sanders coming out of Kentucky wreaked havoc on the East Tennessee & Virginia Railroad between Lenoir and Strawberry Plains. Jackson in late July was made responsible for security of the subject railroad from Knoxville to Bristol and established his command post at Zollicoffer.

The long anticipated and often delayed Union offensive, aimed at the capture of Chattanooga and

No uniformed image of Jackson has been found. This is a postwar portrait. (Miller, *Photographic History*)

driving the Confederates from East Tennessee, began in mid-August 1863. Major General William S. Rosecrans' army by September 9 had crossed the Tennessee River on a broad front and occupied Chattanooga. Burnside's columns, advancing southward from Kentucky, bypassed Cumberland Gap and entered Knoxville on September 3. General Buckner, accompanied by most of his troops, had gone to Georgia to reinforce the army that General Braxton Bragg was assembling to lash back at Rosecrans. This left the defense of East Tennessee to Jackson's understrength brigade and Brigadier General John W. Frazier's twenty-three hundred men, the latter of whom were compelled to surrender at Cumberland Gap on September 9.

At Knoxville the Federals captured two locomotives and a number of cars. Troops were entrained and sent up the railroad to Morristown and on to Greeneville. At Limestone Depot on September 8 General Jackson with his brigade, reinforced by a regiment of Kentucky cavalry, engaged the 100th Ohio infantry—350 strong—led by Lieutenant Colonel Edwin L. Hayes, and compelled them to surrender. Arrival of Union reinforcements enabled the Yankees to continue their offensive, and on the 19th, Union cavalry advancing by way of Kingsport dashed into Bristol, damaged the railroad, and returned to their camp. General Jackson meanwhile had skirmished with the Yankees at Zollicoffer, six miles west of Blountsville. Following a fight at Blountsville on September 22, Burnside, apprised of the stunning defeat suffered by Rosecrans' army at Chickamauga two days before, recalled to Knoxville the troops who threatened to drive Jackson and his brigade, along with reinforcements rushed from southwest Virginia and Richmond, out of East Tennessee.

During the winter of 1863–64 Jackson from his Zollicoffer camp employed his understrength command in pursuit of bushwhackers and to harass Union parties foraging in the area south of the French Broad River. In early May he was alerted that Union raiders led by Brigadier General William Averell were striking south from West Virginia en route to Saltville and was told to hold his men ready to hasten to the point of danger. The march orders never came, as Averell, informed that the Confederates were expecting him, lashed out toward Wytheville instead.

On September 30 Jackson hastened to Saltville and took initial command of the defense of the vital salt works against Union cavalry led by Brigadier General Stephen G. Burbridge. The Yankees attacked on October 2 and were repulsed in a bitter day-long fight that cost them 350 casualties.

Jackson's health now failed, and on November 23, listed as unfit for field duty, he reported to Major General John C. Breckinridge, commanding the Department of Western Virginia and East Tennessee, then headquartered at Wytheville, for light duty. There is no documentation concerning a parole, and Jackson probably just went home, if not already there, at the breakup of the Confederacy in the spring of 1865.

In 1866 Jackson, financially ruined by the war, rented land in Virginia's southwest Washington County and, despite his age, farmed it himself. He was pardoned by President Andrew Johnson for kindnesses shown the latter's kin during the war. He gradually recovered economically and returned to Tennessee, settling in Jonesboro. He died on October 30, 1889, and was buried there.

Edwin C. Bearss

Porter, James D., *Tennessee*, Vol. VIII in Evans, *Confederate Military History*.

✳ *Henry Rootes Jackson* ✳

Jackson was born on June 24, 1820, in Athens, Georgia, where his father taught mathematics at Franklin College (now the University of Georgia). In 1839 he graduated first in his class at Yale University. Jackson studied law after he returned to his native state and was admitted to the bar at Columbus in 1840. He soon moved to Savannah and opened his practice. He received an appointment as U.S. district attorney in 1843, serving until 1847. During the Mexican War Jackson was colonel of the 1st Georgia Volunteers and led his regiment throughout the conflict. He was appointed as a judge of the Georgia supreme court in 1849 and held that office until 1853. He then served as U.S. charge and minister to Austria, leaving that post in 1858. Jackson returned to his law practice and in 1859 participated in the Federal government's unsuccessful case against the captain and owners of the slave ship *Wanderer*.

Jackson was a delegate at the Democratic conventions in Charleston and Baltimore in 1860 and voted for secession in the state's convention early the next year. Governor Joseph E. Brown appointed him as colonel and aide-de-camp, and under Brown's orders Jackson demanded the surrender of the Augusta Arsenal and seized several ships belonging to citizens of New York. When the Civil War began, Jackson became judge of Confederate courts in Georgia. He resigned that position to accept an appointment as brigadier general in the Confederate army on June 4, 1861, effective immediately. Jackson went to Virginia and was assigned to command of a brigade in the western part of that state.

Following the death of Brigadier General Richard H. Garnett on July 13, he assumed temporary command of the Army of Northwestern Virginia and helped stabilize what could have been a disastrous situation. Douglas Southall Freeman wrote: "...in a new capacity and in an unfamiliar country, he had kept his head, had used his strong, native intelligence, and had made in the crises what were, all things considered, probably the best dispositions possible with the small force at hand." Brigadier General William W. Loring relieved Jackson as army commander on July 25, but the latter continued to lead a division of two reduced brigades. He participated in the Cheat Mountain campaign September 11–17, and his troops successfully repulsed an attack on their camp at the Greenbrier River on October 3.

Governor Brown offered Jackson command of the Georgia state forces with rank of major general in November. He asked for a leave of absence to accept this position but was refused. As a result Jackson resigned his commission on December 2 and went to Savannah. When the state forces were organized, he became head of the 1st Division Georgia Troops, which consisted of three brigades. In this capacity Jackson assisted in the fortification of Savannah during the next several months. Passage of the Conscription Act in April 1862 resulted in Brown having

No genuine uniformed photo of Jackson has been found. The uniform on this postwar portrait has been clumsily added by the artist. (Warner, *Generals in Gray*)

to turn these troops over to Confederate service, thus depriving Jackson of his command.

Jackson was an aide to General William H. T. Walker for a while. In December 1862 Brown hoped to organize his new state guard regiments into a brigade under Jackson but did not push the plan before the legislature because it would have endangered the governor's efforts to get that body to approve the creation of the regiments.

On September 21, 1863, Jackson was again commissioned as a Confederate brigadier, effective immediately. He served under Major General Howell Cobb, commander of Georgia State Troops, in northern Georgia after the Chickamauga Campaign. Later he led various units of the Georgia State Guards at Savannah. On July 9, 1864, he was assigned to command the District of Georgia, with headquarters at Savannah. General Braxton Bragg informed Jefferson Davis on July 27 that he had ordered Jackson to Atlanta because of the need for brigade commanders. Two days later Jackson was assigned to the Georgia brigade formerly commanded by Brigadier General Clement H. Stevens. The brigade had recently been transferred to the division of Major General William B. Bate.

Jackson first led his men in the Battle of Jonesborough August 31–September 1. Bate's division accompanied the Army of Tennessee on its campaign into northern Georgia and Alabama September 29–November 13. Jackson's brigade fought in an engagement at Decatur, Alabama on October 27–28. During the second day's action, a Union force drove back part of a neighboring brigade's skirmish line. Jackson personally led the 29th Georgia Infantry Regiment in retaking the lost skirmish pits. His brigade was in the front line of Bate's division when it attacked the Federal entrenchments at Franklin on November 30. Jackson and his men reached the enemy works but were pinned down there until the Federals retreated that night. Bate's division was sent on December 2 toward Murfreesboro to destroy the railroad between there and Nashville. Jackson's brigade was put to work tearing up the tracks near Overall's Creek on December 4. A Union attack threw back Brigadier General Robert Bullock's brigade, but Jackson's men were able to repulse the attack. Shortly after the division rejoined the army at Nashville, Jackson wrote a letter to Major General Benjamin F. Cheatham criticizing the conduct of Bate's other two brigades at Franklin and near Murfreesboro

and asking that his brigade be assigned to another division.

One day while he, several other generals, and their staffs were observing the Federal works at Fort Negley, Jackson had a close call. A Union cannon crew fired a shell that exploded under Jackson's horse, killing it but not harming the general. Jackson's brigade was lightly engaged in the Battle of Nashville on December 15, but Federal troops overran the division the next day. Jackson was captured while attempting to walk to where he had sent his new horse; he became bogged down in the mud and could not escape onrushing Union soldiers. He was sent to prison at Fort Warren and not released until July 1865.

After the war Jackson resumed his law practice in Savannah. President Grover Cleveland appointed him as minister to Mexico in 1885, but he resigned two years later. Jackson was president of the Georgia Historical Society from 1875–1898, acted as a trustee of the Peabody Educational Fund, and became a director of the Central Railroad and Banking Company of Georgia in 1892. He died of a paralytic stroke on May 23, 1898, in Savannah and was buried there in Bonaventure Cemetery.

Arthur W. Bergeron, Jr.

Coleman, Kenneth, and Charles S. Gurr, eds., *Dictionary of Georgia Biography* (Athens, 1983), Vol. I.

Myers, Robert Manson, *The Children of Pride: A True Story of Georgia and the Civil War* (New Haven, 1972).

Northen, William J., ed., *Men of Mark in Georgia* (Atlanta, 1911), Vol. III.

⋆ *John King Jackson* ⋆

The only known wartime uniformed portrait of John K. Jackson shows him as a brigadier in 1862 or later. (Virginia Historical Society, Richmond, Va.)

Born on February 8, 1828, in Augusta, Georgia, John King Jackson was educated at Georgia's Richmond Academy and the University of South Carolina. After graduating with honors from the latter in 1846, he studied law and was admitted to the bar in 1848. Settling in Augusta, Jackson practiced law and served first as a lieutenant, then as a captain in the Oglethorpe Infantry before being elected lieutenant colonel of the city's militia.

Jackson was one of the first to volunteer for service after Georgia seceded. He was elected colonel of the 5th Georgia Infantry at Macon in May 1861 and was ordered to Pensacola, Florida. There on the night of October 18, 1861, Jackson led one of three Confederate columns that attacked the Federal force on Santa Rosa Island. Although Jackson saw little fighting, his commander, Brigadier General Braxton Bragg, was impressed with him. When Bragg was transferred to the Army of Tennessee, he asked to take with him Jackson's well-trained 5th Georgia and recommended Jackson be promoted. Jackson briefly commanded Pensacola after Bragg departed and was promoted to brigadier general, to rank from January 14, 1862.

Upon his promotion Jackson was ordered to take command of Grand Junction, Tennessee, where he went to work organizing troops for shipment to Corinth, Mississippi, and the Shiloh Campaign. He led a brigade of Alabama and Texas infantry at Shiloh, with his old 5th Georgia being attached to him for the battle. His brigade saw heavy action during the second wave of attacks on April 6. Placed on the Confederate right near Wicker Field, Jackson expended almost all of his ammunition during the day and sometimes advanced with only the bayonet.

After Shiloh Jackson moved to Bridgeport, Alabama, where he guarded the railroad there. He had a brigade of Georgia and Mississippi infantry during the 1862 Kentucky invasion but was not heavily engaged again until the Battle of Murfreesboro. On December 31, 1862, Jackson's brigade, a part of Major General John C. Breckinridge's division, was marched to several points on the field before being sent to Lieutenant General Leonidas Polk on the right. Upon its arrival Polk ordered the brigade to attack the Yankee line near the Cowan House. Major General J. M. Withers' division had just been repulsed, and Jackson asked if it would not be best to wait until all of Breckinridge's brigades were ready for the assault. Polk cut him off by snapping, "Jackson, there's the enemy, go in." Jackson complied, attacked twice, and finally withdrew after running out of ammunition. He lost approximately three hundred men.

Jackson returned to Bridgeport for railroad guard duty after the Murfreesboro bloodletting. By September 1863 his brigade was in Major General Benjamin Cheatham's division and saw action at Chickamauga, where around noon on September 19 it helped stop a Union thrust that threatened the Confederate line. The Yankees were beaten back, and Jackson captured three cannons. Late that afternoon he was engaged in another bloody fight when his brigade advanced with the entire division. On September 20 the brigade attacked again on Brigadier General Patrick Cleburne's right and drove the Federals from their trenches. During the two days Jackson suffered heavy casualties, with one of his regiments losing sixty-one percent of its men, the second-highest casualty rate of any Confederate regiment at Chickamauga.

Jackson seems to have performed capably in all of his battles up through Chickamauga. But in November 1863 his tactical ability was questioned during the battles around Chattanooga. Placed in command of an improvised division that was responsible for defending Lookout Mountain, Jackson was attacked on November 24 by Union Major General Joseph Hooker's corps. Throughout the "Battle Above the Clouds" Jackson's brigade commanders complained that they could never find him and that his only order during the day was to hold all positions. Jackson failed to inspect his lines or closely supervise the fight and seems to have stayed on top of the mountain for the duration of the battle. The bitter complaints about him almost led to Jackson challenging more than one of his officers to a duel. This animosity surfaced again after the Confederate disaster at Missionary Ridge, where Jackson resumed his role as brigade commander. After the Federal breakthrough on November 25 Jackson's brigade aided Cheatham in holding back the Union onslaught while Bragg withdrew the army. Brigadier General John C. Moore's brigade fought alongside Jackson's, but Moore wrote after the battle, "I did not see General Jackson or any of his staff whom I recognized...." This prompted Jackson to respond that since Moore was not under his command, "I did not think it necessary for me to show myself to him...."

Jackson later served in the Atlanta Campaign in Major General W. H. T. Walker's division. In July 1864, however, his brigade was broken up and Jackson and two of his regiments were sent eastward. He briefly commanded the center of Major General William Hardee's line. After Savannah's fall Jackson was dispatched to Branchville, South Carolina, where he established supply depots for Major General Lafayette McLaws' division and later for Lieutenant General John B. Hood's army when it marched through. In the last months of the war he moved to Goldsboro, North Carolina, and was on his way to Augusta, Georgia, when the war ended.

After the war Jackson returned to practicing law in Augusta and later became employed as a lobbyist for several banks. While on a trip to Milledgeville he developed pneumonia and died on February 27, 1866. He was buried in an unmarked grave in the City Cemetery of Augusta, Georgia.

Terry L. Jones

Derry, Joseph, *Georgia*, Vol. VI in Evans, *Confederate Military History*.

McDonough, James Lee, *Chattanooga: A Death Grip on the Confederacy* (Knoxville, 1984).

✳ *Thomas Jonathan Jackson* ✳

"Stonewall" seems to have found little time to pose for the camera. This is the famous "Winchester" photograph, made in that Shenandoah city in February 1862, and reportedly his wife's favorite. (Cook Collection, Valentine Museum, Richmond, Va.)

Rarely has a great soldier come from humbler origins. "Stonewall" Jackson was born January 21, 1824, in the mountain hamlet of Clarksburg in what is now West Virginia. Orphaned at an early age by the death of his father and the destitution of his mother, he spent his youth with an uncle at a grist and lumber mill near the town of Weston. In 1842 he entered the U.S. Military Academy. Although lacking in education and social graces, Jackson believed firmly that "you may be whatever you resolve to be." By sheer determination he graduated seventeenth in the class of 1846.

Jackson entered the Mexican War as an artillery lieutenant. Gallantry in action at Vera Cruz, Contreras, and Chapultepec ultimately brought him brevet promotion to major. He then served three years garrison duty at Fort Hamilton, New York, and Fort Meade, Florida. In 1851 following a bitter disagreement with his post commander, Jackson resigned from the army and accepted a professorship of natural and experimental philosophy and artillery tactics at the Virginia Military Institute in Lexington, Virginia.

The ten years he spent at V.M.I. shaped Jackson's life both personally and professionally. There he acquired the strong Presbyterian faith that became the cornerstone of his life. In 1853 he married Elinor Junkin, daughter of the president-minister of nearby Washington College. Fourteen months later she died in childbirth. Jackson resumed the life of a bachelor until 1857, when he married a longtime friend, Mary Anna Morrison.

At V.M.I. the tall and rather heavyset Jackson was known as a colorless professor who tolerated neither levity nor laxity from cadets in class. His rigidity in the section room, plus his many eccentricities in daily habits, earned him such nicknames from cadets as "Tom Fool" and "Old Blue Light." Although Jackson was responsible for the expulsion of several students, he also inspired many others who in time became among the Confederacy's most outstanding line and field officers.

Civil war came in April 1861, and Jackson offered his sword to his beloved Virginia. He left Lexington with a contingent of cadets to act as drillmasters for recruits

This variant of the Winchester portrait shows heavy retouching, yet it is possible that it is based upon a genuine seated print that is now lost in the original. (Library of Congress)

gathering at Richmond to defend the state. Jackson had a brief stint as colonel of militia and commander of the Harpers Ferry post. Appointed brigadier general of infantry on June 17, to rank immediately, he assumed command of Virginia's 1st Brigade.

A month later those five Shenandoah Valley regiments and their commander won an immortal nickname. The first major battle of the war occurred July 21, 1861, at Manassas, Virginia. Federal attackers were about to break the Southern line when a South Carolina brigadier pointed to troops atop the hill that was the key to the battlefield. "Look, men!" Brigadier General Barnard Bee shouted. "There stands Jackson like a stone wall! Rally behind the Virginians!" Jackson's stand and subsequent attack helped turn a doubtful outcome into a Confederate victory.

Promotion to major general on October 7, 1861, effective immediately, was a prelude to Jackson's assignment to command the defenses of the Shenandoah Valley. His responsibilities became twofold: to protect the agriculturally rich valley of Virginia and to prevent Union forces in the area from reinforcing the main Northern army driving on to Richmond. To accomplish both objectives, Jackson in the spring of 1862 began a campaign against three different Union columns.

Outnumbered four to one at times, Jackson employed secret plans, rapid marches, circuitous routes, and concentrated attacks to win victories at McDowell, Front Royal, Winchester, Cross Keys, and Port Republic. Jackson's spectacular successes kept the entire Union military effort in the East off balance. In six weeks of operations he became the most famous Confederate general in the field. The self-styled "foot cavalry" composing his small but mobile army had likewise become legendary.

In mid-June Jackson moved swiftly to Richmond and joined with Robert E. Lee for the counteroffensive against General George McClellan's Union army. Tardiness at Mechanicsville and Gaines' Mill, and a strange lethargy at White Oak Swamp, left Jackson with a somewhat tarnished reputation at the end of the Seven Days' Campaign. He recovered in part with a hard-earned victory in the August 9 battle of Cedar Mountain against the van of Major General John Pope's army. Then, with Lee moving north with the main Southern army to confront Pope, Jackson effected a sweeping and secret march that took him around the flank and into the rear of the Federal forces. This move was the first step in a smashing victory for the Confederates at Second Manassas in August.

Jackson played a key role in the 1862 invasion of Maryland. On September 15 his artillery skill against the Federal garrison at Harpers Ferry resulted in the capture of twelve thousand Union soldiers plus valuable guns and stores. Jackson rushed north with part of his command; and at Antietam Creek on September 17 his troops successfully withstood three hours of assaults on the Confederate left in what became the bloodiest one-day battle of the Civil War.

Reorganization of the Army of Northern Virginia occurred in the autumn. On October 11 Jackson was elevated to lieutenant general, to rank from the previous day, in command of the II Corps in Lee's army. At the December 13 battle of Fredericksburg, Jackson commanded the right wing and repulsed a Union attack that momentarily broke through his line. He spent the winter compiling his 1862 official battle reports, becoming more involved in a personal disagreement with his senior division commander, Major General A. P. Hill, and in becoming acquainted with his newborn daughter and only child.

May 1, 1863, found Lee's forces confronting the huge Army of the Potomac massed in the densely wooded Wilderness around a crossroads known as Chancellorsville. After conferring with Lee, Jackson the following day executed his most famous flank march and struck the unprotected Federal right late in the afternoon. Surprise was complete; pandemonium swept through the Union ranks. Jackson continued to press forward after dark. He was returning to his lines from a personal reconnaissance when he was accidentally shot by his own men.

Amputation of his mangled left arm contributed to pneumonia. On May 10, 1863, Jackson died at Guiney's Station, Virginia. He is buried in the Lexington, Virginia city cemetery beneath one of several statues in the South honoring his memory.

Lord Roberts, commander-in-chief of the British armies, observed early in this century: "In my opinion Stonewall Jackson was one of the greatest natural military geniuses the world ever saw. I will go even further than that—as a campaigner in the field he never had a superior. In some respects I doubt whether he ever had an equal."

James I. Robertson, Jr.

Chambers, Lenoir, *Stonewall Jackson* (New York, 1959).

Henderson, G.F.R., *Stonewall Jackson and the American Civil War* (London, 1898).

Vandiver, Frank E., *Mighty Stonewall* (New York, 1957).

The last photo of Jackson during the war is this 1863 view made not long before his untimely death. (Library of Congress)

The only known uniformed view of William "Red" Jackson, made in 1863 or later. (National Archives)

✶ *William Hicks Jackson* ✶

William Hicks Jackson was born on October 1, 1835, at Paris, Tennessee. His parents were Dr. Alexander and Mary W. Hurt Jackson, who five years before had left Virginia to settle in West Tennessee. Dr. Jackson, within the next several years, relocated to Jackson, Tennessee, where his son grew up and attended in succession local common schools and West Tennessee College. On July 1, 1852, Jackson reported as a plebe at the United States Military Academy. He was graduated thirty-eighth in the class of 1856 and commissioned a brevet 2d lieutenant. After pulling a short tour of duty at the Army's Carlisle, Pennsylvania, cavalry school, he headed for Texas, where he joined his unit—the 1st Regiment of Mounted Riflemen. During the next three years—1857–60—he saw duty at three southwestern forts—Bliss, Stanton, and Union. In a hand-to-hand fight with the Kiowas near Fort Craig on December 7, 1859, he saved the life of William W. Averell, who in 1862 became a brigadier general of cavalry in the Union Army.

On May 16, 1861, he resigned his commission in the Old Army and entered Confederate service as a captain of artillery. Jackson and the six-gun company that he had organized were mustered in at New Madrid, Missouri, on August 17. Some three weeks later, on September 5, Jackson and his company were sent to Columbus, Kentucky, and near Hickman had a brush with Union timberclad gunboats. During the Battle of Belmont November 7, Jackson embarked in battery on a steamboat and crossed the Mississippi to support the Confederate troops who had been routed from their camp by Union soldiers led by Brigadier General U. S. Grant. The gangplank was lost in attempting to land, and the steamer had to return to the Kentucky shore. Later in the day Jackson got ashore and, as an aide to Brigadier General Gideon J. Pillow, led a successful Confederate counterattack but received a serious wound.

The Confederates evacuated Columbus on March 3, 1862, and Jackson and his battery accompanied the army to Corinth, Mississippi. On March 18 Jackson was promoted colonel and ordered to take command of the 7th Tennessee Cavalry, then being organized at Union City, Tennessee. On April 1 the regiment's camp was surprised when attacked by a Union column, lost considerable gear, and was compelled to retreat to Trenton. Jackson and his horse soldiers from mid-May until June 4 picketed the approaches to Fort Pillow. He screened the evacuation of Fort Pillow and the retreat of the garrison southward into Mississippi, where he received orders to guard the crossings of the Tallahatchie River. Jackson on June 25 scored a success when he led a raid into Tennessee. Striking the Memphis and Charleston Railroad near LaFayette, the Confederates captured a detachment of the 56th Ohio and destroyed a locomotive and a string of cars.

The last days of August found Jackson leading a two-regiment brigade and participating in a slashing raid by Frank Armstrong's mounted division northward from Holly Springs, aimed at wreaking havoc on the Mississippi Central Railroad between Grand Junction and Bolivar. The raid lasted forty-eight hours, during which Jackson and his people fought three pitched battles and captured 213 prisoners. On September 25 Jackson surprised and scattered a 290-man Union detachment posted at Davis' Mills. He and his brigade were at the Battle of Corinth (October 3–4), where they watched the Confederate right and then screened the army's rear on the retreat to Ripley and beyond.

The seven weeks beginning November 8 and ending December 28 were exciting for Jackson and his brigade of Tennesseans and Mississippians. They clashed repeatedly with Union cavalry at such places as Old Lamar, Lumpkins Mill, Waterford, Water Valley, and Coffeeville as they covered the successive retreats of Lieutenant General John C. Pemberton's army from Holly Springs, the Tallahatchie line, and finally to behind the Yalobusha. Jackson's was one of the three mounted brigades that Earl Van Dorn led on the devastating Holly Springs raid, resulting in destruction of a major Union supply depot. Jackson's leadership and gallantry on the raid led to his promotion to brigadier general on January 9, 1863, with rank to date from December 29, 1862.

In late January 1863 Jackson and his brigade accompanied Van Dorn's cavalry corps on the long march that detached it from Pemberton's army in north Mississippi to join Braxton Bragg's army in Middle Tennessee. While in Tennessee, he commanded one of the two divisions constituting Van Dorn's corps and played an important role in the Battle of Thompson's Station March 5, where a Union column was annihilated with the loss of 1,446 officers and men. Mid-May found the Union army led by General U.S. Grant east of the Mississippi River, victorious in five battles in seventeen days and closing in on General Pemberton's army as it retreated into the Vicksburg fortifications. Joseph E. Johnston was assembling an army near Jackson to raise the siege of Vicksburg, and Jackson and his division returned to Mississippi, reporting to Johnston at Canton on June 3. The next seven weeks were active but frustrating for Jackson and his troops. First they screened the army's build-up; next they spearheaded Johnston's march toward the Big Black; then, following the July 4 Vicksburg surrender, they covered Johnston's retreat, before the advance of a powerful host led by William T. Sherman, into the Jackson earthworks; and finally the evacuation of Jackson and the retreat forty miles farther eastward to Morton.

Sherman's army by the end of July returned to the Vicksburg area west of the Big Black, and Jackson and his hard-riding cavalry picketed the approaches to the enclave. In mid-October a ten-thousand-man column commanded by Major General James B. McPherson crossed the Big Black en route to Canton. Jackson hit back vigorously and so slowed the Union march that McPherson lost his nerve and returned to Vicksburg. On February 3, 1864, General Sherman crossed the Big Black with more than twenty thousand men on a massive raid to Meridian. Once again, as in October, Jackson and his four-brigade division clashed repeatedly with Sherman's hydra-headed vanguard, as they covered the withdrawal of Leonidas Polk's Army of Mississippi from Jackson through Meridian and into Alabama. Sherman returned to Vicksburg with Jackson nipping at his flanks and rear. Jackson's conduct during the Meridian Campaign was noted by his immediate superior—Major General S. D. Lee—who called attention to Jackson's "good conduct and soldierly qualities" and stated that to his "assistance and action much of the credit of the recent campaign is due."

In mid-May Jackson and his division, reorganized into three brigades, were transferred from Mississippi to northwest Georgia to reinforce General Johnston's Army of Tennessee, which since May 7 had been engaged against General Sherman's "army group." Jackson reported to Johnston at Adairsville on May 17. The Confederate army on the 20th retreated across the Etowah River, and Johnston posted Jackson's division on the army's left and Joseph Wheeler's cavalry corps on the right. From that date until the September 1 evacuation of Atlanta, Jackson's horse soldiers guarded the army's left. Jackson skirmished with Union columns advancing south from the Etowah on May 24. On the 28th his troopers, fighting dismounted, precipitated prematurely the Battle of Dallas, a grim day for the Confederates; from June 5 through the end of the month he took up successive positions, always close to the foe, at Lost Mountain, and behind Noses and Olleys creeks, as Sherman's troops pushed closer to Atlanta; and on July 14 at Moore's Bridge he battered and turned back Union cavalry as they tried to slip across the Chattahoochee. On two occasions during the six weeks that Atlanta was under siege, Jackson helped defeat or checkmate strong cavalry forces sent by Sherman to break up railroads—at Newnan on July 30–31 and near Fairburn in the third week of August.

Jackson accompanied the Army of Tennessee, now led by General John B. Hood, when it recrossed the Chattahoochee September 29–30 and on to Tuscumbia, Alabama. Jackson crossed the Tennessee River and entered Middle Tennessee at the head of one of the three divisions constituting Nathan Bedford Forrest's cavalry corps. At Rally Hill on November 28 Jackson hammered Union cavalry, and on the 29th he was back at Thompson's Station, three miles north of Spring Hill. He was unable to hold the roadblock established there, and John M. Schofield's army succeeded in reaching Franklin. Hood's Middle Tennessee campaign now soured. Jackson was with Forrest near Murfreesboro during the Battle of Nashville. On December 15 at Christiana, Jackson captured a locomotive and seventeen cars loaded with rations en route from Stevenson to Murfreesboro. Jackson rendezvoused with Hood's shattered army at Columbia on the 18th and joined the rear guard in fending off pursuing Yankees, enabling the Confederates to escape across the Tennessee River.

Jackson and his two-brigade division were not with General Forrest when he was defeated by Major General

James H. Wilson's corps at Selma on April 2. The day before, after a sharp fight near Centreville, Jackson had scattered one of Brigadier General John T. Croxton's regiments, capturing a number of prisoners. After Lieutenant General Richard Taylor's May 4 surrender of Southern troops in the Department of Alabama, Mississippi, and East Louisiana, General Jackson was commissioner for the parole of Confederate soldiers at Gainesville, Alabama, and Columbus, Mississippi. He signed his parole at Columbus on May 18.

The war over, Jackson oversaw his father's West Tennessee cotton plantations. In December 1868 he married Selene Harding, daughter of William G. Harding of Belle Meade, near Nashville, and entered into a partnership with his father-in-law in breeding and racing thoroughbreds. After Harding's 1886 death, the general was joined by his younger brother, and they prospered. Belle Meade became one of the best-known horse farms in the nation, with an outstanding stable of stallions. His leadership in agricultural affairs was recognized by election to the presidency of the National Agricultural Congress and the Tennessee Bureau of Agriculture. He died at Belle Meade on March 30, 1903, and was buried in Nashville's Mount Olivet Cemetery.

Edwin C. Bearss

Cullum, George, *Biographical Register, U.S. Military Academy* (New York, 1891).

Nashville, *American*, March 31, 1903.

Porter, James D., *Tennessee*, Vol. VIII in Evans, *Confederate Military History*.

William Lowther Jackson ✳

No uniformed photo of Jackson has been found. This is a considerably postwar portrait. (Warner, *Generals in Gray*)

William L. Jackson was born in Clarksburg, West Virginia in February 3, 1825. Educated as an attorney, Jackson was admitted to the bar in 1847. For the next fourteen years he combined a successful legal practice with an outstanding political career. He served as a commonwealth's attorney for his county, was elected as a member of the state's house of delegates for two terms, held the office of superintendent of the state's library fund, and served on term as Virginia's lieutenant governor. In 1860 he won election to the bench of Virginia's Nineteenth Judicial Circuit.

When Virginia seceded in April 1861, Jackson resigned his judgeship and enlisted as a private in the state forces. His political connections, however, resulted in an officer's commission. Jackson was, according to an officer in the region, "a gentleman of great personal popularity, not only with his own party, but with those opposed to him politically, and devoted to the interests of Virginia, to the last extremity." By June he had reported to Huttonsville, where he was commissioned a lieutenant colonel and assigned to command of the 31st Virginia.

Jackson's regiment participated in the disastrous West Virginia campaign of Brigadier General Robert S. Garnett during the summer of 1861. For the next several months the 31st Virginia fought in the mountainous region. It was engaged at Greenbrier River on October 3, and at Camp Alleghany on December 13. With the rank of colonel Jackson relinquished his command of the regiment during these months and accepted a position of volunteer aide-de-camp on the staff of his second cousin, Major General Thomas J. "Stonewall" Jackson.

Jackson served on the staff of his cousin throughout all the major campaigns of 1862. On February 13, 1863, the War Department authorized him to recruit and organize a regiment within Federal lines in West Virginia. By mid-April Jackson had organized the ten companies, and the regiment was designated the 19th Virginia Cavalry. Assigned to the brigade of Brigadier General Albert G. Jenkins, the regiment participated in the raid against the Baltimore & Ohio Railroad later that month. While most of Jenkins' units joined Robert E. Lee's army in the Gettysburg Campaign, Jackson's troopers remained in West Virginia, operating against Union forces at Beverly and at Huttonsville.

Jackson continued his recruitment of Confederate sympathizers in the region until he had gathered nearly a small brigade of men under his command. In the spring of 1864 he was assigned the command of Major General John C. Breckinridge and given a brigade of cavalry. On May 9 his brigade fought at Cloyd's Mountain and during June resisted the advance of Union Major General David Hunter's army on Lynchburg. His brigade—the 2d Maryland Cavalry Battalion, the 19th and 20th Virginia Cavalry, and the 46th and 47th Virginia Cavalry Battalion—then participated in Lieutenant General Jubal Early's raid on Washington, D.C.

Jackson led his unit in the engagements of the 1864 Shenandoah Valley Campaign. The record of the Confederate cavalry in these operations was dismal as Union mounted regiments, possessing superior numbers, arms, equipment, and horseflesh, routed the Confederate troopers on a number of occasions. At the end of the campaign on January 12, 1865, Jackson was promoted to brigadier general, to rank from December 19, 1864. On April 15, 1865, he disbanded his brigade and started westward for Mexico. On July 26 at Brownsville, Texas, Jackson was paroled.

Jackson returned to his home, but a law forbade ex-Confederates from practicing law in West Virginia, so he moved to Louisville, Kentucky. He opened a law office but within a few years was appointed a circuit judge, a position he retained until his death on March 24, 1890. He was buried in Cave Hill Cemetery in Louisville.

William L. Jackson had a less than distinguished career as a Confederate general. Perhaps nothing remains more controversial about his military service than his nickname of "Mudwall." The evidence indicates that Alfred E. Jackson, who served mainly in East Tennessee, was justifiably given the dubious appellation. As for William L., the evidence is vague and conflicting.

Jeffry D. Wert

Hotchkiss, Jedediah, *Virginia,* Vol. III in Evans, *Confederate Military History.*

Wert, Jeffry D., *From Winchester to Cedar Creek: The Shenandoah Campaign of 1864* (Carlisle, 1987).

The only wartime uniformed portrait of Jenkins to come to light, taken between August 1862 and May 1864. (National Archives)

✳ Albert Gallatin Jenkins ✳

Albert Jenkins was born in Cabell County, West Virginia, on November 10, 1830. After attending the Virginia Military Institute, Jenkins was graduated from Jefferson College in Pennsylvania in 1848 and from Harvard Law School in 1850. Returning to his native state, he prospered as an attorney and as a farmer on his Greenbottom plantation on the south bank of the Ohio River. He served as a delegate to the 1856 Democratic national convention and two terms, 1857–61, as a United States congressman.

When Virginia seceded in April 1861, Jenkins embraced the Confederate cause and organized the Border Rangers, which became Company E, 8th Virginia Cavalry. With the rank of captain, Jenkins showed daring and ingenuity during the early weeks of action. In late June he led approximately fifty men on a a raid from Charleston to Point Pleasant, capturing a number of prominent Union sympathizers. On July 11 at Scary Creek Jenkins rallied a portion of the Confederate troops and secured the victory. Promotion to lieutenant colonel and then colonel of the 8th Virginia Cavalry followed during the next several months.

In February 1862 Jenkins relinquished his command to serve as an elected delegate to the First Confederate Congress. He maintained his seat until August 5, when he secured an appointment to brigadier general, effective immediately. Assigned to western Virginia, he led a five-hundred-mile mounted raid through West Virginia and across the river into Ohio. His men seized three hundred prisoners, stands of arms, government records, and destroyed garrisons and large quantities of military stores. Major General William W. Loring reported that Jenkins exhibited during the incursion "a policy of such clemency as won us many friends, and tended greatly to mitigate the ferocity which had characterized the war in this section. The conduct of his officers and men has received my unqualified approbation, and deserves the notice and thanks of the government."

The following spring, in March 1863, Jenkins conducted another raid through the state but did not penetrate across the river. Then in May Robert E. Lee attached Jenkins' brigade to the Army of Northern Virginia for the invasion of Pennsylvania. Although Jenkins had proved an able raider, he was a poor disciplinarian and lacked administrative ability, despite his prewar career. Lee warned Lieutenant General Richard S. Ewell, to whom Jenkins was assigned, to watch the brigadier and his independent-minded mountain men.

Jenkins was a colorful officer with a reputation as a raider, not a combat officer. An acquaintance described him as of "medium size, with a flat but good head, light brown hair, blue eyes, immense flowing beard of a sandy hue, and rather a pleasant face." His beard was so long, in fact, that when the wind blew, he tucked its end into his belt.

Jenkins' brigade—the 14th, 16th, and 17th Virginia Cavalry, and the 34th Virginia cavalry battalions—roamed along the front of Lee's vanguard as it marched into Pennsylvania. The veteran raiders scoured the countryside for food and livestock and ransacked buildings in Chambersburg. When they encountered opposition, Jenkins tended to panic and withdraw. It was not an enviable performance for the command and its brigadier. On July 2 while on a reconnaissance on Benner's Hill during the Battle of Gettysburg, he suffered a scalp wound and concussion from a shell fragment.

Following the campaign, Jenkins' brigade returned to duty in southern and western Virginia. On May 9, 1864, at the Battle of Cloyd's Mountain Jenkins fell wounded and was captured. A Union surgeon amputated an arm at the shoulder, but the Confederate raider never rallied, dying on May 21. Today, he is buried in Huntingdon, West Virginia.

Jeffry D. Wert

Dickinson, J. L., *Jenkins of Greenbottom: A Civil War Saga* (Charleston, 1988).

Lowry, Terry, *The Battle of Scary Creek* (Charleston, 1982).

Nye, Wilbur S., *Here Come The Rebels* (Baton Rouge, 1965).

✷ *Micah Jenkins* ✷

On December 1, 1835, a third son was born to John and Elizabeth Clark Jenkins at their "Brick House" plantation on South Carolina's Edisto Island. The father—planter and land baron—named the baby Micah. In 1851 Jenkins matriculated at South Carolina Military Academy, from which he graduated in 1854 at the age of nineteen, at the head of his class. The following year, he and a classmate founded King's Mountain Military School at York, South Carolina. In 1856 he married Caroline Jameson, whose father in December 1860 presided at the South Carolina secession convention, and by her he fathered four sons. He continued his association with the school as a teacher and administrator until the winter of 1860–61, when his native state withdrew from the Union.

A states rights enthusiast, Jenkins helped organize, and on June 4, 1861, was elected and appointed colonel of, the 5th South Carolina Infantry Regiment. Jenkins and his unit departed the Orangeburg camp of instruction for Virginia, reached Manassas Junction on June 21, and were assigned to the newly constituted brigade commanded by Brigadier General David R. Jones. At First Manassas on July 21 Jenkins first led troops into battle as his South Carolinians crossed McLean's Ford and attacked the Union left near Little Rocky Run. The unit earned a commendation from General Jones.

In mid-April 1862, five weeks after General Joseph E. Johnston's army evacuated its Centreville camps while en route to the Peninsula the troops were reorganized in accordance with the Bounty and Furlough Act. Colonel Jenkins took advantage of this to recruit and organize the Palmetto Sharpshooters, an elite regiment that included a hard core of officers and men

who had served under him in the old 5th. Jenkins' regiment was assigned to Brigadier General Richard H. Anderson's South Carolina Brigade. Jenkins and his sharpshooters reinforced the Confederate troops holding the Yorktown-Warwick Line. Johnston's army abandoned these works on the night of May 3, and at Williamsburg—on the 5th—Jenkins led a brigade in battle and was charged with the defense of Fort Magruder and several nearby redoubts.

At Seven Pines on May 31, Jenkins again commanded Anderson's South Carolina Brigade in a slashing onslaught against Brigadier General Darius N. Couch's IV Corps division; he broke the Union lines, reached Seven Pines, and slugged his way eastward for one-half mile. These actions earned for him and his troops ringing commendations from General Johnston and Major General James Longstreet.

Jenkins—with Anderson again in charge of the brigade—commanded the Palmetto Sharpshooters in the Seven Days' Battles that saw General Robert E. Lee and his Army of Northern Virginia drive the Army of the Potomac from the gates of Richmond into a fortified camp at Harrison's Landing. At Gaines' Mill, June 27, Longstreet divided Anderson's Brigade, sending Jenkins and the Palmetto Sharpshooters and other units to the right. Jenkins participated in the all-out attack that broke the Union line. He and his South Carolinians surged across Boatswain Swamp, overwhelmed the 16th Michigan, and captured their colors. At Glendale on June 30 Jenkins again led Anderson's brigade into a desperate fight, and

A beautiful portrait of Brigadier General Micah Jenkins taken between July 1862 and May 1864. (Confederate Museum, Charleston, S.C.)

Colonel Jenkins of the 5th South Carolina, probably in 1861. (Library of Congress)

Jenkins in regulation Confederate uniform as a colonel, probably not long before his July 1862 promotion to brigadier. **(Library of Congress)**

Brigadier General Jenkins. (Chicago Historical Society)

A rare variant portrait made at the same sitting as the previous image. (Erick Davis Collection)

General Longstreet once more called attention to his gallantry and skill.

General Lee in the weeks after the Seven Days,' reorganized his army into two corps. On July 22 Jenkins was promoted to brigadier general, effective at once, given command of Anderson's South Carolina Brigade, and assigned to the division in Longstreet's right wing led by Brigadier General James L. Kemper. Jenkins was with Longstreet on his mid-August redeployment from the Richmond area to northern Virginia and on the march through Thoroughfare Gap. On August 30 at Second Manassas in the desperate struggle for Chinn Ridge, Jenkins was severely wounded.

In November Jenkins returned to duty and found that his brigade was now one of the four constituting Major General George E. Pickett's Division. At the Battle of Fredericksburg Jenkins' brigade was present but, except for receiving some artillery fire, saw no combat. Jenkins and his brigade then accompanied General Longstreet to Virginia south side and participated in the Suffolk siege, April 11–May 4, 1863. When Longstreet was recalled by General Lee and abandoned the siege, Jenkins and his South Carolinians remained on the Blackwater and were not with Pickett at Gettysburg.

On September 11 Jenkins and his troops—then posted at Petersburg—were assigned to Major General John B. Hood's division and ordered to accompany Longstreet to northwest Georgia to reinforce Braxton Bragg's Army of Tennessee. Jenkins arrived at the Chickamauga battlefield on September 22, too late to participate in the Confederate victory. General Hood had been seriously wounded, and Jenkins, as senior officer, assumed command of the division. Bragg's army occupied Missionary Ridge and Lookout Mountain, investing the defeated Union army in Chattanooga. Union forces on October 28 bridged the Tennessee River at Brown's Ferry and occupied Lookout Valley. After the ensuing night attack by Jenkins, he and his principal subordinate—Brigadier General Evander M. Law—each held that the other was responsible for the Wauhatchie defeat.

Jenkins was with Longstreet in East Tennessee in November and through the winter of 1863–64. He was commended by Longstreet for his vigorous pursuit of the enemy from Lenoir Station to the Knoxville approaches, November 15–17. But his relations with General Law were further soured when he blamed

Law for their failure to block the Federals' retreat into the Knoxville defenses at Campbell's Station on the 16th.

Jenkins participated in the siege of Knoxville, November 17–December 4, the retreat to Rogersville, December 4–9, and the engagement at Bean's Station, December 14, as Longstreet lashed out at the Federals and checked their pursuit. Cold weather put a stop to the campaign and Jenkins and his division went into winter quarters at Russellville, Tennessee.

In early March 1864 Jenkins, despite the plea of General Longstreet that he retain command of Hood's division, was replaced by Major General Charles Field, and he resumed command of the South Carolina Brigade, then posted near Greeneville, Tennessee. Jenkins and his unit returned with Longstreet to the Army of Northern Virginia, arriving at Gordonsville on May 2. This was forty-eight hours before the Army of the Potomac took the field, crossed the Rapidan, and entered the Wilderness. At 4:00 P.M. on May 4 Jenkins turned out his brigade for the last time. At noon on the 6th Longstreet called up Jenkins and his South Carolinians to exploit the success scored by a devastating flank attack on Major General Winfield S. Hancock's II Corps.

As Jenkins and Longstreet rode eastward on the Orange Plank Road, Jenkins remarked, "I am happy; I have felt despair of the cause for some months, but am relieved and feel assured that we will put the enemy back across the Rapidan before night." Moments later a crash of musketry fired by some of Brigadier General William Mahone's Virginians milling about in the woods south of the road felled Jenkins and Longstreet, critically wounding the latter and mortally injuring the former. A Minié bullet lodged in his brain, Jenkins continued in delirium to urge his veterans forward. He died before dark. He was buried in Charleston, South Carolina.

Edwin C. Bearss

A faded portrait of Jenkins either as a colonel or a brigadier, but in any case an early war image. (Museum of the Confederacy, Richmond, Va.)

Capers, Ellison, *South Carolina*, Vol. V in Evans, *Confederate Military History*.

Charleston, *Mercury*, May 9, 12, 1864.

Thomas, John P., *Career and Character of Gen. Micah Jenkins, C.S.A.* (Columbia, 1903).

A remarkable portrait of "Stovepipe" Johnson made after his August 21, 1864, wounding in the eyes. Interestingly, he has a major general's buttons, though he was only a brigadier. (William C. Davis Collection)

⭐ *Adam Rankin Johnson* ⭐

Of all of the colorful sobriquets borne by Confederate generals—"Stonewall," "Mudwall," "Neighbor," "Shanks," and more—none was more unusual, or more apt, than the nickname given to Adam Rankin Johnson—"Stovepipe."

He was born in Henderson, Kentucky, February 8, 1834, but at the age of twenty he moved west to Texas. There he prospered at a variety of trades—surveyor, contractor to the Overland Mail stagecoach line, erstwhile Indian fighter. When the Civil War erupted, he returned to his native Kentucky and put his frontier skills to use as a scout, first for John Hunt Morgan's Kentucky cavalry, and later with Colonel Nathan B. Forrest. Serving with the latter, he rode out of the trap at Fort Donelson, and before long secured permission to go into Kentucky to raise volunteers for a partisan command of his own. He rode into Kentucky in June 1862 and remained for several months, penetrating to his old home town of Henderson, where with a handful of adherents he commenced harassing Yankee installations. Johnson was especially effective in raising recruits among Kentuckians anxious to avoid the Union draft, and funneled many of them back to Morgan.

It was during his recruiting days that Johnson earned his nickname. With a mere thirty-five men at his command, he crossed the Ohio—he believed it to be the first Rebel "invasion" of the North—and attacked the town of Newburgh, Indiana, on July 18. There were two hundred or more Federals in the town, though mostly convalescent soldiers in hospitals. To bluff them into surrendering, Johnson mounted two stovepipes on an old wagon and paraded it around to look like artillery. The ruse worked, the town gave up, and he became ever after Stovepipe Johnson.

By August Johnson had enough men to organize the 10th Kentucky Cavalry in Hopkins County, equipping it out of captures he had made from the enemy. He was commissioned colonel of the regiment, after which he attacked and took the Federal garrison at Hopkinsville, then repeated the feat at Clarksville, Tennessee, capturing it on August 18, 1862, and with it most of the 71st Ohio. "It was a fine body of men, and splendidly officered, " Lieutenant Colonel Basil Duke said of Johnson's regiment. Morgan, now a colonel commanding an oversized brigade of Kentucky regiments, apparently agreed. That fall, when Johnson joined the main body, Morgan split his command into two brigades and offered Johnson the command of one. For unknown reasons, however, Johnson declined, and the command went instead to Colonel John C. Breckinridge.

Johnson served with the combined command through the rest of the summer and fall of 1862 but then went to Texas briefly on detached service, probably related to recruiting. As a result, he missed being formally assigned—whether he liked it or not—to command of a brigade composed of the 3d, 8th, 10th, and 11th Kentucky Cavalry. Colonel Richard Gano took it instead. But when Johnson returned in February 1863, the command was his, and this time he did not attempt to decline. In his new command he rode off into Kentucky with Duke leading the other brigade and Morgan in overall command, bound on the great raid into Ohio and Indiana. Johnson fought at Green River Bridge and Lexington, Kentucky, and in the severe fight at Buffington Island on July 19, 1863. When Morgan was surrounded and forced to surrender, Johnson and a few hundred others managed to escape across the Ohio River and into the mountains of West Virginia.

As a result, Johnson was left the senior officer of the remnant of Morgan's cavalry division, and commanded it. He rendezvoused them all at Morristown, in East Tennessee, that fall, eventually collecting about five hundred. Ordered to report to Forrest, now a brigadier, Johnson commanded his demi-brigade during the Chickamauga fighting in September as skirmishers in advance of Lieutenant General James Longstreet and Major General John Bell Hood, and then saw his command split between Forrest and

Major General Joseph Wheeler for the operations around Knoxville and Chattanooga.

When Morgan escaped and returned to his command in spring 1864, Johnson reverted to command of a subdistrict in southern Kentucky, engaged chiefly in the recruiting at which he had proven so effective. By the summer he and a small band were operating in home ground around Union and Henderson counties, and threatening once more to lead a new regiment across the Ohio into Indiana and Illinois. But then on August 21, when Johnson led his command in an attack on a Federal camp at Grubbs Cross Roads, in Caldwell County, one of his own men misdirected a shot that sent a bullet crashing through his eyes. It was said then and later in many sources that Johnson's eyes were completely destroyed. However, an extant photograph shows him wearing crude goggles with what appear to be lenses. Certainly there would be little need for such unless he still had at least some limited sight remaining, but the wound certainly put him out of the war for good. Small compensation may have come on September 6, 1864, when President Davis commissioned him a brigadier general, to rank from June 1.

Johnson went back to his adopted Texas after the war, founded the town of Marble Falls, and spent the next fifty-seven years prospering. He finally died October 20, 1922, at Burnet, Texas, one of the last remaining Confederate generals. He was buried in Austin.

William C. Davis

Duke, Basil W., *A History of Morgan's Cavalry* (Bloomington, 1960).

Johnson, Adam R., *The Partisan Rangers* (Louisville, 1904).

Johnston, J. Stoddard, *Kentucky*, Vol. IX in Evans, *Confederate Military History*.

Adam Johnson, probably as colonel of the 10th Kentucky Cavalry. (Barker Texas History Center, University of Texas at Austin)

General Bradley Johnson, late in the war. (Museum of the Confederacy, Richmond, Va.)

✴ *Bradley Tyler Johnson* ✴

Bradley Johnson was born in Frederick, Maryland, on September 29, 1829. An 1849 graduate of Princeton, Johnson was a prominent state's attorney, noted orator, and chairman of the Democratic state committee in his native state during the 1850s. In the 1860 election he supported John C. Breckinridge, and when the Civil War began, Johnson supported the Southern cause. Virginia Governor John Letcher offered the Marylander a commission as lieutenant colonel, but Johnson declined, assisting in the organization of Maryland units for the Confederacy.

By June 1861 Arnold Elzey, George H. Steuart, and Johnson—all future Confederate generals—recruited and organized the 1st Maryland, holding the ranks of colonel, lieutenant colonel, and major, respectively. Assigned to the brigade of Brigadier General E. Kirby Smith, the Marylanders fought at First Manassas, launching an attack with the other regiments at a critical point in the action. Elzey led the assault as Smith fell wounded. Elzey earned a brigadiership and command of the brigade, and Steuart was promoted to colonel, Johnson to lieutenant colonel.

During the spring of 1862 Steuart was promoted to brigadier general, and Johnson assumed command of the regiment, with the rank of colonel. Ordered to the Shenandoah Valley, Johnson's regiment was assigned to Steuart's brigade, participating in Major General "Stonewall" Jackson's brilliant campaign in that region. On May 23 at Front Royal the 1st Maryland and a battalion of Louisiana troops spearheaded Jackson's attack on a Federal garrison in the village. Johnson's men opposed the 1st Maryland (U.S.), capturing numbers of their fellow Marylanders. Johnson's regiment also fought in the Seven Days' Campaign during the last week of June.

On August 17, because of Confederate conscription laws, the 1st Maryland was disbanded, and Johnson was without a command. Jackson, however, assigned him to temporary command of Brigadier General John R. Jones' brigade, which he led with skill and bravery during the Second Battle of Manassas, August 29–30, 1862. On September 4 Jackson recommended Johnson for promotion, adding, "I regarded him as a promising officer when he first entered the army, and so fully did he come up to my expectations that when his regiment was disbanded I put him in command of a brigade, and so ably did he discharge his duties in the recent battles near Bull Run as to make it my duty, as well as my pleasure, to recommend him for a brigadier-generalcy."

Jackson's recommendation was not enough, however. With a number of Marylanders holding the rank, and with Confederate authorities preferring to match officers with troops from the same state, Johnson had no units for a command. For nearly a year Johnson, with the rank of colonel of cavalry, performed various duties, including a long stint on a court-martial in Richmond. On February 4, 1863, Jackson reiterated his recommendation, saying of Johnson that "I do not know of any colonel who, in my opinion, is so well qualified for the position in question."

Johnson rejoined the army on July 2 at Gettysburg and served as temporary commander of Jones' brigade during the retreat to Virginia. In the fall he commanded the so-called Maryland Line, composed of artillery, cavalry, and infantry units from his native state. During the first three days of March 1864 Johnson's troops assisted in the repulse of the Kilpatrick–Dahlgren Raid on Richmond. Major General Wade Hampton praised Johnson for his performance in this action.

During May and June 1864 Johnson fought under Major General J. E. B. Stuart and Hampton in the cavalry engagements of the Overland Campaign. On June 28 Johnson was finally promoted to brigadier general, effective immediately, and assigned to command of the brigade of Brigadier General William E. "Grumble" Jones, who had been killed on June 5 at Piedmont. Johnson reached the Shenandoah Valley in time to advance northward with his brigade on Lieutenant General Jubal Early's raid against Washington, D.C.

During Early's operation Johnson led fifteen hundred men on an impossible operation to free the thousands of Confederate prisoners at Point Lookout, Maryland. When the Confederate returned to Virginia, Early ordered Brigadier General John McCausland and

A portrait of Johnson during his days as colonel, this one probably made in 1863. (Museum of the Confederacy, Richmond, Va.)

Brigadier General Johnson, taken some time after June 1864.
(U.S. Army Military History Institute, Carlisle, Pa.)

Johnson sat for the camera much during the last year of the war, probably during his months in North Carolina. (William A. Turner Collection)

There may have been nothing else for him to do before the surrender. (Virginia Historical Society, Richmond, Va.)

Johnson to raid into Pennsylvania and, if they could not secure $100,000 in gold, to burn the town of Chambersburg. Johnson objected to McCausland's methods and subsequently filed a highly critical report of the operation. On August 7 Union cavalry overtook the raiders at Moorefield, West Virginia, and routed most of McCausland's and Johnson's commands.

Johnson remained in the Shenandoah Valley and fought under Early in the campaign of August to October. The Confederates were outmatched in these engagements, but Johnson performed capably under the circumstances. When the cavalry units were consolidated in the fall, Johnson as a junior officer lost his command. In November 1864 he was assigned to command of the prison at Salisbury, North Carolina, a post he retained until the end of the war in April 1865. Johnson relocated to Richmond after the conflict, opened a law office, and served in the Virginia Senate from 1875 to 1879. He returned to his native state after his term, settling in Baltimore, spending his final years writing historical and legal papers. An excellent infantry officer and a capable cavalry commander, Johnson was perhaps the finest Marylander who cast his lot with the Confederacy. He died in Amelia, Virginia, on October 5, 1903, and was buried in Loudoun Park Cemetery in Baltimore.

Jeffry D. Wert

Goldsborough, W. W., *The Maryland Line in the Confederate Army 1861–1865* (Baltimore, 1869).

Tanner, Robert G., *Stonewall in the Valley* (New York, 1976).

Vandiver, Frank, *Jubal's Raid* (New York, 1964).

A reverse pose made at the same sitting as the first portrait of Johnson. (Erick Davis Collection)

Brigadier General Bushrod Johnson, probably taken in 1862. (Cook Collection, Valentine Museum, Richmond, Va.)

⭒ *Bushrod Rust Johnson* ⭒

Johnson as a major general, presumably taken after May 1864, by Hall of Nashville. (William A. Albaugh Collection)

Of all the men in gray who presented anomalous contrasts, few could compare with this Northern-born Quaker who became a Confederate fighting general. Johnson was born October 7, 1817, on the family farm outside Morristown, Ohio. The family were Hicksite Quakers, confirmed pacifists, and antislavery advocates. The family later moved to Belmont, where Johnson attended what schools he could, including the Marietta Academy. His father's abolitionist politics made the family unpopular in the area, however, and in 1838 they removed to Wayne County, Indiana. Young Johnson had meanwhile become a schoolteacher when seventeen, but decided to break with his Quaker heritage by seeking an appointment to the United States Military Academy at West Point. He matriculated in 1836 and graduated four years later along with William T. Sherman, George H. Thomas, and Richard S. Ewell. He finished twenty-third out of forty-two in his class and was posted to the 3d U.S. Infantry, Company E, at Fort Jessup, Louisiana. When he reached his company, however, it had removed to Fort Brooke, on Florida's Tampa Bay. Thereafter he acted in minor staff assignments at several Florida posts, seeing no action in the desultory fighting with the Seminoles, and was reposted to Jefferson Barracks, Missouri, in 1843.

Following promotion to 1st lieutenant in 1844, Johnson was reassigned to Fort Leavenworth, Kansas, then returned to Fort Jessup in time for the start of the Mexican War. He fought at Palo Alto, Resaca de la Palma, and Monterrey, but missed Vera Cruz thanks to being stuck with commissary duty. Then he blighted his career when he tried to engage in a profiteering

A variant portrait made at the same sitting. (Department of Archives and Manuscripts, Louisiana State University, Baton Rouge, La.)

Johnson late in the war, probably in 1864. (U.S. Army Military History Institute, Carlisle, Pa.)

Probably Johnson's last wartime portrait. (New-York Historical Society, New York, N.Y.)

scheme using government ships to bring contraband goods into Vera Cruz. Quickly summoned back to the United States, he was asked to resign his commission, and he did so on October 21, 1847.

For the next fourteen years Johnson worked as a teacher, first at the Western Military Institute at Georgetown, Kentucky, where he was for a time superintendent, and then president with the rank of colonel. When the institute failed, Johnson took a position with the Military College of the University of Nashville in 1855, acting as superintendent. When the sectional crisis came, he faced a difficult decision. As a Northerner and anti-slavery man, he would be expected to side with the Union. But his friends and fortune were now firmly planted in the South. Moreover, he may have resented his forced resignation from the Old Army. As a result, when the war came, he offered his services to Tennessee in his currently held militia rank of colonel, though he immediately began soliciting an appointment as brigadier in the Confederate Provisional Army.

Johnson was involved in the early location and construction of Fort Henry in his role as chief of engineers, and also in raising and organizing Tennessee regiments. He also inspected Fort Donelson, and briefly commanded it in January 1862, finding it in a sad condition to meet an attacker. Promoted by President Jefferson Davis to brigadier general on January 24, 1862, to rank immediately, Johnson would find out just how vulnerable the fort was when it fell to Grant a few weeks later. Johnson himself managed to escape and joined General Albert Sidney Johnston's army for the Shiloh campaign in April. He commanded a brigade in Major General Benjamin F. Cheatham's division, with the 2d, 15th, and 154th Tennessee; a Mississippi battalion; and a Tennessee battery. An early wound on April 6 put him out of most of the battle, however. He returned to duty in May and got a new brigade, the 17th, 23d, 25th, 37th, and 44th Tennessee Infantry, along with the 5th Confederate Infantry and an artillery battery. He led his brigade in the Perryville campaign, having five horses shot under him during the climactic battle.

There followed service at Stone's River, December 31, 1862–January 2, 1863, where Johnson's troops broke under fire on the first day, and after that Johnson spent much of 1863 campaigning for promotion to major general, with considerable support but no success. But then came Chickamauga, and the attack on September 20. Johnson, now commanding a division, led the attack that penetrated the gap in Major General William S. Rosecrans' line, precipitating the utter rout of the Yankee army. Still promotion did not come immediately, and meanwhile Johnson went off with Lieutenant General James Longstreet on the ill-fated Knoxville Campaign in November and December. The following spring, when Longstreet returned to the Army of Northern Virginia, Johnson was soon ordered to follow. The Senate had only just confirmed at last his appointment as brigadier, on February 17, 1864, and now Davis yielded to the importunities of the army of supporters Johnson had mustered, by appointing him major general on May 26, to rank from May 21. This time the Senate confirmed it immediately.

Johnson gave good service in Virginia, first on the James River defenses, and then at Petersburg. When General Lee attempted to break out in April 1865, Johnson's division was caught in the Federal vise at Sayler's Creek. Once again he managed to escape himself, but Lee relieved him of the remnant of his command on April 8. Johnson gave his parole at Appomattox the next day.

He returned to Tennessee and to education, though he tried real estate in Nashville at first, then dabbled in banking, and even cement making. In 1870, along with Kirby Smith, he helped found the University of Nashville, becoming its chancellor. The school failed in 1874, and Johnson moved to St. Louis but remained only a year before going to Macoupin County, Illinois, where he owned property. There, on a broken-down farm, he lived out the balance of what had been an ill-starred life. He died September 12, 1880, and was buried at the Miles Station Methodist Church near Brighton.

Johnson's whole career seems to have been blighted, in part by bad fortune and in part by weaknesses in his own character. Still, when he fought, he fought well, and the Confederacy owed much of the glorious Chickamauga triumph to the Yankee Quaker.

William C. Davis

Cummings, Charles, *Yankee Quaker, Confederate General* (Cranbury, 1971).

Johnson, Robert U., *Remembered Yesterdays* (Boston, 1923).

✴ *Edward Johnson* ✴

Edward Johnson, known almost universally during the Civil War as "Alleghany" Johnson, was born at the family home, "Salisbury," near Midlothian, Chesterfield County, Virginia, on April 16, 1816. Edward's father and namesake moved the family to Kentucky, and it was from that state that the younger Johnson entered the United States Military Academy. During his first year at West Point Johnson stood within a half-dozen cadets of the bottom of his class, but by graduation in 1838 he had achieved the modestly respectful standing of thirty-second among forty-five graduates. In conduct during his final term the future general rated 127th out of 218 students at the institution (P. G. T. Beauregard was 2d that year, and Irving McDowell 190th).

Johnson's military career began with a promotion far more rapid than the norm. From his July 1838 commission as 2d lieutenant in the 6th United States Infantry he advanced to 1st lieutenant in just over one year. Then the typical antebellum promotion cycle held Johnson in the same permanent rank for a dozen years; he became a captain only in April 1851. Meanwhile successful service in the Mexican War had won two brevet ranks for Johnson. Before the war with Mexico broke out, Lieutenant Johnson had put in nearly a decade on duty in widely separated locations. For three years after graduation he served in the Seminole Wars in Florida. From 1841 to 1846 Johnson was posted to the western and southwestern frontier. In Mexico the lieutenant saw battle action at Vera Cruz, Cerro Gordo, Churubusco, Molino del Ray, and Chapultepec. At each of the last two battles Johnson won brevets, to captain and major, respectively. In recognition of the distinguished performance of her native son, Virginia

voted a sword to Johnson; so did the citizens of Chesterfield County.

Brevet Major Johnson remained in the United States Army until the Civil War broke out. During the 1850s he was stationed on the frontier again at posts in California, Kansas, and the Dakota Territory. He also served at Fort Columbus, New York, for a time. Johnson later declared that he "got Grant a place" after his fellow officer left the army in drunken disorder. Although Johnson's resignation from the U.S. army was not accepted until June 10, 1861, his first Confederate commission, as lieutenant colonel of infantry, took rank from March 16, 1861. That date marked the ranking point for literally hundreds of new commissions, even though many of them reached final fruition at various dates over the next months. Johnson's lieutenant-colonelcy, for instance, was not confirmed until December—by which time he had been promoted twice and was commanding a brigade.

Edward Johnson took command of the 12th Georgia Infantry on July 2, 1861, with the rank of full colonel. That regiment, which he trained and molded into a fighting organization, went on to become one of the most renowned Georgia units in Lee's army. Colonel Johnson took his Georgians into the mountains west of Staunton, Virginia, and established himself during the late fall of 1861 on a crest of a position that he named Camp Alleghany. He and his men by then had earned their battle colors in a series of small and frustrating mountain skirmishes. Their big fight, which won for Edward Johnson both a high reputation and a *nom de guerre*, came on December 13. Federals who

The only known wartime uniformed image of General Johnson, taken probably after his February 28, 1862, promotion to major general. (William A. Turner Collection)

moved against Johnson's regiment and several other Confederate units near the camp met with a sharp repulse. A contemporary account declared that Colonel Johnson "appeared in citizen dress, gave his commands in a most emphatic manner and led the fierce charges in person," sometimes with a club in his hand and sometimes with a musket.

Colonel Johnson was appointed a brigadier general immediately after this success, to rank from the victorious day, December 13. He also became "Alleghany" Johnson or "Old Clubby" Johnson in recognition of the place of his victory and his choice of implements. A Richmond diarist reported popular lore when he wrote that Johnson was "an energetic man, and swears like a trooper" (most observers cited his strong language) while taking a "stout cane" into battle with which to encourage skulkers. One of Johnson's soldiers insisted that the general actually had "seized a fence rail, and springing forward ordered a charge." Whether accoutered with club or fence rail, Edward Johnson had made an impact.

During Major General "Stonewall" Jackson's famous Shenandoah Valley Campaign in the spring of 1862 General Johnson collaborated by resisting a Federal army west of the Valley. Jackson eventually lunged westward to help Johnson and then to absorb the smaller force into his own army. The two generals and their troops joined forces on May 8 to win the Battle of McDowell, but Johnson went down with a serious wound near the end of the fight. By one account, the general had been rolling on the ground in high glee over a humorous remark when a bullet hit one foot sticking up in the air, prompting the general to shout, "Goddamn that Yankee."

Johnson's convalescence took him under the eye of the Confederacy's leading female memoirist, Mary Boykin Chesnut. Mrs. Chesnut left vivid word pictures of the general, whom she styled "a different part of speech." "He had an odd habit of falling into a state of incessant winking as soon as he was…agitated. He seemed persistently winking one eye at you, but…in point of fact he did not know it himself." The wounded general was "as red as a turkey cock in the face," and his head was "so strangely shaped—like a cone, an old fashioned beehive, or, [in the description of another acquaintance]…There is three tiers of it. It is like the pope's tiara.'" To this unusual appearance the general added an "abrupt" personality and a thunderous voice even when courting, ostensibly in private. As might be expected, not everyone appreciated this style. A member of Stonewall Jackson's staff told his sister

that Alleghany made himself "agreeable or odious as the taste of one may determine." Men who fought under the general rather liked him. A Georgian officer who complained about most of his superiors thought Johnson "a stirring old coon, always on the alert."

General Johnson's long absence from the army ended just before Gettysburg, where he commanded as major general (appointed April 22, to rank from February 28, 1863) the division that originally had been Stonewall Jackson's. After leading that command with much distinction at the Second Battle of Winchester on the way north, Johnson fought on Culp's Hill July 2–3. That fall the general took his division into action at Mine Run, where a horse was shot under him. At the Wilderness and Spotsylvania in May 1864 Johnson and his men stood at the center of several desperate actions. Early on May 12 at the East Angle, near what soon would be christened as the Bloody Angle, a massive Federal assault swept over the Confederate works. Johnson and most of his command fell into enemy hands. A Federal who saw Johnson that morning described the same peculiar winking habit that had caught Mary Chesnut's attention as a "nervous twitching of his ears," as though he were "trying to brush flies off the back part of his head with his ears." A member of Grant's staff described Johnson's appearance vividly: "His clothing was covered with mud, and a hole had been torn in the crown of his felt hat, through which a tuft of hair protruded, looking like a Sioux Chief's warlock."

After he was exchanged, Johnson went to the Western theater "against his will," according to a friend, where he commanded a division in Lieutenant General S. D. Lee's corps of the Army of Tennessee. General R. E. Lee in April 1864 had told President Davis, "I cannot spare General E. Johnson," but now he evidently did not wish to have Old Alleghany back at the head of a division in Virginia. Johnson became a prisoner of war again on December 16, 1864, at Nashville and was paroled only on July 22, 1865. He died in Richmond on March 2, 1873, and was buried in Hollywood Cemetery.

Robert K. Krick

Cullum, George, *Register of the Officers and Graduates of the U.S. Military Academy* (New York, 1891).

Hotchkiss, Jedediah, *Virginia*, Vol. III in Evans, *Confederate Military History*.

Johnson, Edward, Letters, Kentucky Historical Society, Frankfort.

⋆ *Albert Sidney Johnston* ⋆

No photograph of Johnston in Confederate uniform is known to exist. This is the only one known showing him in his prewar U.S. Army uniform as brevet brigadier general, and taken probably in 1857 or later. (National Archives)

Albert Sidney Johnston, an illustrious soldier of three republics, was born February 2, 1803, in Washington, Kentucky, the son of John and Abigail (Harris) Johnston. He attended private lower schools and Transylvania University, and in 1822 entered the United States Military Academy. He was graduated eighth in the class of 1826, having served as adjutant of the Corps of Cadets his senior year. On January 20, 1829, he married Henrietta Preston of Louisville, who died August 12, 1835, the mother of their two living children and one deceased child. In October 1843 Johnston married Eliza Griffin of Louisville, who bore him five children and who survived him by thirty-four years.

Johnston had an unusually diversified military career. In 1832 he served in the Black Hawk War as adjutant to the commanding general. Two years later, urged by his invalid first wife, he resigned his commission, and two years later still, after her death, he went to the Republic of Texas, where he became the senior general of the Texan army and later the secretary of war. In the Mexican War he served with valor on General Zachary Taylor's staff in the Battle of Monterrey (September 20–24, 1846). In 1849 Johnston reentered the Regular Army of the United States as a major with the job of paymaster to the frontier posts in Texas.

In 1855 he was appointed commander of the newly created, elite 2d Cavalry, with the rank of colonel. Among his subordinates were such outstanding officers as Lieutenant Colonel Robert E. Lee and Majors William J. Hardee and George H. Thomas. Two years later Johnston was selected to command the expedition sent to put down the so-called Mormon Rebellion in Utah Territory, a service which gained him a promotion to the rank of brevet brigadier general. In 1860 he became the commander of the Department of the Pacific with headquarters in San Francisco. He was located here at the time of the secession of the seven states of the lower South.

Johnston disliked secession in principle, but he feared and loathed abolitionism, and upon the secession of Texas, his adopted state, he resigned his commission. His wife said that he found it "impossible to beat his sword into a ploughshare," and with profound regret, he decided to join the Confederacy. "It looks like fate," he commented. "Texas has made me a rebel twice." In summer of 1861 he journeyed crosscountry from California to Richmond, Virginia, where he presented his services to the South. By now he was looked upon as being perhaps the nation's foremost living military figure, excepting only the aged and infirm General Winfield Scott. Johnston also enjoyed the advantage of having been a fellow cadet with Jefferson Davis, who on September 10 appointed him to the command of Confederate Department No. 2, the Western theater of operations. Johnston received the rank of general on August 31, dating from May 30, making him second in seniority to the elderly Adjutant General Samuel Cooper.

In February 1862 Johnston lost Forts Henry and Donelson, located in Tennessee on the Tennessee and Cumberland rivers, to a Union army-navy attack led by Brigadier General Ulysses S. Grant. With the advanced Confederate line broken, Johnston withdrew his forces all the way to the important rail center of Corinth, Mississippi, and on April 6 he made a surprise attack on Grant's encampment in the vicinity of Shiloh Methodist Church near Pittsburg Landing on the Tennessee River. The blow almost destroyed the Union force, but in the early afternoon, at the peak of the assault, Johnston was killed and the momentum temporarily lost. General Pierre G. T. Beauregard, second-in-command, took over and in the late afternoon halted the attack until the following morning. That night Grant received heavy reinforcements, and the next day he counterattacked and drove the Confederates back to Corinth.

Johnston's death so near the beginning of the war makes impossible any firm conclusion on his ability as a general. Jefferson Davis considered Johnston to be the Confederacy's most outstanding soldier. When

Johnston was denounced for losing the Tennessee forts, Davis kept him in command and said that if Johnston was not a general the Confederacy had none. Yet unquestionably Johnston was culpable in the defeat at the forts; and at times he appeared to be confused and hesitant in comparison with the brilliant but impulsive and visionary Beauregard. Grant later evaluated Johnston to have been an indecisive and ineffectual leader.

But in the Shiloh campaign Johnston clearly outgeneraled Grant in concentrating his forces and achieving one of the great strategic surprises of military history. Johnston also showed that he was superior to Beauregard in judgment, presence of mind, and tenacity of purpose. Late in the afternoon of the day before the battle, at the point which the famed theoretician Clausewitz identifies as the "moment of truth," when the prospective operation depends solely on the will and character of the commander, Johnston was obliged to overrule his unnerved second-in-command and reaffirm the attack order. All things accounted for, one may reasonably speculate that Johnston would have been a great asset to the Confederacy if he had lived to develop his talents fully.

Johnston is buried in the Texas State Cemetery at Austin.

Charles P. Roland

Johnston, William Preston, *The Life of General Albert Sidney Johnston* (New York, 1878).

Roland, Charles P., *Albert Sidney Johnston: Soldier of Three Republics* (Austin, 1964).

Schaller, Frank, "A Review of the Life and Character of the Late General Albert Sidney Johnston, C.S.A.," in Auguste F. Marmont, *The Spirit of Military Institutions* (Columbia, 1864).

✷ George Doherty Johnston ✷

The uniform is clearly a clumsy artist's addition on this portrait of George Johnston. No genuine uniformed view has been found. (Albert Shaw Collection, Virginia Historical Society, Richmond, Va.)

George Doherty Johnston was born on May 30, 1832, at Hillsborough, North Carolina, but moved with his family to Greensboro, Alabama, when he was two. Upon the death of his father, Johnston's mother moved the family once again to Marion, Alabama. Johnston received a good education at local private schools and at Howard College and later earned a law degree from Cumberland University in Lebanon, Tennessee. After graduation he opened a law practice in Marion in 1855 and immediately moved into politics. Johnston was elected mayor of his home town in 1856 but resigned before serving in the state legislature 1857–58.

At the outbreak of the Civil War, Johnston joined Company G, 4th Alabama Infantry, as a 2d lieutenant. He first saw action July 21, 1861, at First Manassas, where his regiment served with Brigadier General Barnard Bee's brigade. Johnston was appointed major of the 25th Alabama in January 1862 and saw heavy fighting at Shiloh. Colonel Zachariah Deas, Johnston's commanding officer, commended the major's coolness and gallantry in the battle while under the "hottest fire." Johnston was promoted to lieutenant colonel after Shiloh and accompanied his regiment throughout the autumn invasion of Kentucky but saw no serious action. He was confirmed as colonel of the 25th Alabama on October 27, 1862.

Colonel Johnston was in all of the major campaigns of the Army of Tennessee from Murfreesboro to Bentonville, but there is little record of his activities. At Murfreesboro his regiment lost 109 men, but after-action reports do not mention Johnston. Likewise at Chickamauga September 19–20, 1863, Johnston reported losing 106 out of 330 men engaged but gave no details of his regiment's service. It is only known that his brigade (Deas' Alabama brigade) was on the extreme left of the army and was fiercely engaged on September 19.

Johnston served with his men throughout the Atlanta Campaign May 1–September 2, 1864, and it was said that the regiment performed well in the fight at New Hope Church May 25–27. At Peachtree Creek July 20 he led his 25th Alabama in a charge that captured more prisoners than the regiment had men. In addition, two battle flags and 350 stands of arms were taken. His actions throughout the campaign did not go unnoticed. Generals Braxton Bragg, John B. Hood, and Benjamin Cheatham recommended that Johnston be promoted to brigadier general. He was so appointed on July 26, 1864, to rank immediately, and was placed in command of Deas' brigade. On July 28, only three hours after being notified of his promotion, Johnston led the brigade into action at Ezra Church. Although soon hit by a ball that shattered his leg, he stayed in the saddle and supported the wounded leg with his bridle. Johnston continued to lead the brigade in the battle until exhaustion forced him to retire.

Despite his wound, Johnston accompanied Hood's invasion of Tennessee in 1864, spending much of his time on crutches. When Brigadier General William A. Quarles was wounded and captured at Franklin, Johnston was given command of his brigade. He led the brigade December 15–16 at the Battle of Nashville and was selected to be a part of the rear guard during the agonizing retreat. Johnston's brigade was then sent to the Carolinas to help stop William T. Sherman's advance there. On March 20, 1865, on the second day of the Battle of Bentonville, Johnston took command of Brigadier General Edward C. Walthall's division and led it until the army was reorganized at Goldsboro, North Carolina, just prior to the surrender. He was on his way to join Lieutenant General Richard Taylor's force in the West when the war ended. His parole has never been found.

Johnston returned to Marion, Alabama, and practiced law until 1868. He then moved to Dallas County, and later to Tuscaloosa, where he became commandant of cadets at the University of Alabama. Johnston also served as superintendent of the South Carolina Military Academy, was appointed to the United States Civil Service Commission by President Grover Cleveland during Cleveland's second administration, and became very active in the Southern Historical Society. He eventually returned to Tuscaloosa and was elected to the Alabama state senate. Johnston died in Tuscaloosa on December 8, 1910, and was buried there.

Terry L. Jones

Wheeler, Joseph, *Alabama*, Vol. VII in Evans, *Confederate Military History*.

This previously unpublished portrait is the only one known that shows Johnston with the proper collar insignia of his rank. (William A. Turner Collection)

✵ *Joseph Eggleston Johnston* ✵

Born near Farmville, Virginia, February 3, 1807, Johnston was the son of Peter Johnston, who had served with distinction in the War of Independence. Young Johnston grew up near Abingdon in southwest Virginia. His early education came from his parents and then at Abingdon Academy.

In 1825 he entered the United States Military Academy at West Point, New York, where he did well in his studies. In 1829 he graduated thirteenth in his class of forty-six and was commissioned 2d lieutenant of artillery. Except for a few months 1837–38 when he was a civilian engineer, Johnston served in the United States Army from his graduation until 1861.

In 1836 Johnston became a 1st lieutenant, and in 1838 he was transferred to the topographical engineers. He was promoted to captain in 1846 and to lieutenant colonel of voltigeurs in 1848. In both the Florida Indian wars and the Mexican War Johnston's bravery attracted attention. In both conflicts he suffered wounds.

Meanwhile Johnston met, fell in love with, and in 1845 married Lydia McLane. Lydia's father, Louis McLane, was a prominent business and political figure. He served in Congress, as minister to Great Britain, and as President Andrew Jackson's secretary of the treasury and secretary of state. Although childless, the Johnston's marriage was a long and happy one.

In March 1855 Johnston was appointed lieutenant colonel of the 1st U.S. Cavalry Regiment, and in June 1860 he became the quartermaster general of the army. Assignment as quartermaster general was very important to Johnston's Confederate career. The post carried with it promotion to the staff grade of brigadier general. Johnston also retained his permanent grade of lieutenant colonel. He was quartermaster general on April 22, 1861, when he resigned to follow his native state into the Confederacy.

Virginia's governor, John Letcher, appointed Johnston major general in the state army and assigned him to organize and train newly raised troops at Richmond. In a short time, however, Johnston was reduced to brigadier general because the state government decided that it had too many major generals. Johnston was also appointed brigadier general in the Confederate Army on May 14, to rank immediately (then that army's highest grade). He was sent to command the Rebel forces gathering at Harpers Ferry, Virginia.

In July 1861 Johnston moved his forces east to participate in the First Battle of Manassas. Johnston, as the senior officer present, was technically in command of the army that won the battle. Afterward he remained in command of Confederate forces in northern Virginia.

Meanwhile, on August 31 Johnston had been promoted to the newly created grade of full general, to rank from July 4. Confederate law stipulated that Rebel officers would hold the same relative rank in each grade that they had held in the United States Army. Johnston assumed that he would be ranked by his staff grade of brigadier general and would be the highest-ranking officer in the Southern army. President Jefferson Davis, however, based Johnston's rank on his permanent grade of lieutenant colonel. As a result of Davis' decision, Johnston stood fourth in rank among Confederate generals.

Johnston was incensed, and he protested in bitter, angry letters that Davis found insubordinate. Differences about the general's rank were soon exacerbated by others over army organization, logistics, and strategy. Both Johnston and Davis were proud, thin-skinned, petulant men, and their relationship increasingly became one of suspicion and loathing.

Johnston was wounded at Seven Pines in May 1862 and underwent a long convalescence. In November when he returned to duty, Davis sent him to command Rebel forces in the West. Johnston was unhappy at losing command in Virginia, and he believed that Davis' plan to defend the West by shifting troops back and forth between Tennessee and Mississippi would not work. He had also become almost paranoid about Davis, thinking that the President wanted to bring about his defeat to disgrace him.

In April 1863 Johnston, believing that both Tennessee and Mississippi were threatened, was unwilling to take

An early-war pose, Johnston's best-known, showing him with the colonel's collar insignia that he seems usually to have worn. (William A. Turner Collection)

A very slight variant of the previous image, somewhat retouched by an early artist. (Cook Collection, Valentine Museum, Richmond, Va.)

Johnston's most unusual pose, probably made in Richmond very early in the war, and certainly prior to May 1862. (Cook Collection, Valentine Museum, Richmond, Va.)

any meaningful action. On May 9 he was ordered to Mississippi to assume personal command of the Confederate attempt to defend Vicksburg. The feeble Rebel effort in Mississippi ended with Vicksburg's surrender on July 4. Almost immediately Johnston and Davis fell into a long, acrid argument over who was to blame for the disaster. Meanwhile Davis reduced Johnston's command to Alabama and Mississippi. Johnston, his wife, and his friends spent the next several months exchanging letters about how Davis and his sycophants were trying to destroy Johnston.

In December 1863 Davis, viewing Johnston as the least evil of several bad choices, assigned him to command the Army of Tennessee, then defending Georgia. In the following spring and summer Johnston was constantly outmaneuvered by the Yankees and fell back into the heart of the Confederacy, abandoning valuable territory and demoralizing many soldiers and civilians. On July 17 Davis removed Johnston from command and named Lieutenant General John Bell Hood as his replacement.

Johnston spent the next several months without a command. Recalled to active service in February 1865, he sought with little success to rally a Rebel force to oppose the Federal army marching through the Carolinas. On April 26 he surrendered his command near Durham Station, North Carolina.

During the postwar years Johnston supported himself and his wife by working in the transportation, insurance, and communications businesses. In 1878 he was elected to the House of Representatives from Virginia, and in the following decade he served as commissioner of railroads. His main interest, however, was to justify his military career. To this end he wrote *Narrative of Military Operations* (published 1874) and several magazine articles. He died on March 21, 1891, and was buried in Greenmount Cemetery in Baltimore, Maryland.

Johnston was arguably the most controversial of Confederate generals. While reasonably competent at day-to-day administration of an army, he proved unwilling to take the risks that a Confederate general had to take in order to win. Historians long held a very high opinion of Johnston. That judgment was based on a comparison with such obvious failures as Braxton Bragg and John Bell Hood (who preceded and followed him in command of the Army of Tennessee) as well as on Johnston's own self-serving memoirs. In recent decades as historians have begun to study

Johnston's campaigns in depth and to base their conclusions on more reliable evidence, Johnston's reputation has sharply declined.

Richard M. McMurry

Govan, Gilbert E., and Livingood, James W., *A Different Valor: The Story of General Joseph E. Johnston, C.S.A.* (Indianapolis and New York, 1956).

Lash, Jeffrey N., *Destroyer of the Iron Horse: Joseph E. Johnston and Confederate Rail Transport, 1861–1865* (Kent, 1991).

McMurry, Richard M., "'The *Enemy* at Richmond': Joseph E. Johnston and the Confederate Government," *Civil War History*, 1981.

Robert Daniel Johnston ✵

Robert Johnston as a brigadier, taken sometime after September 1863. (Don Tiedeken Collection)

Robert D. Johnston was born on May 19, 1837, in Lincoln County, North Carolina. He received a preparatory education in Rutherfordton before entering the University of North Carolina. Johnston was graduated in 1857 and then studied law at the University of Virginia 1860–61. When his native state seceded in the spring of 1861, Johnston was a practicing attorney and a 2d lieutenant in the Beattie's Ford Rifles, a local militia unit.

Upon the organization of North Carolina volunteers in May and June, Johnston's militia company was designated Company K, 23d North Carolina, and he was elected its captain, his commission to date from June 22. In July, seven companies of the regiment rushed northward to Virginia but arrived too late for the First Battle of Manassas. The regiment spent the fall of 1861 and the winter of 1862 in northern Virginia in the brigade of Jubal Early.

On May 5, 1862, the regiment fought in its first engagement, the Battle of Williamsburg. Johnston distinguished himself in combat, and five days later when the regiment reorganized he was elected colonel, his commission to date from May 21. At the Battle of Seven Pines on the 31st, Johnston fell wounded fifty feet from the Union lines—hit in the arm, face, and neck. He recovered and rejoined his regiment in September 1862.

At the Battle of Sharpsburg, the 23d North Carolina and other regiments of Samuel Garland's brigade under the command of Colonel Duncan K. McRae, held the center of the Confederate line along the sunken road or "Bloody Lane." In the furious fighting, Johnston extricated the regiment, earning the praises of D. H. Hill as "the gallant Lieutenant Colonel." The regiment held a reserve position during the Battle of Fredericksburg.

During the Chancellorsville Campaign in May 1863, Robert E. Rodes temporarily assigned Johnston to command of the 12th North Carolina. On May 2, Johnston led his troops in the Confederate assault, capturing some Union battle flags. Two months later at Gettysburg, on July 1, the 23d North Carolina was shattered in an open field. Losing every commissioned officer except one, Johnston suffered a severe wound that kept him from duty for two months.

On September 2, 1863, Johnston was promoted to brigadier general, effective the previous day, and assigned to command of his old brigade comprised of the 5th, 12th, 20th, and 23d North Carolina and the 2d North Carolina Battalion. Johnston directed the brigade at the Wilderness and Spotsylvania during May 1864. In the latter battle his brigade counterattacked into the vicious struggle at the Mule Shoe on May 12. At one point in the combat, Johnston seized the flag of the 23d North Carolina and leading the men forward, planted the flag on the works held by the Federals. He fell wounded, however, and relinquished command of the brigade.

Once again Johnston recovered quickly and returned to duty by the summer. During the 1864 Shenandoah Valley Campaign, Johnston fought in the battles of Third Winchester, Fisher's Hill, and Cedar Creek. On September 19 at Third Winchester, his brigade fought a brief, isolated action that delayed the Union advance of Phil Sheridan's army. By the campaign's conclusion, Johnston was a capable, gallant brigadier.

Johnston returned with the II Corps to Petersburg in November. For the next three months, his brigade participated in the trench warfare. In March 1865, Confederate authorities assigned Johnston to command along the Roanoke River in his native state. In May he was paroled out at Charlotte.

Johnston remained in Charlotte after the war, practicing law in the city for twenty years. In 1887, he relocated to Birmingham, South Carolina, assuming the presidency of the Birmingham National Bank. He also served as register of the United States Land Office. Late in life, Johnston moved to Winchester, Virginia, where he died on February 1, 1919, and was buried.

Perhaps a slightly later portrait of Johnston. (Cook Collection, Valentine Museum, Richmond, Va.)

Jeffry D. Wert

Clark, Walter, ed., *Histories of the Several Regiments and Battalions from North Carolina* (Goldsboro, 1901).

Hill, D. H., *North Carolina*, Vol. IV in Evans, *Confederate Military History*.

Wert, Jeffry D., *From Winchester to Cedar Creek* (Carlisle, 1987).

✯ *David Rumph Jones* ✯

The only known portrait of David R. Jones, made probably in 1861 or early 1862. (Museum of the Confederacy, Richmond, Va.)

On April 5, 1825, a son was born to Donald B. and Mary Elvera Rumph Jones in their rural home in South Carolina's Orangeburg District. He was named David Rumph, his middle name honoring his maternal grandfather, Captain Jacob Rumph, a revolutionary war soldier. David was educated in the common schools of Georgia, where his parents moved. In July 1842 he became a cadet at the United States Military Academy. During his West Point years Jones demonstrated a proficiency in fencing and as an equestrian. He graduated in 1846 as number forty-one in a class of fifty-nine. Among his classmates were George B. McClellan (number two), Thomas J. Jackson (number seventeen), and George E. Pickett (number fifty-nine). Like U. S. Grant, the best horseman in the class of 1843, Jones was assigned to the infantry, being commissioned a brevet 2d lieutenant in the 2d U.S. Infantry.

When war with Mexico broke out, Jones reported to his regiment, then in the field. He was promoted 2d lieutenant on November 23, 1846, and, as a member of Winfield Scott's army, participated in the siege and capture of Vera Cruz, March 1847. He was appointed regimental adjutant April 15 and took part in the campaign from Vera Cruz to the Valley of Mexico and in the capture of Mexico City on September 14. On August 20, 1847, Jones had been brevetted 1st lieutenant for gallantry and meritorious conduct at the Battles of Contreras and Churubusco.

Jones and his regiment returned to the United States in the summer of 1848 and, on May 7, 1849, he was promoted 1st lieutenant, the regiment then posted in California. He spent two years (1851–53) as an instructor in infantry tactics at West Point, and on March 16, 1853, was transferred from the 2d Infantry to the Adjutant General's Department and made a brevet captain, serving successively as adjutant general of the Western and Pacific departments, acting judge-advocate of the Pacific Department, and assistant adjutant general of the Department of the West. He married well, taking as his wife Rebecca Taylor, a niece of President Zachary Taylor, who was a cousin of Jefferson Davis' first wife, Sarah Knox Taylor Davis.

Jones resigned from the Old Army on February 15, 1861, and on March 16 was commissioned major in the Confederate States army; he quickly reported for duty as chief of staff to Brigadier General P. G. T. Beauregard at Charleston. On April 13 he visited Fort Sumter, then under bombardment, and offered Major Robert Anderson the terms for the fort's surrender, which were accepted, and is said to have lowered the "Stars and Stripes." Promoted to brigadier general on June 17, 1861, to rank immediately, he was assigned to command one of seven brigades in General Beauregard's new Army of the Potomac. His brigade was on the Confederate right at First Manassas on July 21, guarding McLean's Ford, and late in the afternoon crossed Bull Run and clashed with the enemy at Little Rocky Run.

On July 24 the army was reorganized, and Jones, in accordance with the law requiring units from a state to be brigaded together, assumed command of a brigade that included the 4th, 5th, 6th, and 9th South Carolina Infantry. Jones' brigade was assigned to Major General James Longstreet's division and spent the next seven months camped in Fairfax County. On February 16, 1862, Jones was detached from the South Carolina Brigade and relieved Brigadier General Samuel Jones as commander of a brigade that included the 7th, 8th, 9th, and 11th Georgia infantry regiments. The five weeks that began on March 9 and ended in mid-April saw General Joseph E. Johnston redeploy his army from northern Virginia to the Peninsula to confront George B. McClellan's Army of the Potomac in front of the Yorktown-Warwick line.

Late March found Jones in command of a two-brigade division, and on April 5 he was promoted major general, to rank from March 16, although the appointment was not confirmed by the Confederate Congress. Jones and his troops, though frequently close to the enemy, saw little or no action on the retreat up the Peninsula or on the lines before Richmond, until the Seven Days' Campaign. Jones, commanding one of the three divisions of Major General John B. Magruder's corps, fought the enemy at Garnett's and Golding's farms on the 27th and 28th and at Malvern Hill on July 1. When he filed his after-action report, General Magruder commended Jones and his troops for their actions in these engagements.

Robert E. Lee, although successful in driving the Army of the Potomac from the gates of Richmond into a fortified camp on the James River, was dissatisfied with the performance of a number of senior officers. This led to transfers, and in the army's reorganization Jones' command gained a brigade and was assigned to the wing led by Major General James Longstreet.

Jones and his troops participated in the campaign that resulted in the Second Battle of Manassas. He crossed the Rapidan on August 18, maneuvered along the Rappahannock the 23d to the 25th, engaged the enemy at Thoroughfare Gap on the 28th, and on the 30th repeatedly hammered the Union left on Chinn Ridge until it crumbled.

On September 6 Jones crossed the Potomac as General Lee carried the war into Maryland. His division now numbered six brigades. Nightfall on the 13th found Jones camped at Hagerstown. The next day Jones made a forced march with five of his brigades to Boonsboro and provided timely support for Major General D. H. Hill's division in the fight for Turner's and Fox's gaps. At Antietam Jones and his troops held the Confederate right from 9:30 A.M. until 3:00 P.M. against Ambrose E. Burnside's slashing attacks. Time bought by Jones was valuable, because it enabled A. P. Hill's division to reach the field from Harpers Ferry and strike Burnside's corps from an unexpected direction as Jones' exhausted brigades were breaking up. Following the army's return to Virginia, General Longstreet commended Jones for his leadership at "Thoroughfare Gap, Manassas Plains, Boonsboro, and Sharpsburg."

In mid-October Jones was stricken by a heart attack and left the army, never to return. He died in Richmond, Virginia, on January 15, 1863, and was buried in Hollywood Cemetery. There were those who would say that Jones died of a broken heart. His brother-in-law—Colonel Henry W. Kingsbury of the 11th Connecticut Infantry—was killed at Antietam near Burnside's Bridge battling Jones' troops.

Edwin C. Bearss

Capers, Ellison, *South Carolina*, Vol. V in Evans, *Confederate Military History*.

Cullum, George, *Biographical Register, Officers and Graduates, U.S. Military Academy* (New York, 1891).

After spending most of the war on staff duty, Jones can finally pose as a brigadier between May 1863 and May 1864. (Cook Collection, Valentine Museum, Richmond, Va.)

⋆ John Marshall Jones ⋆

John Marshall Jones is memorable as one of very few Confederate generals who won that rank after serving only in staff positions. Jones was born in Charlottesville, Virginia, on July 26, 1820. He attended the United States Military Academy at West Point as a member of the class of 1841, which included a large proportion of cadets who became familiar names during the Civil War—among them Don Carlos Buell; Josiah Gorgas; both Confederate Garnetts, Richard B. and Robert S.; and Horatio G. Wright. Jones finished his first year at the academy standing forty-fourth among seventy-two classmates. He maintained that relative position throughout his four years, graduating thirty-ninth out of fifty-two graduates. Jones managed his highest academic standing in artillery studies, ranking twenty-fifth. He never had much to do with artillery, however, during his career. Young Jones' disciplinary performance at West Point mirrored the mediocrity of his classroom efforts: He stood 129th in "merit in conduct" in his graduation year among 219 cadets rated throughout the academy. Perhaps his standing in conduct was related to the nickname "Rum" Jones, applied by his comrades.

John M. Jones began his military career under a commission as a brevet 2d lieutenant in the 5th United States Infantry. For four years he served at that rank in postings to Fort Mackinac and Detroit, Michigan, and in Florida and Texas. Jones received a commission as 2d lieutenant , unencumbered with the brevet, in the 7th United States Infantry on April 18, 1845. He advanced to 1st lieutenant on August 20, 1847, and to captain on March 3, 1855. Lieutenant Jones did not share the Mexican War experiences of most of his contemporary officers, because he was on duty at his alma mater during that period. Jones' other assignments during the years before the Civil War included duty on a board revising tactical doctrine; service with A. W. Whipple's topographical survey in the West; marching with the Utah expedition and into New Mexico; and the usual stretches of garrison duty.

As secession brought on civil war, Captain Jones took a leave of absence while he prepared to follow his native state's course. His resignation from the United States Army was accepted on May 27, 1861, even though Jones' first Confederate commission—as a major of the artillery corps—dated its rank from March 16. For nearly two years John M. Jones held staff positions of modest rank. From September 4, 1861, to January 14, 1862, he served as adjutant on the staff of John B. Magruder as a lieutenant colonel. For most of 1862, including "Stonewall" Jackson's Shenandoah Valley Campaign, Jones was a.a.g. on Major General Richard S. Ewell's staff. In December 1862 he transferred to duty as inspector general on Brigadier General Jubal A. Early's staff—the same divisional staff, Ewell being absent wounded. Early in 1863 Jones, still a lieutenant colonel, reverted to a.a.g. status under Early and Ewell. His long-delayed promotion on May 16, the first and only one of his Confederate career, came as part of the post-Chancellorsville reorganization of Lee's army. It elevated Jones from staff rank of lieutenant colonel to the substantially higher line rank of brigadier general, to date from May 15, 1863.

The stagnation that beset Jones at his low rank and his role on staff duty rather than in command of troops were fates dramatically different than those of most other professional soldiers situated as he was when war broke out. His West Point education coupled with two decades of credible military service produced an initial early-war rank for Jones at least as high as most of his peers and higher than many. Assignment to staff duty during 1861 seems unusual under the circumstances; staying in that duty and at that rank for one-half of the war must be classified as astonishing. Ewell regularly praised Jones in reports for his courage and skill, and the army seemed to like him. A Louisiana staff officer who knew Jones called him "one of the best officers & most thorough gentlemen in the Army." Another staffer described him as "very gallant and efficient." The problem clearly lay in Jones' personal habits: The boy known as "Rum" Jones in 1840 had grown into a man who had serious difficulties with alcohol. At Cross Keys in 1862 Jones

Captain Jones sits in the center of this image, which may possibly have been taken in the early days of the war, or else just before his resignation from the Old Army. (William A. Turner Collection)

had a flask of whisky handy to share with a wounded comrade but "had been quite sober for two or three months" himself. Two days later the wounded officer came across Jones in a hotel inebriated and "in a perfectly limp state." By early 1863 there was evidence that Jones had control of himself, or at least enough strong hope to warrant entrusting him with a brigade of Virginians. General R. E. Lee told President Davis that Jones had promised to resign at once if his problem flared up.

Jones' new assignment was as difficult as could be imagined. He took over the second brigade of Stonewall Jackson's old division, which for the past year had languished under the most spectacularly unsuccessful general officer in the army's history, John R. Jones —no relation to John M. Jones applied a rigid discipline to the brigade's problems, combined with solicitous concern for the men. One of them, a free spirit not inclined toward regimentation, admitted that the effect was salutary. Jones "was a strict disciplinarian," the soldier wrote, "and inaugurated several plans for the benefit of his men....He was the only officer who made the men take care of themselves as far as they could." Jones fought straggling and other marching abuses in traditional ways, as well as by demanding the constant presence of bandsmen to play on the march as needed.

The brigade badly needed good leadership within weeks after Jones assumed command, when it fought in July 1863 as part of Major General Edward Johnson's division at Gettysburg. General Jones led his men in the assault on Culp's Hill on July 2 and fell at their head "near the first line of the enemy's entrenchments" with a severe thigh wound. He returned to command during September and led the brigade during the October operations north of the Rapidan. At Payne's Farm near Mine Run Jones suffered another wound on November 27, 1863. This head wound kept him off duty only briefly.

Jones' brigade participated in the fighting on May 5, 1864, on the Orange Turnpike that opened the Battle of the Wilderness. Federals of Major General G. K. Warren's V Corps stopped the Confederates, then drove into Jones' right flank with devastating impact. The brigade, still not recovered from its shaky experiences in 1862 and 1863, fled precipitately. Jones calmly watched the approaching Federals until they shot him dead, together with his aide Robert Davies Early. The word in the army was that Jones, having valiantly failed to rally his men, "rather than survive the disgrace of his command, preferred death." In the words of a surviving staff member, the general, "apparently disdaining to fly, was killed while sitting on his horse gazing at the approaching enemy."

In fitting encomium, General Ewell declared in an official document, "I consider his loss an irreparable one...." Unfortunately, "a stone on the south side of the Pike...marking the spot where he fell," has not been seen in living memory.

Robert K. Krick

Brown, G. Campbell, Memoir, Tennessee State Library and Archives, Nashville.

Cullum, George, *Register of the Officers and Graduates of the U.S. Military Academy* (New York, 1891).

⋆ *John Robert Jones* ⋆

No uniformed photo of Jones has been found. This was taken several years after the war. (Miller, *Photographic History*)

"Stonewall" Jackson's numerous military virtues did not include an aptitude for identifying and nurturing promising subordinates; in fact, most of his proteges failed signally. None was more disappointing than John Robert Jones. Jones was born in Harrisonburg, Virginia, on March 12, 1827. He attended Virginia Military Institute and graduated with distinction in the class of 1848. Cadet Jones stood seventh among twenty-four graduates that year (second in tactics), and he also earned the high honor of appointment as 1st captain.

For a few months after graduation Jones taught school in Staunton, then in January 1849 he moved to Rappahannock Academy to teach mathematics. The next fall he was back at the Staunton school, though applying eagerly for a position at the South Carolina Military Academy. A few months later Jones had returned to Rappahannock Academy. His peripatetic teaching career took Jones to Quincy, Florida, during the 1850s to run two seminaries. He also established a boys' military school in Urbana, Maryland, in a building that later became famous because of J.E.B. Stuart's associations with it in September 1862.

When war broke out in Virginia, Jones organized a Harrisonburg company and commanded it as captain when it was mustered into service on June 22, 1861. Captain Jones' men became Company I of the 33d Virginia, one of five regiments that made up the famous Stonewall Brigade. They fought at First Manassas July 21 with the brigade on Henry House Hill. Jones became lieutenant colonel of the 33d a month later, to rank from August 21, 1861. Lieutenant Colonel Jones went with his regiment and the brigade to the Shenandoah Valley that fall. He succeeded in winning the confidence of Major General Stonewall Jackson during the campaigns in that region. Perhaps Jones impressed Jackson because of his VMI associations, though the two men had not been contemporaries there. More likely, though, the senior officer appreciated Jones' zealous treatment of anticonscription insurrectionists in the Rockingham County mountains. Jones took some artillery and a few infantry into the hills, shelled the rebellious militiamen, killed one of them, and captured the rest. That treatment was precisely what the stern Stonewall would have prescribed.

Soon after he routed the dissident militia, Jones had need of Jackson's help. The spring elections in the 33d Virginia went poorly indeed for the lieutenant colonel. He aspired for the colonelcy but was defeated; then he ran for a renewal of his post as lieutenant colonel and lost; an attempt to win the majority met the same fate. Jones was out on his ear. But at Jackson's urging, the President promoted Jones over all of the victorious field officers to rank of brigadier general on June 25, effective June 23, 1862, on the eve of the Seven Days' Campaign. This unsettling result "surprised our officers very much," a member of the regiment wrote disgustedly. General Jones actually never achieved the full status of his new rank, because the Senate failed to act to confirm the appointment during two consecutive sessions.

The new general took command not of the famous Stonewall Brigade containing his old regiment, but rather of the 2d Brigade of that division, which included the 21st, 42d, and 48th Virginia Infantry and the 1st Virginia Battalion. He led this brigade during the Seven Days' and was engaged at Gaines' Mill and Malvern Hill. A slight wound suffered near the end of the campaign kept Jones out of the fighting at Second Manassas August 29–30. At Sharpsburg on September 17 he entered the battle at the head of Jackson's old division as its senior brigade commander. Early in the action that day Jones left the field, complaining that a nearby shell explosion had disabled him, although no fragments struck him. Men in the ranks began to talk of cowardice. In December at the Battle of Fredericksburg, where his command did but little fighting, reports circulated of the general "getting behind a tree."

During the winter after Fredericksburg, talk of misbehavior by Jones reached such a pitch that it resulted in the unprecedented measure of a formal court-martial for cowardice of a general officer in Lee's army. Captain (later Colonel) William Addison Witcher of the 21st Virginia came to Stonewall Jackson's attention as being among those talking about the subject. Jackson typically insisted that Witcher either prefer charges or himself be charged with misconduct for his remarks. When the captain sought to avoid the issue by resigning, Jackson refused to accept that settlement of the issue; the corps commander also denied Witcher's request for leave of absence pending the court. On March 17, 1863, an army general order announced the court's composition. It would include Generals A. P. Hill, Jubal A. Early, Isaac R. Trimble, Robert E. Rodes, Henry Heth, James J. Archer, and William D. Pender, with Major William Ruffin Cox of the 2d North Carolina as judge advocate. Although the general charge of cowardice was made public, the high command delicately dropped a veil over the particulars with the subterfuge that they were too long to be printed: "The Specifications being lengthy and minute, are omitted in this order." On April 18 another general order reported the result: Jones was not guilty of the four unpublished specifications, nor of the charge. He was, the order said, "honorably acquitted...and will resume his sword."

Two weeks later Jones led his brigade briefly onto the field of Chancellorsville, but he soon headed for the rear, "owing to the ulcerated condition of one of his legs." Lee quickly faced the necessity of finding a new leader for the brigade and relieved Jones of his command. Apparently the timid general accompanied the army toward Gettysburg in some supernumerary capacity, perhaps even under arrest, because he was captured at Smithsburg, Maryland, on July 4, 1863. Under the circumstances no one in a position of authority sought Jones' parole and exchange, so he remained a prisoner of war for more than two years. After several months at Johnson's Island the unfortunate officer was moved to Fort Warren, in Boston harbor. He was finally released from imprisonment there on July 24, 1865.

Jones returned to Harrisonburg after the war and established a farm equipment dealership. In 1887 he became commissioner in chancery of the county court and held that post until his death. During his later life the former general suffered some personal difficulties and eventually made domestic arrangements decidedly unusual under the circumstances. Jones died in Harrisonburg on April 1, 1901, and was buried there in Woodbine Cemetery.

Robert K. Krick

Jackson, Thomas J., Letterbook and other material in the Jedediah Hotchkiss Papers (Washington, D.C., Library of Congress).

Jones' alumni file (Virginia Military Institute, Lexington).

Superintendent's Records (Virginia Military Institute, Lexington).

Major General Samuel Jones, in profile. (Cook Collection, Valentine Museum, Richmond, Va.)

⭐ *Samuel Jones* ⭐

Samuel Jones was born in Powhatan County, Virginia, on December 17, 1819. A Virginia appointee to the U.S. Military Academy in 1837, he graduated nineteenth out of the fifty-two cadets in the class of 1841. Brevetted a 2d lieutenant in the 1st U.S. Artillery on July 1 of that year, he was promoted to that full grade on September 28. He served on the Maine frontier during the boundary dispute with Great Britain until 1843 and in Florida 1845–46. From 1846 to 1851 Jones held the position of assistant professor of mathematics and instructor of infantry and of artillery tactics at West Point. Although he missed serving in the Mexican War, the army promoted him 1st lieutenant on March 3, 1847. Between 1851 and 1858, his duty stations included New Orleans, Fort McHenry, and various posts on the Texas frontier. He achieved the rank of captain on December 24, 1853. Assigned in November of 1858 as assistant to the judge advocate of the army, Jones remained in Washington, D.C., until the secession of Virginia.

Jones resigned from the U.S. army on April 27, 1861, and entered the Confederate Regular Army as a major of artillery. Promoted to lieutenant colonel, he was appointed assistant adjutant general of Virginia forces. By July he was serving as chief of artillery and ordnance on the staff of Brigadier General P. G. T. Beauregard at Manassas, Virginia. He had been elevated to the rank of colonel. Beauregard and others commended him for his performance during the First Battle of Manassas on July 21. President Jefferson Davis appointed him brigadier general on August 28, to rank from July 21.

Until January of 1862 Jones remained under General Beauregard but now in command of a Georgia infantry brigade deployed along the Potomac River. Transferred to the Gulf Coast, Jones relieved Major General Braxton Bragg in command at Pensacola on January 27, 1862. On March 3 he replaced Bragg as commander of the Department of Alabama and West Florida and established his headquarters at Mobile. He was promoted to major general on March 14, to rank

from March 10, with the appointment being confirmed on March 14.

In mid-April, because of complaints made against him, Jones was ordered to report to Beauregard, who now commanded the Western Department with headquarters at Corinth, Mississippi. On April 29 Jones commanded a division in Major General Earl Van Dorn's Army of the West, but a month later Van Dorn relieved Jones of that command. Even though Jones' request for a court of inquiry was denied, General Braxton Bragg gave him command of a division in the II Corps, Army of Mississippi, on June 2. Apparently the controversy with Van Dorn was dropped.

Apparently Bragg quickly concluded that Jones was unsuited for field command. On July 26 he ordered Jones to resume the command at Mobile, now designated the District of the Gulf and a part of Bragg's command. President Davis overruled this order. The President, unlike Bragg, knew of the opposition to Jones that existed in Mobile.

On August 17 and just prior to his invasion of Kentucky, Bragg removed Jones from field duty by placing him in command of Chattanooga. On September 19, however, Secretary of War George W. Randolph instructed Jones to move his headquarters to Knoxville and assume command of the Department of East Tennessee, which he did four days later. On September 27 Bragg assigned Jones to command the District of Middle Tennessee. The district included that portion of Alabama north of the Tennessee River; Chattanooga remained part of the Department of East Tennessee. Bragg further instructed Jones to gather recruits and conscripts and hurry them to the Army of Mississippi in Kentucky. At the same time he instructed Jones to press forward and capture Nashville—an impossible task for the limited number of troops available to Jones.

The conflicting instructions from Bragg in Kentucky and the War Department in Richmond ended with Jones remaining in Knoxville and having his department expanded to include all the territory between the

Jones was a frequent sitter for the camera, probably during his days in Charleston in 1864. (Library of Congress)

Jones, in fact, was one of the most photographed generals of the Confederacy. (Cook Collection, Valentine Museum, Richmond, Va.)

The progress of the war can be seen in his receding hairline. (William A. Turner Collection)

Tennessee and Cumberland rivers. More importantly, Jones now withheld, with the approval of the War Department, troops that Bragg desired to have join him in Kentucky. When the infuriated Bragg returned to Tennessee, he secured a transfer of Jones out of his department. On November 4, 1862, the War Department ordered Jones to report for duty to Lieutenant General John C. Pemberton at Jackson, Mississippi.

Unwanted or unneeded by Pemberton, Jones was assigned to command the Department of Western Virginia on November 25. He assumed his new post on December 10 and established his headquarters at Dublin Depot. He lost favor with General Robert E. Lee by failing to furnish troops and supplies during the invasion of Pennsylvania in 1863. Nevertheless, his department was expanded on September 6 to include that portion of western Virginia that had previously belonged to the Department of East Tennessee and command over those troops stationed in Tennessee east of Knoxville. Major General Simon B. Buckner suggested this change when he learned that he was to abandon East Tennessee and reinforce Bragg in northwestern Georgia, prior to the Battle of Chickamauga September 19–20.

Although unsuccessful, Jones' defense of the region, and especially of the Virginia & Tennessee Railroad and of the salt mines, was probably all that could have been expected considering his resources. Nevertheless, he incurred the wrath of the Virginia lawmakers, and the War Department ordered him to be relieved on February 24, 1864. He turned over his command on March 5 and departed for Richmond.

On April 2 the War Department ordered Jones to assume command of the defenses of Savannah, Georgia, in Beauregard's Department of South Carolina, Georgia, and Florida. Upon Beauregard's reassignment on April 20, Jones became commander of the department. He retained control of Charleston harbor until he was relieved on October 12, 1864, at which time he was reduced to commanding the District of South Carolina, which comprised most of that state. Reassigned on December 31 to command the District of Florida, he held that post until May 10, 1865, when he surrendered at Tallahassee and was paroled.

Following the war Jones retired to private life at Mattoax, Virginia, where he engaged in farming until 1880, when he secured a clerkship in the Adjutant General's Office at Washington. In 1885 he transferred to the office of the judge advocate

A previously unpublished late-war image of Jones, with the years showing their toll. (Museum of the Confederacy, Richmond, Va.)

Probably Jones' last wartime photo, with the beard fully grown and the weariness evident on his face. (Cook Collection, Valentine Museum, Richmond, Va.)

general. He died at Bedford Springs, Virginia, on July 31, 1887, and was buried in Richmond.

Lawrence L. Hewitt

Faust, Patricia L., ed., *Historical Times Illustrated Encyclopedia of the Civil War* (New York, 1986).

Heitman, Francis B., *Historical Register and Dictionary of the United States Army, From Its Organization, September 29, 1789, to March 2, 1903* (Washington, 1903).

Hotchkiss, Jedediah, *Virginia*, Vol. III in Evans, *Confederate Military History*.

Only two uniformed views of "Grumble" Jones are known, and neither shows sufficient detail to determine whether it is wartime or prior to his 1857 resignation from the Old Army. This previously unpublished portrait certainly could be of war vintage, though no rank can quite be seen on his shoulder strap. (William A. Turner Collection)

★ *William Edmondson Jones* ★

William Edmondson Jones, known universally by the well-earned sobriquet "Grumble," was born in Washington County, Virginia, on May 9, 1824. Young Jones attended Emory and Henry College, then entered the United States Military Academy. He quickly established himself in the top quarter of his class, finishing the first year tenth among fifty-seven classmates. After posting excellent grades in engineering, ethics, and English—offset by standing nearly last in drawing—Jones graduated tenth in the thirty-eight-member class of 1848. Classmates destined for Civil War prominence included N. G. "Shanks" Evans, George H. "Maryland" Steuart, and John Buford. In his final year Jones ranked 133d in conduct among 230 cadets at West Point.

Graduating just as the Mexican War ended doomed Jones to a dreary professional experience bereft of opportunities for advancement. His initial rank of brevet 2d lieutenant in the Mounted Rifle Regiment, dated July 1, 1848, was not even converted to regular rank as 2d lieutenant until November 30, 1850. Four years later Grumble Jones crept up one notch to the rank of 1st lieutenant. During these years the lieutenant served in Missouri and Kansas, but he was posted most of that time in Oregon. A disaster that permanently and drastically changed Jones' life struck him in 1852. Early that year he returned home on furlough to marry Eliza Dunn. Soon after the newlyweds took ship from New Orleans for the West Coast, their vessel foundered off the coast of Texas and Mrs. Jones drowned when waves swept her from her husband's arms. Jones, in the gentle understatement of a biographer, "returned to his command with a sad and broken heart." After unhappy and desultory postings over the next five years, mainly in Texas, Jones resigned on January 26, 1857. Later that year the grieving widower visited Europe. For the rest of his years before the war Jones operated his farm and estate in Washington County, Virginia.

When war broke out, William E. Jones led the Washington Mounted Rifles to Richmond for Confederate service as the company's commander and captain. The unit, which had been formed in 1859, became Company D of the 1st Virginia Cavalry on July 9, 1861. Less than two weeks later it fought at First Manassas. When the regiment's first colonel, J. E. B. Stuart, won promotion to brigadier general on September 24, Jones received commission as colonel to replace Stuart.

Grumble Jones enjoyed a very warm reciprocal friendship with Major General "Stonewall" Jackson, but his Confederate service was deeply marred by a dislike for Stuart so violent that it interfered with both men's official duties. One of Stuart's staff described Jones' initial dislike for the senior cavalryman in Lee's army as "a feeling which ripened afterwards into as genuine a hatred as I ever remember to have seen in my…life." The 1st Virginia had been fond of Stuart, and also liked Lieutenant Colonel Fitzhugh Lee, but "Colonel Jones was not popular with his regiment, and the contrast between our ugly, surly Colonel" and the "handsome, dashing" Lee was hardly to Grumble's credit. In consequence, the regimental elections during the spring of 1862 displaced Jones. A few weeks later, on June 20, Jones became colonel of the 7th Virginia Cavalry—Brigadier General Turner Ashby's old unit.

When Jones moved to command of the 7th Cavalry, he began a successful association with mounted units from the Shenandoah Valley and western Virginia. Many regiments from those areas suffered from lack of organization and discipline so extensively as to render them all but worthless. Grumble Jones managed to instill firm principles of command and control in that sort of cavalry better than any other officer who performed in Virginia. He dressed like they did, wearing "a home-spun suit and a broad yellow hat" and riding an "old yellow mare" to match. The net effect that this outfit produced was of "a rough, seedy-looking individual, without any insignia of his rank." Some of the men inevitably complained about the stern discipline, but one trooper who thought Jones "a brave, cautious man" concluded that though "he was very strict...I thought he was very humane." Anyone identified with Stuart could expect rough treatment from this sworn enemy of their general. One of Stuart's aides complained that Jones "blazed all sorts of language at me." Another recorded with chagrin the egregious lies that Jones employed to discredit him. The cold-hearted dishonesty witnessed by another officer who observed Jones from a disinterested position suggests that this peculiar and misanthropic general was so consumed by bitterness that he was immune to conscience in some matters.

Jones fought under his patron Jackson during the Cedar Mountain campaign as colonel of the 7th. Soon thereafter, at Jackson's insistence, he received promotion to brigadier general on October 3, to rank from September 19, 1862. Near the end of the year, again with Jackson sponsoring him, Jones was posted to command of the Valley District. The enormous task of disciplining troops unaccustomed to strictures of any sort took much effort, but Jones succeeded to some degree. Men grumbled savagely about such measures as sharpening the sabers that they thought to be all but useless. Many, though, came to respect their general when they found that in action "he made every lick count," in the words of a private in the 8th Virginia Cavalry. Major S. P. Halsey of the 21st Virginia Cavalry (who would become the last surviving field officer of the Confederacy) wrote after the war that Jones "came nearer being a Jackson (when independent) than any other officer we had."

Jones' first major venture in the Valley, a raid toward Moorefield in January 1863, failed completely. In April and May, however, he collaborated with Brigadier General John D. Imboden on a highly successful month-long raid that took him west of Cumberland, Maryland, against Federal railroads and property. Jones moved his brigade back to the Army of Northern Virginia on October 9. In that theater the general again displayed his unique ability to organize irregular cavalry into an effective force. He cooperated with Lieutenant General James Longstreet during that general's disastrous campaign in East Tennessee and then assumed the defense of southwestern Virginia against Federal raiders. In May 1864 Grumble Jones foiled Federal designs on Saltville and Wytheville, then he moved down the Valley to resist the destructive march of Federal Major General David Hunter toward Staunton and Lynchburg. On June 5, 1864, Jones opposed Hunter at the battle of Piedmont. The polyglot Confederate force was a weak mixture of units drawn from several forces. A major part of Jones' little army was made up of the sort of unreliable cavalry he had done so much to organize. The cavalry failed in its assigned role, and Grumble Jones fell dead when a Federal bullet struck him in the head as he sought to rally his infantry fragments. A Louisiana officer who had no part in the controversies surrounding the dead general wrote feelingly: "He was one of the bravest, most skillful & active Cavalry commanders in the Confederate service." Jones was buried beside the remains of his drowned wife in the Old Glade Spring Presbyterian Churchyard in his native county.

Robert K. Krick

Blackford, W. W., *War Years with Jeb Stuart* (New York, 1945).

Colley, Thomas W., "Brig. General William E. Jones," *Confederate Veteran,* XI (1903).

Dabney, C. W., Papers, West Virginia University Library, Morgantown.

Nor can rank be made out on the epaulettes in this well-known portrait of Jones. (Library of Congress)

✷ *Thomas Jordan* ✷

A soldier and journalist, Thomas Jordan was born September 30, 1819, in Luray, Virginia. His parents were Gabriel and Elizabeth Ann Sibert Jordan. He received an education in the common schools of Page County and was appointed to and entered the United States Military Academy in the summer of 1836. He graduated as number forty-one in the class of 1840, which included William Tecumseh Sherman (one of his roommates), George Henry Thomas, and Richard S. Ewell. He was commissioned brevet 2d lieutenant in the 5th U.S. Infantry, and on December 1, 1840, was promoted 2d lieutenant and transferred to the 3d U.S. Infantry, then stationed in Florida Territory.

Jordan participated in the Second Seminole War, and was with the detachment that surprised and captured Chief Tiger Tail, near Cedar Key, Florida, in November 1842. Along with his regiment Jordan was ordered to Corpus Christi, Texas, to join Zachary Taylor's army. He was with Taylor at the battles of Palo Alto and Resaca de la Palma, and his unit was the first to cross the Rio Grande. Jordan was promoted 1st lieutenant June 18, 1846.

The 3d Infantry, along with most of the regular army units, was detached from Taylor's army and joined Winfield Scott's army that was to campaign from Vera Cruz to Mexico City. On March 3, 1847, before the capture of Vera Cruz, Jordan was promoted captain and assigned duty as a staff quartermaster. Following the peace treaty ending the Mexican War, he was posted at Vera Cruz with the responsibility of procuring transportation and arranging for the embarkation by sea of thousands of Scott's soldiers who were returning to the United States—the volunteers to be mustered out and the regulars for redeployment. He earned a commendation from Brigadier General David E. Twiggs for this duty.

Ordered back to Florida on return from Mexico, Jordan pulled two years of duty as staff quartermaster during the Third Seminole War. His next assignment took him to the Pacific Northwest. There he participated in the Steptoe War, 1857–58. While stationed at Fort Dalles, Oregon, 1856–59, he introduced steamboat navigation on the upper reaches of the Columbia River above the Dalles. Taking an extended leave of absence in 1860, he authored his first book, *The South, Its Products, Commerce, and Resources,* published the following year.

On May 21, 1861, less than five weeks after Virginia's secession, Jordan resigned his commission in the old army, tendered his sword to his native state, and was commissioned lieutenant colonel of Virginia troops. He was ordered to Manassas Junction, and when Brigadier General P. G. T. Beauregard assumed command of Confederate forces on the Alexandria Line, he was promoted colonel and made adjutant general of the Confederate Army of the Potomac. On July 21 at the First Battle of Manassas, when Beauregard rode to Henry Hill, Jordan remained at the general's McLean House command post and directed the march of reinforcements from the army's left to the point of danger. Upon the arrival of President Jefferson Davis by rail from Richmond, Jordan accompanied him on his ride to Henry Hill.

The only known uniformed portrait of Thomas Jordan was made sometime after April 1862. (Library of Congress)

In January 1862 General Beauregard was ordered to report to General Albert Sidney Johnston as second in command of the vast Department No. 2. Jordan accompanied Beauregard as his senior staffer. He was named assistant adjutant general of the Army of Mississippi on March 30. He played a major role as the army's chief of staff at Shiloh, first under Johnston and under Beauregard after Johnston's death. He was omnipresent, giving orders in the names of the commanding generals, and in recognition of his valuable services he was made a brigadier general September 26, to rank from April 14, 1862. Jordan continued as the army's chief of staff under Beauregard and then under Braxton Bragg, who replaced Beauregard as commander of Department No. 2 on June 17. As such, Bragg wore a second hat; he had been commander of the Army of Mississippi since May 6.

As Bragg's chief of staff, Jordan participated in the opening and successful phase of the Kentucky Campaign—the transfer of the Army of Mississippi by rail from Tupelo, Mississippi, to Chattanooga. On September 24, 1862, Beauregard, recovered from the illness that had cost him his army, returned to duty as commander of the Department of South Carolina and Georgia, headquartered at Charleston. Jordan, having had personal difficulties with the acerbic Bragg, on September 26 rejoined Beauregard—to wear three hats—as "adjutant and inspector general and chief of staff of the department." The previous week he had accompanied Beauregard on an inspection of the defenses of Charleston and Savannah. In mid-December the department was enlarged to include all of Florida except the panhandle. Earlier Jordan had shed his duties as Beauregard's inspector general.

A facile write, excellent manager, and loyal subordinate, Jordan served Beauregard and the Confederate well in the twelve months from April 7, 1863, to April 20, 1864, during which the Union committed major naval and army forces in a futile effort to capture Charleston. On April 20 Beauregard was ordered to proceed to Weldon, North Carolina, and assume responsibility for defense of the Departments of North Carolina and the Cape Fear. On doing so, he was replaced as commander of his former department by Major General Samuel Jones. Jones had his own team and on May 16 Jordan was reassigned by Jones to command the Third Military District, headquartered at Pocotaligo, South Carolina. Before the end of the month, the War Department notified Jordan that he was to turn over command of the district, travel to Richmond, and await orders. He remained in the capital city until early February 1865, when he rejoined General Beauregard, then commanding the Military Division of the West, as aide-de-camp. Jordan was surrendered and paroled at Greensboro, North Carolina, May 1, 1865.

A few months after his parole, Jordan again took up the pen. The October 1865 issue of *Harper's Magazine* carried an article by him on Jefferson Davis that attacked the former Confederate president, then imprisoned at Fort Monroe. He pictured Davis as imperious, narrow, and lacking in administrative talents and statesmanship. In 1866 Jordan became editor of the *Memphis Appeal* and in 1868, in collaboration with J. B. Pryor, wrote and published *The Campaigns of Lieutenant-General N. B. Forrest.*

Jordan, a romantic, became interested in the Cuban independence movement. In May 1869 he landed in Cuba at Mayari with three hundred men and weapons and ammunition for six thousand and became successively chief of staff and then commander of forces in rebellion against Spain. Troops led by Jordan in January 1870 met and defeated a numerically superior army at Guaimaro. With a price of $100,000 on his head, supplies nearly exhausted, and strict enforcement of the neutrality laws by the Grant Administration, Jordan in February 1870 resigned his commission, returned to the United States, and escaped prosecution for his violation of the nation's neutrality laws.

Later that year, he organized and became editor of the *Financial and Mining Record of New York,* a journal championing free coinage of silver. He held this position until 1892, when failing health compelled his retirement. Meantime, in 1887 his article "Notes of a Confederate Staff Officer at Shiloh" was included in Volume I of *Battles and Leaders of the Civil War.* He died on November 27, 1895, and was buried in Mount Hope Cemetery, near Hastings-on-the-Hudson.

Edwin C. Bearss

Cullum, George, *Biographical Register, Officers and Graduates,* *U.S. Military Academy* (New York, 1891).

Frank Leslie's Illustrated Newspaper, February 26, 1870.

Hotchkiss, Jedediah, *Virginia,* Vol. III in Evans, *Confederate Military History.*

New York Times, November 28, 1895.